THE PSYCHOLOGICAL DEVELOPMENT
OF GIRLS AND WOMEN

In this book, Sheila Greene presents a challenging new perspective on the psychological development of girls and women which emphasizes the central role of time in human development. She critically reviews traditional and contemporary theoretical approaches – ranging from orthodox psychoanalysis to relational and postmodern theories – and argues that even those claiming to be focused on development have presented a view of women's lives as fixed and determined by their nature or their past. These theories, she believes, should be rejected because of their inherent lack of validity and their frequently oppressive implications for women.

Greene's approach places primary importance on temporality itself and on the competing discourses on time, age and development which play an active role in the construction of the lives of girls and women. Essential but often neglected insights from the more compelling developmental and feminist theories are woven together within a theoretical framework that emphasizes temporality, emergence and human agency. The result is a liberating theory of women's psychological development as constantly emerging and changing in time rather than as static and fixed by their nature, socio-cultural context and personal history.

The Psychological Development of Girls and Women will be essential reading for students and researchers in the psychology of women, developmental psychology and women's studies.

Sheila Greene is a senior lecturer in psychology at Trinity College Dublin and co-founder and Chair of its Children's Research Centre. Her research interests cover developmental psychology, the psychology of women and the psychology of personhood.

WOMEN AND PSYCHOLOGY
Series Editor: Jane Ussher
School of Psychology,
University of Western Sydney

This series brings together current theory and research on women and psychology. Drawing on scholarship from a number of different areas of psychology, it bridges the gap between abstract research and the reality of women's lives by integrating theory and practice, research and policy.

Each book addresses a 'cutting edge' issue of research, covering such topics as postnatal depression, eating disorders, theories and methodologies.

The series provides accessible and concise accounts of key issues in the study of women and psychology, and clearly demonstrates the centrality of psychology to debates within women's studies or feminism.

The Series Editor would be pleased to discuss proposals for new books in the series.

Other titles in this series:

THE THIN WOMAN
Helen Malson

THE MENSTRUAL CYCLE
Anne E. Walker

POST-NATAL DEPRESSION
Paula Nicolson

RE-THINKING ABORTION
Mary Boyle

WOMEN AND AGING
Linda R. Gannon

BEING MARRIED. DOING GENDER
Caroline Dryden

UNDERSTANDING DEPRESSION
Janet M. Stoppard

FEMININITY AND THE PHYSICALLY ACTIVE WOMAN
Precilla Y. L. Choi

GENDER, LANGUAGE AND DISCOURSE
Ann Weatherall

THE SCIENCE/FICTION OF SEX
Annie Potts

THE PSYCHOLOGICAL DEVELOPMENT OF GIRLS AND WOMEN

Rethinking change in time

Sheila Greene

 Routledge
Taylor & Francis Group

LONDON AND NEW YORK

First published 2003 by Routledge
27 Church Road, Hove, East Sussex, BN3 2FA

Simultaneously published in the USA and Canada
by Routledge
29 West 35th Street, New York, NY 10001

Routledge is an imprint of the Taylor & Francis Group

© 2003 Sheila Greene

Typeset in Times by Regent Typesetting, London

Printed and bound in Great Britain by TJ International, Padstow, Cornwall
Paperback cover design by Terry Foley at Anú Design

British Library Cataloguing in Publication Data
A catalogue record for this book is available
from the British Library

Library of Congress Cataloging in Publication Data

Greene, Sheila, 1946-
The psychological development of girls and women: rethinking change in time / Sheila Greene.
p. cm. – (Women and psychology)
Includes bibliographical references and index.
1. Women–Psychology. 2. Girls–Psychology. 3. Developmental psychology.
4. Feminist psychology. I. Title. II. Series.

HQ1206 .G767 2002
155.6'33–dc21

2002068746

ISBN 0-415-17861-4 (hbk)
ISBN 0-415-17862-2 (pbk)

To Paul

CONTENTS

ACKNOWLEDGEMENTS

I would like to thank the following people who have helped me in the writing of this book, whether by providing me with ideas or by encouragement and support: the many students who have participated in my classes in life-span developmental psychology and in the psychology of women and gender; my friends and colleagues in the Centre for Gender and Women's Studies and the Children's Research Centre in Trinity College Dublin; Mary McDermott; Annie Rogers; Gisela Schmidt; Marian Moylan (for the sanity-restoring walks!).

In relation to the preparation and production of this book I would like to thank Jane Ussher for her positive, unfailingly encouraging attitude, Lucy Farr and the helpful staff at Routledge and Tony Murray for permission to use his photograph, 'Time passing', taken on a country road in Kerry.

My family has been very patient with this project and I would like to thank my mother, Myrtle Greene, my children, Kit and Helen O'Mahony, and my husband, Paul O'Mahony, for their loving support. This book is dedicated to Paul, fierce critic and astute psychologist, who read and improved the final manuscript and, in many different ways, made this book possible.

1

INTRODUCTION

Building blocks for a critical analysis

The focus of this book

To date, mainstream developmental psychology has failed to provide an adequate theoretical base for describing changes in the psychology of girls and women across the life span. There is certainly a long history of developmental theorizing about the psychology of women, but even the more recent theories show little sign of being influenced by the conceptual insights that have emerged from life span developmental psychology and from important critiques of developmental psychology from both inside and outside this discipline. In addition, within the discipline which has come to be known as the psychology of women, there is a failure to confront developmental issues, associated with an over-reliance on social psychological frameworks. Feminist psychologists demonstrate either an acute wariness of all developmental theory – understandable given the way it has been traditionally defined and practised – or a questionable fixation on psycho-analytic approaches to development.

This book represents an attempt to identify the parameters of a contemporary framework for understanding the psychological development of girls and women. Such a framework should provide a better basis for analysis of the sources and meaning of psychological change across the life span and the significance of the passage of time, of timing, age, growth, ageing and mortality to girls and women. I question the adequacy of historical and contemporary theoretical accounts of female psychological development, while arguing that it is important to retain a developmental perspective on the lives of girls and women and their experience of being in the world.

In this book, I am not arguing for a new life span developmental psychology of women, complementing the existing life span developmental psychologies of men, as critics of androcentric theories of development such as Carol Gilligan (1979) have done, but for the importance of a critical developmental perspective on the psychology of girls and women (and ultimately on that of boys and men also). The answer to dissatisfaction with current developmental theorizing is neither to adopt its traditional framework and apply it to women nor to abandon the developmental perspective altogether as unredeemable. If we fail to take on board the dynamic and diachronic nature of human psychology, we have an inadequate picture of our subject matter – a picture which is doomed to be static and fixed in time and fails in its project of being capable of understanding the origins of the self, the complexities of selfhood and subjectivity, and the factors involved in psychological change with time and the person's changing relationship to a changing world.

Developmental psychology is one of the central disciplines engaged in explaining the nature of human personhood, whether it does so explicitly or by implication. I consider that the depiction of the human person that emerges from most traditional and some current developmental theorizing is one which is incomplete, restrictive and ultimately demeaning to the human person. This is particularly evident in psychology's views on the restraints imposed on humans by their gender and even more so in its views on the psychology of women. Thus we have many theories which see women as the victim of their anatomies, their genes, their social conditioning or, more recently, the discourses which constitute their subjectivity. Theorizing the nature of personhood is an extremely important task for contemporary psychology and for an adequate psychology of women. Drawing out the extent to which women can and cannot function as agents in their own life stories is a central aim of this book.

I am also arguing that gender is a central feature of the processes entailed in the production of persons and the experience of being a person. These processes will differ for males and females, I propose, as long as societies divide humans into two sexes along the lines of the male–female biological division and then build constructs and practices around that division. A developmental perspective on the gendering process draws attention to the shifting, complex and multi-faceted place of gender in the person's psychological functioning over the life course.

This book concentrates on the psychological development of girls and women for the following reasons:

- To date, developmental psychology – with exceptions which will be discussed later – has offered a restrictive and, at times, oppressive account of the development of girls and women.
- Developmental psychology is permeated in some areas with gender bias and in others with gender blindness.
- For understandable reasons, many feminist researchers and theorists in psychology and the social sciences have turned their backs on the developmental perspective.
- Notwithstanding this history, there is a need for a critical developmental perspective on human psychology and on the psychology of girls and women.
- Approaching the psychology of girls and women from a developmental orientation provides a foundation for the understanding of the sources of personal change and transformation in the life course. Such understanding is necessary for a complete perspective on human psychological change and is

potentially useful to the feminist project, which is also fundamentally about change.

- Life span developmental theory tends to neglect gender, race, sexuality, class and other major categories of difference, and thus this book is an exercise in the application of the developmental perspective to the processes involved in the production and shaping of difference.
- Developmental psychology, while being the study of psychological change in time, has not adequately explored the significance of time in human experience and in psychological change across the life course.
- This neglect of the significance of our temporal existence is also a feature of the psychology of women as a discipline and feminist scholarship in general.

Construction of a new framework entails the combination of theories, findings and insights from several sub-disciplines of psychology including developmental psychology, the psychology of women, feminist psychology and critical theories of psychology. Many of the most interesting recent developments within these sub-disciplines are due to the influence of intellectual and political movements outside psychology such as feminism, women's studies and postmodern theoretical movements. I will first outline in summary form the different psychological traditions, which are central to the subject matter of this book.

Developmental psychology

Developmental psychology encompasses the study of psychological development across the life course, although some psychologists still use the term to apply only to the study of the psychological development of children, and, perhaps, adolescents. To date, the formal study of the development of children has been more extensive and more influential than the study of later parts of the life course or those studies which attempt to understand the life span in its totality.

For many years life span developmental psychology was seen as the poor relation of child developmental psychology, borrowing its clothes and its ideas and owning very few of its own. To a large extent this is still the case, as a perusal of popular life span developmental textbooks would demonstrate. Stage theories, for example, which are popular ways of expressing developmental changes in children, have been extended to cover the life span, the most notable example of this being Erik Erikson's doctrine of the Eight Ages of Man (Erikson, 1950). Principles such as universality and unidirectionality, which are inherent in the thinking of child developmentalists, have been applied to thinking about life span issues. Despite the fact that such thinking is still apparent, opposition to the thoughtless extension of theories which originated in attempts to understand child development has grown and, even more importantly, a new critical perspective on the nature of development and on the concept of development itself has had an increasing influence.

Recent struggles for theoretical ascendancy within developmental psychology have been, to summarize drastically, between those who adopt an organismic approach versus those whose perspective is socio-cultural. In other words, one camp is seeking causative mechanisms within the organism and the other from without. Both perspectives are inadequate and incomplete. I will adopt the view, now well articulated by a number of theorists like Susan Oyama (1993) and Richard Lerner (1998), that developmental theories must abandon dysfunctional dualisms, most particularly the nature–nurture dualism which underpins the perennial competition between biological and social theories of development. The emerging developmental systems perspective is an advance on the dualistic perspectives fostered in traditional developmental theories and will be discussed in more detail in Chapter 2. It provides one of the central theoretical strands in a new and integrated account of developmental processes and the nature of change in time (Lewis, 2000).

Developmental psychology's perspective on time has been unduly restrictive in that developmental theory has tended to be almost entirely past-oriented. Developmentalists tend to search for explanation or understanding of human psychological change in the history of the individual. In many ways, despite the fact that developmental psychology is that branch of psychology which most clearly deals with the person's existence in time, it may be argued that developmental psychology has failed to develop a satisfactory account of human existence in time – past, present and future. In a paper published in 1985, James Faulconer and Richard Williams argued that the human sciences are in thrall to two linked epistemological positions: positivism and historicism. Critiques of positivism abound in contemporary scientific literature and elements of the anti-positivist argument willl be addressed in Chapter 2. Historicism on the other hand is less often examined and it is historicism which has particular relevance to developmental psychology. Historicism entails the objectification of history or events in history and their use in a causal account of behaviour. As it applies to the psychology of the individual it implies that 'early events cause later events to be as they are'. Faulconer and Williams argue that both positivism and historicism 'contain an assumption about time that prevents them from doing what their adherents would like them to do, namely, render human behaviour intelligible' (p. 1180). The assumption about time which these authors question is the view of time as a dimension without content. As an alternative they promote the view of time offered by Heidegger (1962), that 'time is *essentially* content' (p. 1184). For biological organisms time is irreversible; it is intrinsic to their existence in this world, not a phenomenon which can be separated from the fact of their existence.

All things are temporal, including our understanding. As the philosopher Hans Gadamer (1975) has elaborated, atemporal causal certainty is an impossiblity. Our interpretations are therefore both situated, culturally and historically, and provisional in that what we are attempting to describe does not stand still.

Developmental psychology poses itself the challenge of explaining life course change. It is necessary also to explain or further our understanding of the relative stabilities and continuities which are also a feature of human development; that is, we rely upon a certain level of predictability in ourselves and others and in the character of our material world. Nonetheless it will be a central theme of this book that the existence of flux, the unrepeatability of life, must be central to our understanding of who we are. Psychology and developmental psychology fail to address unpredictability and novelty adequately. As Jaan Valsiner (2000) comments, there is a tendency within the sciences to represent phenomena as static rather than as dynamic or processual. 'Most of psychology', he states, 'is built on non-developmental premises, utilizing representations of the object-like kind' (p. 8). Thus we have explanatory terms like 'intelligence', 'personality' or 'cognition'. He continues, 'A developmental scientist necessarily rejects the "object-like" construction of stability, yet remains open to the opposition between "dynamic stability" and "change"' (p. 9). While the living organism is never the same as it was before, relative stability is essential for all organized life forms. Developmental psychologists need to find a vocabulary for dealing with the relative stabilities which are a key feature of the organization of living systems, systems which are inevitably changing through time.

Two concepts which may assist developmentalists to disentangle their discipline from the strictures of history are emergence and agency. Complex organic forms, which have complex relationships with their environments, change in ways which are characterized by the emergence of novel and often unpredictable structures and processes. Developmentalists in the biological sciences as well as in psychology are attempting to grapple with the significance of this new conceptual framework for understanding change. When the focus is on humans, an additional layer of complexity enters the equation, which is the self-creating, self-directing power of the human mind. To what extent humans are indeed agents in their own lives has been the subject of many philosophical debates. The capacity of humans to act with a degree of agency is, however, ungainsayable. Agency can be regarded as a very significant emergent process, an outcome of the interactions of a highly complex organism and its elaborate culture. The positing of agency is in some ways a moral as much as a scientific stance, for it may be considered as fundamental to a respect for the rights and dignity of all persons.

Aside from the necessity to reorient developmental thinking towards a more satisfactory explanation of the causes and nature of developmental change, it is also the case that developmental psychology tends to underestimate the importance of time psychically; that is, in the thought and actions of the person living her life. One of the few developmental psychologists to recognize the centrality of time in human life was Bernice Neugarten who asserted that psychologists should pay attention to 'what the person selects as important in his (*sic*) past and in his present, what he hopes to do in the future, what he predicts will occur, what strategies he elects and what meanings he attaches to times, life and death' (1977, pp. 639–640). Writing also in the 1970s, the developmental psychologist Klaus Riegel concludes a paper on the dialectics of time by saying: 'I should like to propose that life span developmental psychology deals with the interlude between conception and death and with the efforts of the individual to reconcile himself to these two poles of existence' (1977, p. 51). The work of Neugarten and Riegel on time is rarely cited today, but the issues they attempted to place centre-stage have not gone away. The meaning to the person of time, age and the passage of their own life course are all germane to the construction and interpretation of each individual life story and therefore to the subject matter of developmental psychology.

Many of the traditional theories about the development of women's personalities and psychological characteristics in general have been critiqued and rejected by feminist psychologists as hostile to a feminist standpoint. Some of these critics would argue that developmental psychology as a whole is fundamentally flawed and has little to offer to our understanding of the psychology of women. As Erica Burman states, 'It is difficult to think of any two more unlikely allies than developmental psychology and feminist research' (Burman, 1992, p. 49). Burman argues that developmental psychology promotes a model of child psychology which is prescriptive and oppressive, which claims a neutral, supposedly scientific status but which in fact is tied into oppressive political systems and ideologies. Her critique of developmental psychology is focused mostly on child development and 'developmentalism' against which, in recent years, a number of critics like John Morss, Ben Bradley, Valerie Walkerdine and Burman herself have mounted convincing attacks (see Bradley, 1989; Morss, 1990, 1996; Walkerdine, 1984). As used by these critics the term 'developmentalism' covers theories that ascribe to human psychological change a predictable, universal and sequential character which is fallacious and prescriptive. Many of the arguments which have emerged from this critical developmental psychology perspective will be taken up and used in this book. However, developmental psychology does not stand still, and some more recent attempts to theorize development provide the basis for a less flawed and oppressive developmental psychology of girls and women.

The psychology of women and feminist psychology

As a distinct discipline within psychology, the psychology of women has a short history, shorter than that of life span developmental psychology. It is the case that views on the psychology of women can be extracted from the pronouncements of the earliest psychologists and their intellectual progenitors but the formal birth of a distinctive sub-discipline of psychology did not take place until the 1970s (see e.g. Parlee (1979) and Unger (1997) for historical accounts of the emergence of the psychology of women). The psychology of women and feminist psychology may be assumed superficially to focus on the same subject area; however, there are important differences. The psychology of women, as a term, simply identifies a subject area, whereas feminist psychology identifies with feminism as a political and value base which influences theory, method and practice. The psychology of women is of central interest to feminist psychologists, but when the psychology of women is conducted from an explicitly feminist perspective, a number of consequences may follow. As Stephanie Riger (1992) states, a feminist psychology of women is 'a study not just *of* women but *for* women'. Identification with feminism implies also a particular (albeit multiply elaborated) approach to psychology in general. Clearly, then, some students of the psychology of women would not identify themselves, nor be identified, as feminist. Some writers (e.g. Rhoda Unger) seem to think that the psychology of women is transforming itself over time into feminist psychology. She says, 'the shift from a psychology of women to a feminist psychology is a gradual one and the paradigm shift is not complete' (1997, p. 21). Although it is the case that the emergence of feminist psychology as a detectable movement within psychology came after the establishment of the psychology of women as a discipline, I would maintain that they are separable and are likely to remain so.

Feminist psychology belongs to a different intellectual tradition to that of mainstream psychology. Its blatant partiality is an affront to the objective, avowedly value-free standpoint of mainstream psychologists, which is strongly represented in the academy despite recent challenges to positivism and empiricism. Feminist psychology consists of many different strands, but most feminist psychologists would be united in their opposition to psychology's androcentrism and failure to recognize the extent of plurality in human experience and behaviour, its treatment of the people who are the focus of research as 'subjects' rather than thoughtful participants, and its adherence to methods of study which fail to respect and capture the viewpoint of the research participants. In principle, at least, feminist scholars have a commitment to promoting social and structural changes which will benefit the life situation of women and an interest in the analysis of the political and socio-cultural factors which help to determine the shape and colour of women's lives.

Aside from these broad parameters, a variety of feminist theories exists (see Tong, 1989) and feminist psychologists also vary in their orientation. It should be noted, also, that studies by Michele Fine (1985, 1992), and by Brinton Lykes and Abigail Stewart (1986), have found that self-identified feminist researchers often employ methods which are no different from those used by mainstream researchers.

Critical psychology

Within psychology, feminist psychology may be seen as but one of a number of recent critical movements which have challenged the discipline's fundamental value assumptions. One of the key assumptions under challenge is psychology's claim to be politically and morally neutral and uncommitted, the traditional claim of the natural sciences. This view of science has been thoroughly undermined by a number of philosophers of science and critics from within psychology (e.g. Rorty, 1979; Gergen, 1982). The pretence of objectivity and neutrality was always more difficult to maintain and more specious in the human and social sciences.

From a political perspective the value-system espoused by mainstream psychology is one which is conservative at best and oppressive at worst. Critical psychologists on the other hand attempt to be morally and politically aware and to make an explicit commitment to the goals of increasing human welfare and promoting social justice.

As Fox and Prilleltensky (1997) point out, there is a variety of approaches clustered under the umbrella of critical psychology. The term 'critical theory' was used originally in social science with reference to the Marxist theorizing of writers such as Habermas and Holzcamp who promoted 'emancipatory social enquiry'. Contemporary critical psychologists do not all adhere to a strictly Marxist worldview but do share an interest in emancipation, although they may use other terms, such as 'liberation' or 'empowerment'. Feminist psychology aligns itself with critical psychology since it offers a critique of mainstream psychology's biased and oppressive stance towards women. This book advances a critical perspective, entailing critique of the assumptions, both epistemological and political, which underpin widely cited theories about the development of girls and women.

The developmental psychology of girls and women

The developmental psychology of girls and women is by no means a new area of activity; it has been the focus of numerous different theoretical and empirical studies. This work will be discussed in some detail in later chapters of this book. It is the case that some of these approaches belong to a traditional and questionable orientation towards developmental psychology. It is also the case that in much of the developmental psychology literature, which may not have focused explicitly on girls and women, there are strong implications about the psychology and social roles and status of women. For example, a great deal of the research on the development of children includes value judgements and exhortations aimed at women who are mothers. However, I would argue that much of the developmental psychology which is seen to be unhelpful, damaging or misconceived arises from a particular, once powerful, but now increasingly undermined, theoretical tradition. A central question for this book is the extent to which a developmental perspective on the psychology of the female person is informative and helpful. I believe that a reconstructed developmental perspective is both essential to an understanding of the psychology of girls and women and compatible with a feminist standpoint.

There are potentially many different expressions of the developmental orientation, a fact that is recognized even by Erica Burman. In the same paper where she dismisses developmental psychology as an unlikely ally of feminist psychology she expresses the view that 'there must be a place for developmental psychology, an alternative developmental psychology that can theorize how we can create, and can become, the people who can bring about and can inhabit a very different world' (1992, p. 50).

In both developmental psychology and the psychology of women, comfortable assumptions about the nature of psychological science, what it can claim, what it cannot claim, its methods and its uses, are under challenge. In attempting to approach the psychology of women from a broadly developmental perspective, I will argue that it is necessary to critique the assumptions underpinning both developmental psychology and the psychology of women. Such a critique will lean heavily on recent developments in feminist psychology, feminist theory, particularly social constructionist perspectives, and critical psychology in general. I will argue also that, although many contemporary developmental psychologists and critical theorists are very good at pointing to the influential and indeed constitutive role of the social and cultural context, they have been less effective in theorizing the role of time – historical, social, personal and biological – in the patterning of the life course, and that any comprehensive approach to explaining women's psychology and how and whether it changes with age must take into account social-spatial context *and* time. Time and the interpretation of time are part of an individual's total culture.

Developmental psychology and the psychology of women: separate paths

On both sides of the developmental psychology–psychology of women divide there seems to be evidence of resistance to incorporating the methods or insights of the other discipline. To start with the literature on the psychology of women: there is little evidence that writers and researchers working in the psychology of women or feminist psychology or women's studies in general pay much attention to recent developments in life span psychology or in critical developmental theory. In modern texts, women's lives are contextualized in terms of place and social identity (i.e. race, class, sexual orientation) but not so much in personal and historical time. As a source of evidence for this proposition, I will survey briefly the coverage offered in current psychology textbooks. Such texts may be seen as indicative of the prevalent attitude to any particular issue within a discipline. It could, of course, be argued that textbooks are not representative of the cutting edge of a discipline, but I would agree with Jeanne Maracek (1993) who says, 'Textbooks do more than shape students' knowledge of the discipline. . . . They regulate psychological knowledge by drawing the boundaries of the field . . . [and] in codifying knowledge' (p. 551). Textbooks claim to summarize the current state of knowledge in a particular area in a form that is accessible to under-graduate or postgraduate students. From this point of view, it is especially instructive to examine the coverage of developmental psychology in psychology of women textbooks.

Most psychology of women texts in the English language are from the USA but sell widely in the English-speaking world. A popular psychology of women text now in its fourth edition, Margaret Matlin's *The Psychology of Women*, claims to offer a combined developmental and topical approach. Matlin states:

'the combination of life-span and topical approaches seems to provide a cohesive framework my own students appreciate' (Matlin, 2000, p. viii). The life span approach may be seen in the loose chronological organization of the topics covered in the book. Thus some of the chapters relate to recognizable phases of the normative life cycle, some do not. Chapters on physical health, psychological disorders, violence and so on are interspersed with chapters on infancy and child-hood, adolescence and older adulthood. Each chapter stands alone and there is no attempt to link one phase of the life cycle to the other; nor is there any overarch-ing theoretical framework. There is no discussion of the issues which arise when approaching psychology from a developmental perspective, rather than, say, a social or a clinical perspective. There is no acknowledgement of the disagree-ments between developmental psychologists or of the critiques of traditional developmental psychology and its assumptions from feminist and other theoreti-cal standpoints.

Mary Crawford and Rhoda Unger's *Women and Gender: A Feminist Psychol-ogy* is in its third edition (2000). It has a much stronger commitment to theory than Matlin's text but it incorporates a similar lukewarm identification with a developmental perspective. The authors suggest that their text may be used in a chronological developmental sequence and that 'chapters 3, 6–8, 10, 11 and 13 have a developmental approach that covers the life-span'. The other chapters are seen, by the authors, to fall into the social psychological cluster or the clinical/personality cluster. In fact, the most relevant chapter from a develop-mental point of view is Chapter 2, which provides an interesting and critical account of theories concerned with women's personality development.

Recent texts by Janet Hyde (1996, 5th edn) and Michele Paludi (1998) do not claim a developmental or life span approach but it is interesting to note their treat-ment of life span issues and how they implicitly define them. Hyde includes a chapter called 'From infancy to old age: development across the life span'. In this chapter, she moves straight into a coverage of infancy and gender without any preliminary delineation of issues or approach. Different consecutive stages of the life course are described in under thirty pages, the content being basically what we think we know about what (some Western) women do at different ages. After the description of women in old age, there is a brief section titled 'In conclusion' which reads as follows:

> I have traced female development across the lifespan. Gender similarities seem to be the rule in infancy and childhood with many gender differences not emerging until adolescence. The femininity–achievement incompatibility exerts an important force on female development. Declines in girls' self-esteem in adolescence are cause for concern.

> (Hyde, 1996, p. 155)

This could be seen as a very restricted vision of the psychological development of girls and women and what we understand about it.

Paludi, on the other hand, seems to see development primarily in physical terms, including just one chapter with a developmental focus, called 'Physical development across the life cycle'. At the beginning of this chapter she talks about women's development as a process, saying, 'This process includes a variety of interacting complex factors – involving psychological, physical, cognitive and social domains – that continues (*sic*) throughout the life span'(1998, p. 122). Paludi then claims that she will cover 'cognitive development', 'socialization agents contributing to girls' and women's development across the life span' and 'developmental discontinuities and continuities across the life span' (ibid.). In fact, she does not address any of these topics in any recognizable form. The nod in the direction of developmental psychology remains just that, a nod, and a rather baffling one at that.

Of course, there is no reason why textbooks should adopt an explicitly developmental approach to the psychology of women. A broad approach, incorporating social, cognitive, clinical and other perspectives, makes sense since most textbooks aim to be comprehensive. What I am concerned to identify is the impoverished and confused approach adopted to the coverage of developmental issues by authors who, at the same time, claim that a developmental perspective is useful or central to their project.

Turning, then, to the other side of this relationship: the absence of a gendered perspective in life span psychology is striking, if one accepts the view that 'gender is deeply implicated in any account of developmental psychology and any claims the discipline might make to be neutral in this regard can only be fraudulent' (Morss, 1990, p. 219).

Despite the trenchant critiques of psychology's gender blindness and gender bias, current life span psychology texts still seem to display elements of both. For example, in an analysis published in 1992 of the treatment of gender issues in textbooks on life span human development and on introductory psychology, Sharyl Peterson and Traci Kroner reported fewer descriptions of women psychologists' work in comparison to the work of male psychologists. This finding needs to be seen in the context of the American Psychological Association's statistics, which show that in the field as a whole women outnumber men (Ostertag and MacNamara, 1991). Only one of the texts which Peterson and Kroner reviewed mentioned sex or gender as a general concern when carrying out research, and more texts failed to mention the sex of subjects than reported it. Regardless of the sex of subjects, findings were generalized to all people more often than they were limited to people of the appropriate sex. The authors conclude that 'Many forms of gender bias exist in contemporary textbooks for introductory psychology and life-span human development courses' (Peterson and Kroner, 1992, p. 290) and that 'females tend to be portrayed in negative and gender-biased ways'. This conclusion emerged despite the fact that most of the authors of the developmental psychology texts that were appraised were women.

Peterson and Kroner's study was based on the content of the twelve best-selling texts in the USA at that time. Although they looked for reference to gender issues, their study was quantitative and they did not pay much attention to how theoretical issues were treated. My own perusal of a number of popular life span and adult psychology texts such as those written by Bert Hayslip and Paul Panek (1993), Kelvin Seifert, Robert Hoffnung and Michele Hoffnung (1997), and John Santrock (1999) revealed a reasonably frequent reference to gender differences and to gender roles but an almost total absence of theory in relation to gender, whether from a feminist or any other perspective.

In these texts, gender is seen typically as an unproblematic term and, where gender is mentioned at all, there is an unquestioning commitment to the description of gender differences and similarities as stable features of male and female individual psychology. Hayslip and Panek (1993), authors of *Adult Development and Aging*, typify this point of view when they say, 'Gender roles are formed or acquired early in life and maintained until death' (p. 274). Santrock summarizes gender role acquisition as follows:

> Boys and girls learn gender roles through imitation or observational learning, by watching what other people say or do. In recent years, the idea that parents are the crucial agents in gender role development has come under fire. Parents are only one of many sources through which the individual learns gender roles. Culture, schools, peers, the media and other family members are others. Yet it is important to guard against swinging too far in this direction because, especially in the early years of development, parents are the important influences on gender development.
>
> (1999, p. 248)

In this passage, there is no reference to theories of gender role acquisition which present a view different to that of social learning theory, and the picture painted is of a thoroughly unproblematic, unambiguous process, as simple as learning how to tie one's shoelaces. Santrock follows his discussion of social learning theory with descriptions of cognitive-developmental and gender schema theories of gender development. Typically, all examples relate to children and the discussion of gender role development is placed in the part of the book dealing with early childhood, reinforcing the assumption that gender is neatly fixed at an early stage and does not change. Seifert *et al.* (1997) place their discussion of gender role development in a chapter on early childhood, and later mention of gender is mostly in relation to sex differences or gender differences, as 'discovered' in empirical studies.

If one turns from the chapters on childhood to those dealing with development in adulthood one finds that most texts will pay respectful attention to the theories of Erikson, Levinson and Vaillant. As I will point out in more detail later, these theories present considerable difficulties from both a psychology of women perspective and a critical developmental perspective.

12

In developmental theory generally there is a failure to integrate gender into the discipline. Thus much of the discussion about the developing individual takes as its subject a non-sexed, non-gendered person. (I am leaving equally important issues to do with neglect of racial, class and other differences to one side.) In reality, such a creature does not exist. Many developmental theorists are gender blind; that is, they fail to mention gender as an issue. I will take as an example a theory which is contemporary and very influential: the ecological model of development associated with Urie Bronfenbrenner. Bronfenbrenner's (1979) book *The Ecology of Human Development: Experiments by Nature and Design* was emblematic of a new awakening of interest in context and culture among developmental theorists. Bronfenbrenner proposed that the developing child should be seen as immersed in a complex environment, and that it made little sense to talk about the child without reference to his or her ecology and made little sense to take the child out of his or her everyday environment to study him or her, as was the prevalent practice in psychology. He conceptualizes the environment as a set of nested systems: the microsystem, mesosystem, exosystem and macrosystem. Bronfenbrenner recognizes the importance of not just the immediate but also the wider social context in influencing the child's development. Thus, the ideologies of the culture, its mores and values are all seen to be of major importance. This should open the door to an analysis of prevalent discourses and their constitutive role in forming the child's psychic life, but this is not the language employed by Bronfenbrenner.

Bronfenbrenner's model is also wedded to a transactional view of the relationship of the child to his or her environment. The child is seen as active and as acting upon the environment, influencing it as much as being the recipient of influences. The interchange is represented as an unending process of mutually influential transactions. However, sex or gender are not seen as central features of this transactional process. The inference one may draw is that gender is seen as a fixed property of the child (most of Bronfenbrenner's work focuses on children) rather than as a social process. Nonetheless, this remains an inference since gender is not discussed by Bronfenbrenner, perhaps because his major concern was the development of a framework for thinking about development rather than dealing with specific matters of content.

In a relatively recent collection of papers, published by the American Psychological Association in 1995 to celebrate the life and work of Urie Bronfenbrenner, two papers dealt with topics related to gender. Neither mentioned any reference by Bronfenbrenner to sex or gender issues and both take gender as an unproblematic, unchanging descriptor of male and female individuals. Where there is no effort to theorize gender, what can be said about gender becomes uninteresting. It rests at the level of 'Some men did this and some women did that'. Questions of why and how are not addressed. I will argue in Chapter 2 that, while ecological theories within developmental psychology provide a more useful theoretical foundation for thinking about development than traditional organismic theories, they too have a number of limitations.

A central question, then, is whether the sex of the person should always be taken into account when one attempts to understand their psychology. Carol Gilligan and colleagues ask: 'How can sex be a difference that makes no difference for personality and development?' (1990, p. 123). On the other hand, Sandra Bem would reply that the relevance of sex to a person's psychology has traditionally been overstated, that many people in the West are socialized into thinking in ways which place sex and gender at the centre of attempts to explain and predict human behaviour. Bem argues that to a greater or lesser extent we insist upon gendering ourselves and others and that many people over-extend their gender schemas to encompass facets of life which basically have nothing whatsoever to do with sex and therefore should not be gendered. She rejects 'the gender polarizing conception of the natural link between the sex of the body and the gender of the psyche' (Bem, 1993, p. 209). Bem's point of view is highly aspirational. What she is saying is that gender *should not* be a feature of so many aspects of human psychology. The reality however is that, in Western society as we find it at the beginning of the twenty-first century, it is. There is also, of course, an ongoing debate as to the advantages or disadvantages for women of working with the gender polarity rather than trying to dismantle it.

Another issue that must be addressed is the extent to which developmental theories, while failing to explicitly address the sex of the human beings who are the focus of these theories, are in fact promoting a gendered – male – version of what psychological development is or should be about. This point has been made very clearly by Erica Burman:

> Psychology has trouble recognizing that the implicit gender informing its models is the Western world's culturally normative masculine subject. In developmental psychology this norm is given new life in the trajectories it traces: development is structured to mark a move from the culturally feminized qualities of attachment, relationship, concrete connectedness and cultural dependency to autonomy, detachment and dispersion. The gendering of the term 'mastery' that characterizes developmental accounts of progress is apt.
>
> (Burman, 1997, p. 143)

It is important to be alert to the way in which stereotypically masculine values and goals, which exclude women's experiences and perspectives and serve the political ends of patriarchal social systems, have been enshrined in developmental theory. The androcentrism of developmental psychology is not surprising when seen within the context of the gender bias which has permeated the discipline as a whole. As Wine argued in 1985, psychology has adopted models of the subject which highlight individualism, rationalism, goal pursuit and egocentrism. By contrast, the opposite qualities of dependency, irrationality, passivity and selflessness are either pathologized or demeaned. They are also more likely to be associated with femaleness or the feminine. As Simone de Beauvoir asserted as long ago as 1949, women are seen as 'the Other', and 'defined with reference to man and not he with reference to her' (1997, p. 16). 'The Other' is by definition opposite, lesser, incidental. Androcentrism reflects a long tradition in Western thought on the subject matter of women and the feminine. The possible responses to the androcentrism of traditional developmental theories are various and will be discussed later in this book.

It is also the case that even the critics of the gender bias that exists in mainstream developmental psychology often exhibit very localized conceptions of masculinity and femininity. For example, the 'relational self' is a popular focus of study and discussion among social psychologists and feminist psychologists alike (Curtis, 1991; Jordan *et al.*, 1991). The orientation towards others exhibited in the relational self is commonly described as feminine. In other cultures, such as India and Japan, the concept of self and enactment of self is far more relational than that in Western cultures and interdependency and reciprocity are typical of the self systems of both men and women (Roland, 1991).

A recent edited collection of papers entitled *Toward a Feminist Developmental Psychology* has addressed the failure to integrate developmental psychology and feminist scholarship. In relation to the impact of feminist scholarship, the editors, Patricia Miller and Ellen Scholnik, note that 'developmental psychology has remained almost untouched by this influential intellectual movement' (Miller and Scholnik, 2000). In their introductory chapter, the editors state that their goal is 'to inspire developmental psychologists to read feminist literature and feminist scholars to read developmental literature, for we see much of value in each perspective for the other'. This is a sentiment that I would strongly echo, and Miller and Scholnik's book provides interesting examples of the potential for cross-fertilization between the two disciplines. It includes developmental psychologists viewing their subject matter through a feminist lens and feminist psychologists examining developmental issues. The book's main emphasis is on the application of feminist theory and scholarship to developmental psychology and it pays less attention to how feminist theory might be made more developmental. The latter goal is central to this book. My main emphasis is on how our understanding of women's psychology may be informed by the adoption of a developmental perspective and on the need to rework developmental theory to be adequate to the task of enhancing our understanding of the psychology of girls and women.

I have chosen to place an emphasis on time as a conceptual linchpin for understanding development. Time is central to both our being and our becoming. As Heidegger stated, time is 'the horizon for all understanding of Being and for any way of interpreting it' (1962, p. 39). Time is central to our scholarly understanding of development, but it is also central to the individual's understanding of her daily life and her location in the life course. In attempting to address the temporality of our existence, its continuous and inevitable movement towards an incompletely predictable future, an immediate question mark is placed over theories which confine their approach to time and change to the analysis of what is past and the quest for historical cause or causes. As Elizabeth Grosz asserts, 'Determinism is the annulling of any concept of temporality other than the one structured by the terms and conditions of the past and present' (1999, p. 4). The intrinsic determinism and rigidities of traditional developmental psychology have not served anyone well but have done a particular disservice to women.

2

DEVELOPMENTAL PSYCHOLOGY

Some promising perspectives

The history of developmental psychology as a discipline is complex and has been written in a number of different forms ranging from the congratulatory to the critical (Bradley, 1989; Parke *et al.*, 1994; Greene, 1997a). As is the case for psychology in general, mainstream developmental psychology in the early years of the twentieth century adopted a positivist, natural science epistemology. As the century progressed, theories emerged which competed with each other, but these theories shared common ontological and epistemological assumptions: the quarrels were not, to quote Teo (1997), at the level of meta-theory, and the underlying commitment to the assumptions and methods of the natural sciences was rarely challenged. The dependence on positivist ideology and methodology was very widespread.

The questioning of these cherished assumptions in recent years has not arisen from one source but from numerous sources. Much of the current challenge to developmental psychology has its origins in movements outside the discipline whose influence has gradually percolated through to the centre. A new self-critical tone and form of discourse is very apparent in the writings of some of the major and most influential researchers working at the heart of the discipline. Examples which come to mind are Bruner (1990) and Bronfenbrenner (1979), as well as critics like Morss (1990, 1996) and Burman (1992) who adopt an explicitly anti-developmentalist standpoint. In the latest *Handbook of Child Psychology*, the Editor-in-Chief, William Damon (1998), makes reference to recent perturbations in child psychology's relationship to the concept of development. He says,

> Another pattern that emerges [in the Handbook] is a self-conscious reflection about the notion of development. . . . We have just passed through a time when the very credibility of a developmental approach was itself thrown into question.

This 'crisis of faith' as Damon calls it – an interesting term for a devotee of the scientific method to use – has supposedly passed. Damon continues,

> Fortunately, as the contents of this Handbook attest, such doubts are

waning. . . . After all, the story of growth during infancy, childhood and adolescence is a developmental story of multi-faceted learning, of acquisitions of skills and knowledge, of waxing powers of attention and memory, of transformations of character and personality, of increases of understanding of self and others, of advances in emotional and behavioral regulation, of progress in communicating and collaborating with others and a host of other achievements that are chronicled in this Handbook.

(Damon, 1998, p. xvii)

Damon shows at least an awareness of the kinds of questions which have been raised about development as the foundational metaphor of his discipline, but many other developmental psychologists, perhaps the majority, seem to be caught in an epistemological time-warp, never questioning for a moment the particular kind of developmentalist assumptions which direct their thinking.

It is difficult to share the totally sanguine view represented by Damon. A very basic question which persists is the extent to which the whole notion of development and thus, perhaps, the use of the word 'development', provides an inappropriate metaphor for describing human psychological change across the life course and the person's relationship with time, age and ageing. It is useful to remind oneself of the etymology of the word 'development'. The *Shorter Oxford Dictionary* gives the primary definition of develop as 'To unfold, unroll, to unfurl'. Development is defined as 'A gradual unfolding, a fuller working out of the details of anything'. As applied to psychological development the notion of unfolding or realization of latent or inherent potential has been fundamental to the usage of this word and to the thinking of developmental psychologists. The idea of development was a powerful concept at the end of the nineteenth century and was a core principle in the biological sciences, but also in social sciences such as history and economics. Morss (1990) makes a strong case that developmental psychology is permeated with biological thinking, largely expressed in the adherence to the development metaphor.

From this point of view, *developmentalism* may be defined as a commitment to the view that psychological change is to a large degree biologically determined, natural, universal, predictable and in the process of moving towards a final definable end-point. This is not the understanding of development which I wish to promote in this book. I will argue for a view of development as constrained rather than determined, emergent not given, historically and culturally contingent not universal, more constructed than natural (in the traditional sense in which natural has been used). However, I will use the term *development*, since it maps on to the subject matter of this book, if not the assumptions traditionally associated with its use. Psychological development will thus be defined very broadly as qualitative and quantitative psychological change associated with age, ageing and the passage of time. Nonetheless, it is clear that anti-developmentalism arguments represent a timely and important dismantling and deconstruction of some of the many unexamined, flawed and sometimes pernicious assumptions of developmental psychology as practised to date.

Accordingly, it is important to recognize the need to theorize life span psychological change and also to be open to the view that change may at times be directional and linked to innate capacities and maturation, particularly in childhood. Thus, for example, it would be difficult to resist a traditional developmental orientation to explaining the core features of children's acquisition of language, a capacity which is dependent on the maturational level of the child, moves from a rudimentary to a sophisticated form and is in many aspects universal in our species. At the same time the meaning systems and uses of language may be less usefully explained by theories which are geared to find universal and natural principles underpinning their changing manifestation with age. In any particular culture, age may be the organizing principle which triggers certain practices, expectations and opportunities for children which produce the kinds of changes and advances which we choose to construe as the result of *development*. From this point of view, the insights offered by the 'new sociology of childhood' with its emphasis on the social structuring of childhood are a welcome counterbalance to the traditional developmental psychology perspective (James and Prout, 1997).

A further major challenge to traditional psychological theories of development has come from movements which have drawn attention to the white, male, middle-class, Western assumptions and values enshrined at the heart of the discipline. Among those external movements which have had an impact on some developmental theorists and practitioners are feminism and feminist theory. The second-wave feminist movement of the late 1960s and early 1970s arose after or in tandem with a number of other civil rights movements involving people who belonged to a marginalized and disempowered class, religion or race. These eruptions, of varying degrees of ferocity, occurred in both the USA and Europe. Those involved demanded an end to exclusion from the resources, privileges and centres of power in society and from the formal academic and scientific systems of knowledge. Within the academy, the first demand was for the voices of these silenced people to be heard and represented. For such a demand to be met required recognition of the invalidity of the traditional claims for universally applicable truths about the nature and experience of man, now revealed to be a white, middle-aged, middle-class, Western man. From this point of view, feminism was allied to a critical approach, which Teo has classed as the multiple voices discourse (Teo, 1997).

The core principles of developmental psychology have been challenged, therefore, by the emergence of the multiple voices discourse and also by other critical schools, some of which have also shaped the making of a variety of identifiably distinct voices within feminist psychology. Aside from the multiple voices critique, Teo identifies the German critical-theoretical tradition of Habermas and Holzkamp and the postmodern critiques of French theorists such as Derrida and Foucault.

In his critical accounts of developmental psychology, Morss (1990, 1996) covers somewhat similar territory to Teo. He discusses the critiques of developmental psychology inherent in or explicitly mounted by alternative movements such as social ecology developmentalism and social constructionism. A historian of ideas would probably readily concede a level of cross-fertilization between the different strands so that what we are dealing with at this point is a tangled skein. It is therefore difficult very often to identify the intellectual provenance of a particular critique.

Rather than providing a systematic history of recent developments in critical developmental psychology and in critical epistemologies, which may have relevance to developmental psychology – this task has been accomplished elsewhere by people such as Bradley, Morss and Teo – I will attempt to outline some of the tensions within developmental psychology, which have surfaced as a result of dissatisfaction with simplistic unidimensional models of development and of the new mood of criticism and deconstruction. I will pose these tensions as polarities, one pole representing the position of traditional developmental psychology and the other the recently emerged, or recently rediscovered, counter-motion. In each section I will mention some of the critical theoretical influences which have particular relevance.

Prescription vs. deconstruction

One of the primary concerns of child development this century has been the delineation of 'normal development'. The testing movement, for example, was built around statistical notions such as the intelligence quotient, which permitted a judgement as to whether the child was above or below average and compared the individual child's score with established norms. Aside from the psychometric movement in which children's intelligence and personality characteristics were measured and compared to the norms for children of their age, there was a strong interest in the comparison of children's rate of development with that of the 'average child'. Arnold Gesell would be one of the most influential of those psychologists committed to charting the course of normal development from birth to adolescence. Gesell's work (e.g. Gesell and Ilg, 1946) involved mapping the developmental milestones of children in order to establish what was average or typical. Gesell was very explicitly concerned with norms, but in fact a great deal of child psychology shares the same concern in a more hidden form. Thus much of developmental psychology and its clinical offshoots has been concerned with defining the conditions associated with optimal development, whether that development is related to the achievement of heterosexuality, concrete operational intelligence or secure attachment.

Part of the antagonism expressed by feminists towards developmental psychology resides in its *normalizing* intentions directed at children, and also very often at mothers who have been made responsible for the proper growth and development of their children. Valerie Walkerdine has written extensively on the pernicious consequences of normalization for those children – indeed the major-ity of children – who do not fit the norms, and Cathy Urwin has written about the normalization of motherhood (Walkerdine, 1984, 1993; Urwin, 1985). Both writers would see the normalization process, as originally delineated by Foucault, as coercive, in that it dictates standards which influence and intimidate parents and children. In many ways this process is subtle and hard to pinpoint, for it is the case that people come to 'willingly' accept and promote these values as their own.

Theories and models within developmental psychology, which their authors may naively propose as simply descriptive of reality, quickly take on the charac-ter of prescriptions rather than descriptions. For example, Erik Erikson's Eight Ages of Man may have the appearance of describing 'the' life course but in fact lays down what ought to occur as the individual journeys through the life course, and this is undoubtedly the sense in which his work has been understood and employed. The stages are presented as non-negotiable and the final goal, ego integrity, as a highly desirable fulfilment of a person's psychological life. Not proceeding through the stages to the final point and veering to the negative pole in the eight crises is seen as failure. Erikson may be seen as a prototypical exam-ple of what Levenson and Crumpler have termed the ontogenetic perspective within developmental psychology, which promotes a view of development as 'driven by and constrained by age-linked intrinsic imperatives' (Levenson and Crumpler, 1996). As Jerome Bruner notes, 'these are developmental psychologies which assume that there is one way up, one kind of human nature that will express itself but for the fact that there are interfering injustices, degra-dations or differential opportunities that prevent its coming up' (1986a, p. 104).

Levenson and Crumpler (1996) are among those who use the term 'ontogentic' to describe those theories which emphasize internal origins and determinants of change (see also Dannefer, 1984; Featherman and Lerner, 1985). It is perhaps not the most useful term to cover this theoretical perspective, since ontogenetic, in its more familiar genetic context, refers to the genesis (origin and development) of the individual and does not necessarily carry the baggage of fixed assumptions about the nature of the origins or the nature of development. *Organismic* is a more apt term which has also been used to describe this theoretical perspective, for example, by Lewis (1997). It is developmental theories of this (organismic) type which are prescriptive and which carry implicit but oppressive value pre-suppositions. The values operate oppressively partly because they are neither open to inspection nor easily challenged and partly because they are the adopted frameworks of the professional and powerful in our society.

Developmental psychology has failed to recognize the extent to which value-laden assumptions have shaped its selection of behaviour worthy of its attention and coloured its definition of what is *normal*. Behaviour, which is seen as reflective of *natural* and appropriate development, is very often simply that which is normal in the sense of corresponding to the current norms and mores of a particular society. This is not to say that developmental theory should be

21

value-free; far from it. It should be recognized that, as Jerome Bruner (1986b, p. 20) says, 'developmental theory is impossible without a base of valuational axioms'. He argues that human development should be seen as a 'policy science, a science whose intrinsic object is not simply to describe but to prescribe alternative optimal ways of achieving certain outcomes' and, he continues, 'this deep truth is frequently disguised (and well disguised at that) by choosing the growth patterns of particular children or children in particular milieux and holding those patterns up as normal or, worse, as "natural" with the heavy implication that other patterns of growth are in some manner deviant' (1986b, pp. 21–22).

I have accused ontogenetic/organismic models of being prescriptive but their kind of prescriptiveness is very different from the kind of prescriptiveness acknowledged by Bruner to be at the very heart of any application of developmental psychology. Erikson and other like-minded theorists assume that what they are describing is natural and good. Those who question such theories know that they are describing what is constructed and that as far as values are concerned what is seen to be good must be negotiated – not asserted from hegemonic positions of authority. Clearly, then, there is no one definitive policy but a highly diversified engagement with policy-making. Our notions, of what is desirable and what is undesirable for persons in our society, inevitably influence our theorizing and our practice. What we are obliged to do, once our awareness of the dangers of unexamined ideological and ontological assumptions has been raised, is to make our assumptions and our policies clear – in the way that ontogenetic theories about universal pathways and end-points do not. This process entails a recognition that our values may be very different from those held by others.

Numerous examples may be given of psychology's prescriptiveness in relation to female psychology and the development of female personality, and some of this work will be reviewed in Chapter 3. Recognition of the extent of developmental psychology's prescriptiveness has, then, been an achievement of those critical theorists who are concerned to examine the way in which developmental psychology's findings are employed in processes of social regulation, whether that regulation is of mothering, schooling or therapy or any other practice. The deconstructive stance and the deconstructive process reveal and examine the assumptions built into the discourses of developmental psychology.

Progression towards an idealistic end-point vs. multiple pathways and multiple goals

Morss has argued that 'the assumption of progress in individual development is probably the most fundamental of the presuppositions of developmental psychology' (1990, p. 175). This is undoubtedly true of most developmental theorizing and has deep historical roots. Developmental psychology as a discipline saw its beginnings at the end of the nineteenth century, a time when the glorious vision of progress was still strongly embedded in the thinking of most intellectuals (Kessen, 1986; Morss, 1996). In his monograph, *The Rise and Fall of*

Development, William Kessen examines the manner in which the concepts of evolution and progress have become central to our thinking about human development. He quotes a noted supporter of Darwin, John William Draper, who stated in 1860: 'man is the archetype of society and individual development the model of social progress and both . . . are under the control of immutable law' (p. 2). Kessen claims that the notion of 'humanity as a steadily ascending progressive species' was widely accepted among intellectuals at the end of the nineteenth century and thus not surprisingly a foundational principle for many of the influential leaders in the fledgling discipline of psychology. Not only were they committed to a view of mankind as an evolving species but also to the pre-Darwinian view that ontogeny recapitulates phylogeny and that each individual life course replays the progressive development of the species. There were some dissenting voices. Kessen quotes William James and John Dewey, who were both uncomfortable with this type of thinking, but mainstream developmental psychology remained firmly wedded to an equation of individual development and progression.

A related issue to that of progression is the assumption about what progression is aiming towards. Clearly the end-point must be superior in some way to the starting point. Developmental theories have varied in their choice of the final end-point. As Piaget noted, this choice is crucial, since 'A developmental theory does not so much rest upon its initial stage as hang from its higher one' (Piaget, cited by Alexander and Langer, 1990). For Piaget this end-point was formal operational intelligence, for Erikson (1950), ego-integrity, for Kohlberg (1976), post-conventional morality. In general, there is an assumption that children are moving towards adulthood and maturity, that they are unfinished and incompetent. This vision of childhood has become so commonplace that it serves as the bedrock for most of our thinking on children and their place in the world. Children are frequently denied rights that are accorded to adults (for example, the right not to be hit), and are spoken about as society's 'investment in the future' rather than being valued for who they are and for what they do now. A positive side to this perspective on childhood is the view that children are in need of protection by adults and the state. But it should be possible to protect children without devaluing them.

Alexander and Langer (1990) also assert the importance of end-points when they say, 'One's conception about the endpoint of development is crucial for it contains one's assumptions about the direction, possibilities and dynamics of human growth' (p. 3). One can accept that – in a theory which sets out to describe a single developmental pathway – the culmination of the path is of defining importance but the question in relation to human life span psychology is whether or not there is one pathway and therefore one end-point for all.

Gisela Labouvie-Vief and Michael Chandler are among those who have argued that developmental psychology's obsession with what they label the 'idealistic end state' is misplaced. Their alternative to the 'youth-centred, unilinear, organismic models of development', which they see as prevalent within developmental psychology and which have dubious relevance to the lives of children let alone adults, is a contextual model which emphasizes plurality and multilinearity. In a paper on this theme they state that 'as the contextualist argues for multiformity of developmental adaptation, no one teleological stage is seen as capping off the process of development' (1978, p. 202).

Such resistance within developmental psychology to 'idealistic thinking' is growing. Levenson and Crumpler label models of development which do not see development as unilinear and progressive as sociogenic theories since, they claim, the emphasis of *sociogenic* theories is all on social determinants which by their nature are various and lead the person into multiple pathways and multiple end-points. This may well be so, but underpinning Levenson and Crumpler's ontogenetic/sociogenic distinction is an unhelpful promotion of the view that biological or organismic variables entail a predictable developmental path for all healthy humans. Genetic and biological differences between individuals also serve to promote diversity in individual characteristics and developmental pathways, and, equally, the social demands of a particular culture may act to enforce uniformity of developmental pathways rather than diversity. More adequate non-deterministic approaches to conceptualizing the relationship of biology to developmental change will be discussed later. For the moment, it is important to appreciate that Western theories of development themselves and the promotion of the concept of development are discourses which may be used to exert pressure towards conformity.

In relation to women, the androcentric nature of many of the desirable paths and goals as laid down by ontogenetic theorists is unmistakable. This fact is not surprising given the now well-exposed sexism behind much psychological theorizing, but the fact that many of these developmental theories may be inapplicable to women or restrict their potential also serves to illustrate the parochial and patriarchal thinking behind these supposedly universal accounts.

Having said this, the issue of goals and their importance to human psychology cannot be brushed aside. Humans are often future-oriented in their thinking. Planning and setting goals are very much a feature of the way people organize their lives and establish meaning for themselves. Women's goals, whether they be short or longer term goals (what one might call *life-goals*), are highly relevant to a full understanding of each woman's psychology. And it is also the case that, where a society sets goals for the women in that society, women may well internalize those goals as their own. It is interesting to consider the role psychology has played in institutionalizing goals for women, such as the goal of being a mother and then of being a good mother or even a 'good enough' mother.

The isolable organism vs. the person in context

In recent years, critics have accused developmental psychology of presenting a view of the child or adult as decontextualized, existing in an environment-free and culture-free vacuum. One of the best known of these critiques came from

William Kessen (1979) who coined the phrase 'the isolable child' to describe the manner in which child psychology has conceptualized children. This reductive, decontextualizing approach to the subject matter of the discipline may be seen as yet another consequence of the positivist orientation which psychology borrowed from the natural sciences.

From this perspective, the child has much the same status as a chemical compound. It is assumed that its properties may be described without reference to its environment. In fact, in many ways the environment has been treated as though it were a collection of confounds getting in the way of our true picture of the child itself. Prediction and control are held up as highly desirable aims. Prediction and control will follow from an understanding of the causes of behaviour. It is assumed that the only way to establish the causes of behaviour is through carefully controlled experiments in controlled environments and that the findings from these experiments can be generalized back to real life.

Within developmental psychology, Urie Bronfenbrenner has provided one of the most effective critiques of psychology's practice of isolating humans from their context both at the level of theory and at the level of research. In his 1979 book, he famously accused developmental psychology of being 'the science of the strange behaviour of children in strange situations with strange adults for the briefest possible periods of time' (p. 19). Around this time there was a detectable change in the writings and research of many developmental psychologists as reference to ecological validity and to context became more and more frequent. One of the major theorists whose work has been central to this shift was Lev Vygotsky (e.g. 1978). One might see the popularity of his work as arising from a widespread discomfort with the decontextualized nature of mainstream developmental psychology. The demand from the various human rights movements to take seriously issues of class, race, culture and gender also required a response – it was becoming harder and harder to ignore culture as a defining and integral aspect of children's development.

As John Morss (1996) points out, there are various ways of taking social context into account, some superficial, some thoroughgoing. Theories range from those which take account of the child with little more than a tangential glance at factors of influence in the child's environment, to radical social constructionism, to the Marxist critical psychology of development and developmentalism favoured by Morss himself. Despite theoretical differences, such perspectives have collectively delivered a significant blow to the decontextualized study of the person. 'The isolable organism' so present in the bulk of mainstream developmental theorizing in the twentieth century has been exposed as a sterile and vacuous construct.

One interpretation of the role of context in development is that development is *in* the context; specifically it is defined in those social discourses which are about age, life stages and the differences between the generations in terms of needs, capacities and responsibilities. For example, in Western society we do not expect five-year-olds to have the understanding and sense of responsibility which would enable them to act as caretakers of their infant siblings. So we do not give them the knowledge or the opportunity to learn how to look after babies. In parts of the East and Africa, five-year-old childminders are commonplace and ideas about children's psychological development are correspondingly different to ours (Valsiner, 2000). From this perspective one might say that the child is developed by the context rather than development being intrinsic to the child.

Facts and laws vs. understanding

A central tenet for positivist psychology is that that reality is out there waiting to be revealed and analysed. Much energy has been devoted to the achievement of objectivity and the elimination of the biases and personality of the scientist from scientific procedures. Methods are carefully implemented with the goal of avoiding the intrusion of subjectivity and thus bias. Such bias, it is argued, distorts and colours the true picture. Rorty (1979) labels this view of science 'the mirror of nature', the view that science can capture a veridical image of nature and its workings, uncontaminated by human biases.

Mainstream developmental psychology, like other branches of psychology, has privileged methods, essentially the experiment, which can, it is argued, establish causal relationships and inform us about the laws which govern behaviour. Thus, in the methods adopted in twentieth-century developmental psychology, one has seen the working out of the positivist conviction that there is a reality which is there to be captured and represented in observation and by measurement. The behaviour of the developing person is determined and can be predicted and controlled, if only one knows enough about the determinants and their influence.

In recent years, the core methods employed in developmental psychology, based – sometimes loosely – on the paradigm of the scientific experiment and concerned with establishing facts and laws, have been both challenged and expanded. As in other areas of psychology, where dissatisfaction with the limits of quantification has been articulated, qualitative methods of enquiry have become more popular. For some researchers such methods are seen as an adjunct to traditional quantitative approaches, geared to answer different kinds of questions or to map out a domain before the real business of experimentation or quantitative research can begin. For others the use of qualitative methods represents a shift in epistemological commitment from the goal of accurate measurement of or controlled experimentation with the phenomena of interest to a hermeneutic, interpretive stance towards knowledge and an acceptance that one's interpretation is inevitably shaped by one's standpoint. This shift may be characterized as the elevation of the quest for understanding over the search for 'facts'.

Jerome Bruner is one of the developmental psychologists who has advocated a turn to a hermeneutic orientation and method. In *Acts of Meaning* written in 1990 he says, 'the methodology of causation can neither capture the social richness of lives in a culture nor begin to plumb their historical depth. It is only through the application of interpretation that we, as psychologists, can do justice to the world of culture' (p. 137). In his own work, he has made use of narratives as a method of accessing people's personal stories about their lives, and importantly, from a developmental point of view, their construction through story of their selves.

Although the hermeneutic tradition in philosophy and psychology has a long history, it has had relatively little impact on English-speaking psychologists until taken up by writers such as Bruner in the last decade or so. The number of writers who adopt a hermeneutic standpoint appears to be increasing and the perspective holds promise as a counterbalance both to the extremes of scientism and the extremes of postmodernism. This point of view is strongly articulated by Jack Martin and Jeff Sugarman in their book *The Psychology of Human Possibility and Constraint*, which was published in 1999 and in a later (2001) paper. For Martin and Sugarman scientism entails the overvaluing of natural science, particularly as the best route to psychological knowledge and understanding. 'Progress in psychology will not be achieved if the very nature of the subject matter of psychology is overlooked, misconstrued or ignored' (1999, p. 47). They view psychological phenomena as emergent, dynamic and situated in a changing socio-cultural context. Such phenomena are essentially not amenable to objectification. The hermeneutic method of Hans Gadamer is, from this perspective, best suited to advancing understanding of psychological phenomena.

Gadamer's approach has been criticized as being intrinsically conservative, in that it relies upon existing traditions of interpretation. However, it would appear possible that ideologically and politically creative solutions could emerge from the conversations which occur on the borders of contrasting interpretative traditions, where horizons fuse or conflict.

Value-free science vs. value-laden enquiry

The traditional claim of the natural sciences is that they are value-free. This is a position which has been critiqued as untenable, and is particularly so when we are dealing with the human or social sciences. As Ben Bradley states, 'we can no longer operate as developmental psychologists without a discussion about values' (1993, p. 408).

In fact throughout all of the years when psychologists most loudly trumpeted their impartiality and freedom from ideology they were, to be sure, deeply enmeshed in political and ideological assumptions about the good life and the good person. Psychology was employed frequently and uncritically as a discipline of social control, in schools, in mental hospitals, in prisons and even, most insidiously, in the home.

Those who have attempted to identify the actual value-base of mainstream Western psychology would describe it as conservative, patriarchal, and promoting a version of the person as individualistic and autonomous – the mobile, unrooted worker with his portable nuclear family ideally suited to the requirements of capitalist economies. Rather than pretend to a value-free engagement with scientific practice many modern theorists would argue for the inspection and interrogation of one's essentially and inevitably value-laden standpoint. Thus, as mentioned earlier, in developmental psychology, Bruner asserts that developmental psychology is and always has been a policy science. It is a discipline which has been intimately connected with practice and with setting standards in relation to what is desirable and undesirable about the behaviour and development of people – children in particular (Bruner, 1986b).

From a critical psychological perspective, Burman agrees with the view that developmental psychology is 'shot through with cultural-political assumptions' (1997, p. 136). In her own work she has attempted to uncover some of these assumptions and their oppressive consequences. For example, she has reviewed the implications of developmental psychology's preoccupation with the mother–child bond and its advocacy of perennially attentive, 'sensitive' mothering (Burman, 1994). Developmental psychology, it may be argued, has bolstered policies which serve to keep women in the home, to undermine state commitment to the provision of childcare, to keep men at a distance from their children and to burden mothers with guilt.

Fixed vs. open-ended

The developmental perspective is one which should be inherently dynamic; that is, capable of addressing the fact that human lives are always in process and yet capable of addressing the relative stability that can co-exist with the basic condition of flux. Human psychological development is to an extent open-ended. Attempting to understand the forces involved in maintaining constancy and examining the extent of constancy versus the extent of change are key concerns. Describing the nature of psychological change across the life course has caused developmentalists to resort with varying degrees of success to a number of different models which attempt to capture the essence of development. One of the most important and central dimensions on which these models differ is that of open-endedness-fixedness. Many early developmental theories were pre-formationist, implying that development is the unfolding of a relatively fixed potential and pattern. Pre-formation could be either biological or social. Thus Freud's developmental theory suggests that the basic parameters of an individual's personality are determined by the time the child has progressed up to the Oedipal stage. G. Stanley Hall (1904, 1922) saw development as the recapitulation of the development of the race and thus fixed in pattern and in nature. To early developmentalists plasticity and open-endedness were not features of development. The major concern was the identification of the common course and the promotion of the *natural* or most adaptive pathway.

Because of the conviction that development was predetermined, whether by the genes or by early experience, many psychologists invested a great deal of energy in charting the constancies of development and in establishing predictability. As writers such as Clarke and Clarke pointed out in relation to the role of early experience, 'the belief in the special, disproportionate, long term effects of early experience is deeply embedded in a very common view of development' (2000, p. 10). Such a view, they go on to say, 'obscures the rich interplay throughout life of personal and social influences and can have unfortunate implications'. The unfortunate implications include assumptions about the inevitably disabling effects of early deprivations and trauma, and the pointlessness of later intervention. In relation to biological determinism, belief in, for example, genetically determined lower intelligence in black people led to a perpetuation of poor educational provision and denial of opportunities (Gould, 1996). Developmental models premised either on the unfolding of (genetically) fixed potential or the carry-forward of the consequences of early experiences have been the subject of strong criticism. The biologist Stephen Jay Gould points out that it is a serious misinterpretation of human genetics to think that our genes dictate our development and behaviour. On the other hand, he asserts that 'Biology is not the enemy of human flexibility but the source and potentiator' (1996, p. 390). Alan Clarke and Ann Clarke have, for forty years, been promoting the view that Western philosophy and folk psychology are wedded to a predeterministic model of development which is both not supported by the evidence and in some crucial ways a self-fulfilling prophecy. They have accumulated contrary evidence and have presented an alternative view of development as incorporating 'a degree of unpredictability for the individual, a principle of developmental uncertainty' (Clarke and Clarke, 1976, p. 48).

A key criterion when evaluating any conceptualization of development should be its effectiveness in capturing the dynamic, constrained, but to a degree remarkably open-ended nature of psychological change across the life course. The model of the person promoted by traditional developmental psychology is not one which presents the person as process nor does it emphasize the possibility of radical transformation, that the person could potentially be very different from what they are if located in a different time or place and culture. Furthermore, the preoccupation with determinism does not permit a view of the person as agent, capable, through reappraisals and revisions of her own thoughts, feelings and behaviour patterns, of initiating personal change. There is still an obsession with fixing the individual in terms of traits, genes and capacities. From this point of view a developmental perspective which emphasizes the radical potential for change is necessary and informative. It can speak to the possibilities for transformation in any human life story.

A recent position, which has emerged in the literature perhaps as a reaction to prevalent notions of a fixed pattern to development, is an ahistorical view of the psychology of the life span. From this perspective history is an irrelevance. The person is seen as capable of reconstructing their own history, and shaping their current and future attitudes and responses in the light of that reconstruction. Michael Lewis (1992, 1997) expresses the extreme or strong form of the development as current construction argument. He states:

As a developmental psychologist I have at least until recently accepted the traditional view of the developmental process – that events in the past dictate in some way events in the future. Development is a unidirectionally bounded process . . . movement is from an earlier to a later point in time. More importantly, development is a causally related chain of events; therefore it should have a claim on predictive necessity. This view is taken as a sine qua non of what is meant by development. Recently an alternative view has begun to take shape, one that does not treat development as a unidirectionally bounded process. This view transforms history from past events acting in the present into the present reconstructing the past. With events formed this way we have the capacity to alter the past in the light of the present. History, as a construction, allows for the possibility that our actual histories have relatively little bearing on development. Rather current behavior is influenced by what we think our histories were.

(Lewis, 1992, p. 46)

The view that our current behaviour is influenced not by our actual history but by what 'we think our histories were' begs a lot of questions. Where does one accumulate the attitudes and beliefs that go to make up our current approach to the occurrences of daily life and the qualities associated with the person's sense of self? Undoubtedly, as narrative psychologists have persuaded us, we do play a role in storying our own lives. In fact an awareness of the extent to which we can – in the present – reconstruct our own histories is one of the important legacies of Freud. However, is the idea of personal history, as a major determinant of current and future psychological functioning, bunk? Some of the postmodern theorists like Gergen also seem to adopt this attitude towards development. Gergen says that 'the very idea of development is story' and in some of his writing seems to advocate the view of the person as unfettered by history, free to be whatever she wants to be, engaged in a playful construction and reconstruction of self (Gergen, 1991).

While arguing for the capacity of the individual to be an agent in her own life, the extreme position adopted by Lewis and Gergen is not convincing. People do not exist in historical and social vacuums; their lives and experiences are situated. Although the reflexive capacity of the self to reinterpret its past has often been underestimated, any interpretation conducted by the self has to make sense in terms of the history of the person as understood by both that person and the key people in their lives. We are not slaves of our past but we are expected and therefore come to expect that we will keep faith with it. We are also constrained by our contemporary context.

It is certainly time to rethink in a fundamental way the extent to which we are in the present the product of our past. And certainly part of our imprisonment in the past is due to our being in thrall to theories of the person which are built on historical explanations of who we are. By resisting such views one is not entirely resisting the adoption of a developmental orientation, for I would argue that, in the broadest meaning of the word, any theory, which deals with the sources of psychological change, our relationship to time and age and the way we engage in the construction of our life stories, may be labelled *developmental*. It is important also to keep an open mind about the extent to which our pasts may influence who we are in ways that cannot be altered by rethinking our histories.

There has been a long tradition in psychology of argument between those who see human behaviour as largely determined by current contingencies and those who argue for the central role of inbuilt traits. In the debate between social constructionists and developmentalists one sees perhaps a new version of this old debate. Michael Lewis (1997) argues that we are motivated by our need for predictability and continuity to cling to a deterministic theory about development and the construction of self. Thus developmental theories may be seen as the working out of our desire for explanations that do not threaten our personal sense of identity and meaning. He says: 'We need to preserve our identity and our narratives serve that need' (p. 65). In reality, he argues, our need to adapt to current demands is paramount and the causal force of past events insignificant except insofar as they serve as material for our current story about ourselves. For Lewis, context is crucial but so also is the active role of the person in constructing and interpreting their story of who they are. The title of Lewis's (1997) book is *Altering Fate: Why the Past does not Predict the Future*. He claims that his ahistorical view of the person liberates us to alter our fate – by retelling and revisioning our current and future selves. Whether, Lewis and other like-minded theorists are overstating the dominance of the here and now and the irrelevance of past events is a question that remains to be explored. There is a danger inherent in such a perspective that the lasting effects of earlier experiences could be disregarded. Michael Rutter (1989), for example, is one theorist who has attempted to work through just how early experiences may affect later functioning by setting people on negative or positive pathways. In Rutter's use of terms such as *pathways* and *chain effects* a degree of open-endedness is preserved but also a recognition that where one is situated now makes certain later outcomes more probable and others less probable.

Uni-factorial vs. systemic theories

Developmental psychology has been characterized, as has psychology in general, by thinking of causation in terms of polarities – nature vs. nurture, biological vs. environmental and so on. Clearly there has been recognition for some time that the answer lies in neither of these extremes and that at the very least we must think in terms of interaction. However, it is still the case that when attempting to categorize the grand theories of developmental psychology they can be typically arraigned on one side or other of the biological vs. social opposition. Such oppositions still provide a ready mode of categorizing developmental theories (see Levenson and Crumpler, 1996), but just because it is easy to type current theories in this way does not imply that these theoretical divisions are in any way productive. The more interesting question is: how can developmental theorizing move away from false polarities, in particular that of the nature–nurture dichotomy? Some developmental psychologists have made serious efforts to theorize the nature of development in a holistic and integrated manner. This is a goal which is not specific to psychology. Biologists who are interested in development are confronted with the same theoretical challenges.

One modern response to the need to recognize the role of both biology and social influences is in terms of an essentially additive model. An example of this approach may be seen in the work of behavioural geneticists such as Robert Plomin (1994), who adopts a quantitative approach to the assessment of the relative contribution of heredity and environment. He is to some extent an interactionist in that he recognizes that both sides of the equation must be taken into account. He states, 'modern theory and research in both nature and nurture are converging on the interface between them' (1994, p. 20). A number of developmental theorists adopt an approach in line with Plomin's and have developed a range of concepts to elaborate their theories about nature–nurture interaction, such as niche picking, active, passive and evocative genotype–environment effects and so on. However, the basis of such work is an acceptance of the conceptualization of nature and nurture as separable determinants of development. This is a way of thinking that has been critiqued as being at heart a misleading representation of the living organism and its development.

A more acceptable, contemporary position is articulated by Stephen Rose in his book *Lifelines* (1997) where he says, 'The phenomena of life are always and inexorably simultaneously about nature and nurture and the phenomena of human existence and experience are always simultaneously biological and social. Adequate explanations must involve both' (p. 279).

And within developmental psychology a similar view has been articulated by Richard Lerner, who states that it is 'counterfactual to contend that nature is separable from nurture' (1993, p. 123). Lerner and other developmentalists such as Gilbert Gottlieb (1992) are opposed to the naive genetic reductionism and genetic determinism which are still very prevalent today and are central to the evolutionary psychology movement. Instead they place genes as elements in a complex bidirectional system. Psychology in general and developmental psychology in particular have been bedevilled by unhelpful and misleading dichotomies of which the nature–nurture split is perhaps the most significant. Writers like Lerner and Gottlieb have shown how it is possible to move beyond dichotomous thinking to systemic conceptualizations more adequate to the task at hand.

In particular, a number of developmentalists have argued that systemic theories represent the way forward (e.g. Wapner, 1993; Thelen and Smith, 1994). Richard Lerner has identified a convergence in recent theory-building on what he calls a 'superordinate developmental systems view of human development' (1998, p. 16). The systemic paradigm unifies a number of theoretical perspectives within developmental psychology which attempt to model and theorize the multifaceted, multiply determined nature of development. Such theories are also in line with recent theoretical movements within the biological and physical sciences and indeed in sociology and economics.

Systemic thinking can only take one so far in developmental theorizing. It aids in the conceptualization of dynamic complexity and of the processes by which new forms may emerge from complex systems, but it does not necessarily encompass the self-making (or auto-poietic) and self-aware nature of human being in the world.

Universalizing vs. particularizing

Psychology has always felt embarrassed by its failure to meet one of its most valued aspirations – that of finding universal laws of behaviour. The fact that such laws did not seem to be forthcoming did not prevent a frequent resort to universalizing; that is, to extending findings far beyond their valid reach. Developmental psychology has been very prone to universalizing its findings. Indeed, it has been the explicit goal of many developmental theorists. Piaget, for instance, was not interested in individual differences, nor some might say in child psychology. He was concerned to chart the development of intelligence and knowledge of the world as it was structured during the course of development. His focus, genetic epistemology, was premised on the view that in all children knowledge would be constructed in the same way and in the same sequence. One can see here his commitment to biology and to the theory of evolution since he seemed to believe that studying the child's development gave an insight into the development of knowledge in the species.

Jaan Valsiner is a foremost proponent of cultural psychology and is also a developmental theorist. Despite his close attention to cultural differences he is also committed to the view that 'scientific knowledge needs to be universal rather than particular' (2000, p. 3). He states that he wishes to overcome 'the traditions of 'post-modernism' that have proclaimed the fragmentation of knowledge into locally valid (at best) constructions' (ibid.). He aims to identify common processes underlying apparently different activities – a universal grammar of development. It seems that for Valsiner the point of surveying numerous different cultures is to arrive at a more complete and informative picture of developmental mechanisms and principles. Such knowledge, then, would be generalizable in the way that studies restricted to middle-class children from the USA or Europe are not.

A different response to the reality of human diversity and different ways of framing development and change in time is to abandon all claims to universal knowledge about development. In her paper, 'Beyond developmentalism', Valerie Walkerdine presents a strong critique of developmental psychology, attacking it for a number of deficiencies, one of which is its false claim of universal applicability. She says, 'The very idea of development is not natural and universal but extremely specific' (Walkerdine, 1993, p. 455). With reference to the 'story' of child development she argues that 'the big story is a European patriarchal story' (ibid.), which excludes women and children outside the West. Both are problematic for developmental theory. According to Walkerdine, the failure of developmental theory to incorporate girls and non-Western children demonstrated 'the very specificity of the concepts upon which childhood and development are founded' (p. 459).

Richard Lerner takes a more moderate position in his (1998) chapter in the *Handbook of Child Psychology*. He comments that 'What is seen in one data set may be only an instance of what does or what could exist'. Such a view, which recognizes the specificity of data, is gaining more widespread acceptance. Accordingly, in contemporary research, including that published in the most prestigious journals such as *Child Development,* there tends to be much more attention than there was in the past paid to diversity and to the specific characteristics of a sample, and thereby to the limits of generalization. Lerner claims for his discipline a 'focus on diversity – of people, of relations, of settings and of times of measurement' (p. 13). He is, I think, somewhat optimistic in this statement. Most mainstream developmentalists are still very enamoured with the idea of generalizability. Why, otherwise, would they spend so much time obtaining large *representative* samples and testing significance statistically?

Objecthood vs. personhood

As a student of psychology in the 1960s I was socialized to refer to the human being as 'the organism'. Although personality theory was part of the undergraduate programme on which I was enrolled, there was not much talk about the person or persons. Personality theory was seen as a branch of the study of individual differences which was in the main a distraction forced upon us by the need for the clinical application of the science, a diversion from psychology's true goal which was to establish the laws or principles governing behaviour.

For most of the twentieth century *the child* has been the object of enquiry for developmental psychology. Despite the Freudian legacy of insight into the importance of subjectivity in arriving at an understanding of human psychology, most developmental psychologists have persisted with a peculiarly external objectivist perspective on the person.

The science of 'mind' has in many ways avoided the implications of the reality that each and every human has their own mind, their own perspective on the world and their own subjectivity, taking subjectivity as being the individual's conscious awareness of their own status as a 'thinking and cognizing agent' or subject (*Shorter Oxford English Dictionary*). According to Ben Bradley, 'we remain to be delivered from the absurdity of an intellectual discipline that habitually disowns its defining topic of inquiry' (1998, p. 68).

The effort towards objectivity that has characterized psychology's struggle to be accepted as a scientific discipline has brought with it a distancing from human subjects with their messy, various and unpredictable lives and an investment in humans as objects of investigation which could be studied, weighed and measured in the psychologist's own chosen terms. Quantitative methods have been the chosen research tool of a discipline which defines its subjects as objects. Quantification and the use of large subject pools allow for the creation of the abstracted 'child' or 'adult' of developmental enquiry. Interest has not been focused typically on the person – child or adult – and on their interpretation of their own experience.

Psychology has as a discipline been wedded to a reductionism which has as a major consequence the incapacity to recognize humans as subjects and agents. In recent years, however, a number of strands have come together which have resulted in the recognition of the person as an active agent in their own development whose efforts after meaning and understanding of their own life situations need to be taken into account (Greene, 1997a).

For example, Bronfenbrenner, one of the leading figures in contemporary developmental psychology, places the agentic person at the heart of his ecological theory, stating: 'an ecological view of organism–environment interaction takes as its point of departure a conception of the person as an active agent who contributes to her own development' (1994, p. 203). Arguably, developmental psychology has still some distance to go in terms of theorizing the nature and extent of human agency.

Social contructionism, which stands currently as the major theoretical movement within psychology offering an alternative to scientism, does not support the construct of personhood. In fact it also obliterates the person, seeing the idea of personhood and the idea of self as discursive constructions. While admitting the importance of socio-cultural practices, and language in particular, in the construction of the self, it is surely not necessary to wipe out the psychological from consideration, as an epi-phenomenon of no central importance. My view is that developmental psychology must deal with the psychological; that is, with the experience of self and personhood which is at the heart of each individual's consciousness and relationship to her world.

Developmental psychology – moving on

In 1986 William Kessen proposed that, for developmental psychologists, 'the ultimate scholarly task is trying to understand the circumstances of change with age' (p. 39). If the fundamental task for the developmental psychologist is the explanation or understanding of the roots of psychological change in our passage through life, many of the above-named tensions may be seen to reduce to competing ways of understanding the origins and nature of such changes.

Explanation of human psychological change across the life span is a huge challenge. Given the multiple factors to be taken into account and their constantly shifting patterning and reworking across time and location, there will never be an explanation, only more or less useful efforts after understanding of *this* kind of phenomenon, in *this* kind of life, at *this* time and in *this* place. Uncertainty must be part of the fabric of our understanding since we are attempting very often to project our understanding on to the future which is, in terms of human psychology, radically unpredictable. Deanna Kuhn has hinted at the primitive nature of our current understanding of human psychological development when she says, 'Our existing vocabulary is insufficient to characterize the many forms of change that are part of the human experience' (1995, p. 293). It seems likely that, at the moment, we have neither the words nor the concepts to grasp adequately the complexity and flux which is integral to development.

It would be possible to name and describe more tensions and polarities in the field of developmental psychology, and clearly the issues I have selected are those which appear to me most salient. My prejudices are also on show in that I would, optimistically, identify the recently emerged counter-movement to the traditional assumptions and precepts of mainstream developmental psychology as typically more productive and potentially more fertile.

One must be on guard, however, and be open to the possibility – indeed the probability – that the new counter-movement will in time ossify and become a static polarity equally in need of revision or rejection. The current fashion is just that, a passing fad. As Bruner has stated, when commenting on the effect of the cognitive revolution on developmental psychology, 'we have fallen into a new set of postures in developmental psychology' (1986b, p. 23).

As a historical examination of the discipline readily reveals, there is no one developmental perspective. However, some of the emerging directions within the discipline are more compatible with the goals of a feminist psychology than was traditional developmental psychology.

What contemporary insights offer to our understanding of the psychology of girls and women

I have argued that within those disciplines labelled psychology of women and feminist psychology and by extension in the interdisciplinary field of women's studies there is a need for a clearly articulated developmental perspective. Although developmental psychology has failed to serve women's interests and our understanding of the psychology of girls and women well in the past, there are welcome changes within developmental psychology which may provide the basis for better understanding. The feminist project is at heart transformative, and there is therefore a need to understand the possibilities for life span change and the conditions which bring it about.

It is a fact that all human beings exist in time, that they have a past, a present and a future. Not only are people shaped by past events and by their interpretations of past events, they are also shaped by their expectations of the future. Their experience of being in the world is profoundly influenced by the culture and historical period they find themselves in, by its discourses concerning personhood, the self and the significant achievements and goals expected of a person of their sex, age and social location. The self is experienced as both stable and in flux, and the flow of events and of the changing contents of consciousness are inevitable features of lived experience. Not all branches of psychology incorporate this aspect of human life and experience into their accounts of psychological functioning.

To some extent, what emerges from examination of tensions and debates within developmental psychology is indeed an anti-developmental developmental psychology. It is anti-developmental in not endorsing a view of psychological change across the life course as propelled by fixed and universal internal processes, whether they are genes or cognitive schemas. The need for a developmental perspective remains, however, if one defines the developmental perspective broadly as that associated with the branch of psychology which is attempting to understand the nature of change occurring across the life span and which recognizes the role of history and time in the construction of the person (whether that history be actual events or psychic constructions of events). This history is a complex mix of the personal, the contextual and the transactional. In addition, history is only part of the developmental story since the developmental orientation should also address the time-dependent nature of human existence, the manner in which we all find ourselves located in a stream of time, consisting – in our particular cultural perspective – of the past, the present and the future. No other sub-discipline of psychology other than developmental psychology attempts to deal with the reality of the passage of time and change, and the consequences of past experiences and future prospects as well as current contingencies and the person's responses to them. The sense of being located in time, including our consciousness of our chronological age and our mortality, is arguably a defining characteristic of human consciousness and of our sense of ourselves as persons. Time is also a basic principle of social order, particularly in industrialized societies (Lichtman, 1981, 1987). Our life course is divided into periods according to age, and our opportunities and experiences differ accordingly. The effects of the delineation of the first part of the life course as childhood have been expertly analysed by sociologists such as James and Prout (1997). In fact all periods of the life course carry with them social demands and expectations which radically shape the experience of those caught in that particular life phase. Thus the periodization of the life course has an important role in development. A linked topic is the importance of timing and whether or not an event is considered to be on time or off time and whether a behaviour is considered to be (developmentally) appropriate or inappropriate.

Our culture, committed as it is to the notion of progress and development, shapes our thoughts and social structures in such a way as to embed the notions of progress and development in our consciousness – as persons engaging with our own life stories, as parents, as participants in ongoing social processes. From that point of view many people living in Western cultures are engaged in personal developmental quests, quests which are not the working out of a biological imperative but of a cultural construction and strongly developed subjectivity.

Thus, while the traditional developmental framework presents a number of problems, the developmental perspective broadly defined is important since it can potentially increase our understanding of the sources of psychological change during the life course. The dynamic time-conscious approach, which should be central to the developmental perspective, is missing from much current theorizing on the psychology of women. It is certainly the case that many feminists have embraced psychoanalytic thinking of one denomination or another, but even modern revisions and reworkings of Freud turn on a remarkably deterministic view of the human psyche. From this perspective, the possibilities for change are confined to a reworking of the significance of early and supposedly formative experiences. Anatomy also is accorded a universal significance which is dubious to say the least. Clearly these issues deserve closer attention and the contributions of psychoanalytic theory to a developmental psychology of women will be considered in chapters 3 and 4.

In conclusion, some contemporary life span developmental theorists are attempting to come to terms with the multi-directional, heterogeneous, historically, temporally and culturally situated nature of human life span change. There is from some quarters a clear call for a more systemic appreciation of the complexities of development and a refusal to adopt simplistic models as the basis for the discipline (Lerner, 1998). Some contemporary theories support a psychology which enables an understanding of the person as both embedded in culturally specific meaning systems and as an active constructor of personal meaning. The impact of critical and deconstructive attacks on developmental psychology as practised, while not representing a model of development, has been very useful in placing the discipline politically. Some of this recent theoretical and empirical work in life span psychology – much of which has not had a perceptible impact on theoretical work on the psychology of girls and women – may provide useful insights and the basis for a more adequate conceptualization of the life span psychology of women.

3

FEMALE DEVELOPMENT

Traditional approaches

To provide a historical review of psychologists' pronouncements on the psychology of women would be beyond the scope of this book and has been accomplished by a number of different authors elsewhere (e.g. Parlee, 1979; Lewin, 1984).

In the next two chapters I will therefore concentrate on providing a critical overview of those views which relate to developmental issues specifically, although drawing boundaries between developmental accounts and those which describe personality or social functioning, say, is not always easy. I will examine theories which discuss girls' and women's psychology with reference to origins, formation, socialization, assumed developmental pathways, tasks or goals, and changes with age or in time. In this chapter I will concentrate on theories which do not question their own gender blindness or which seem unaware of their own gender bias or which simply generalize about the psychology of 'man'. In Chapter 4, I will focus on theories which are written from a woman-centred perspective.

Most histories of developmental psychology locate its starting point towards the end of the nineteenth century, although it is undoubtedly the case that philosophers, theologians, educators and others before this date had had plenty to say on developmental issues in general and some things to say on what we might now describe as the developmental psychology of women. However, I will confine my review to the shorter history of psychology as a formal discipline. From the beginning, it was clear that the discipline was divided into a number of different theoretical families which were involved in a struggle for ascendancy. Some theoretical offerings were relatively short-lived, but others established a theoretical standpoint and tradition which have had an enduring influence, traces of which may still be seen in contemporary theorizing. For example, the work of Darwin was highly influential in the early years of child psychology and is the clear intellectual progenitor of evolutionary psychology, which is being widely discussed today.

In fact, as one examines the history of psychology in the twentieth century, many theories of development prior to the second wave of feminism in the late 1960s and early 1970s had little to say about gender or about female psychological development, other than offering explanations about gender role acquisition in early childhood. They had even less to say about adult psychological development, although some relevant work on this topic could be extracted from the field known in the world of English-speaking psychology as personality theory.

Evolutionary theory from the nineteenth to the twenty-first century

The Enlightenment entailed the questioning of many assumptions about the natural order of things and a turning to reason and science rather than theological explanations of the nature of the universe and human activity within it. As Miriam Lewin comments: 'The belief in female inferiority which had once rested more or less comfortably on selected misogynistic teachings within Genesis, Aristotle, St Paul and others now required a scientific base. That intellectual base became Darwinism, the most powerful idea of the nineteenth century' (1984, p. 48). Darwin and other evolutionary theorists provided 'scientific' arguments for the natural place of women as weaker to men and fit for a certain range of activities only. Darwin himself was less of a misogynist than were some of his fellow evolutionists. He certainly saw women as less evolved but believed that this was due largely to environmental factors and that it could be rectified in time by providing different environmental conditions such as the opportunity for improved education (Lewin, 1984, p. 50). Darwin argued that men were more evolved because of the fact that females were motivated to select only the strongest and fittest males as mates. Males, on the other hand, would mate with any female. The fact that males were less selective lessened the likelihood of selection of quality characteristics in the female stock.

The exact nature of Darwin's influence on developmental psychology is difficult to specify. Morss (1990) argues convincingly that much of the developmental theorizing which claims an allegiance to Darwinian tradition is in fact pre-Darwinian. It is certainly the case that G. Stanley Hall (1904), who is widely recognized as the founding father of developmental psychology in the USA, saw himself as a follower of Darwin, but in reality some of his central ideas were derived from Haeckel's views on the development of the embryo. For example, he adopted Haeckel's notion of ontogeny recapitulating phylogeny and applied it to psychological development from conception to maturity. Arnold Gesell (e.g. Gesell and Ilg, 1946) was similarly influenced by Darwin and saw him as the intellectual progenitor of the science of child development. Gesell was a nativist and a leading figure in establishing developmental norms. Others who based their work as developmentalists on evolutionary theories included Piaget and Freud. The key assumption which enshrined and typified their biological orientation was that development in each individual followed a predictable and universal course. Their commitment to evolution was seen in their employment of concepts such as adaptation and ontogenetic progression. Clearly these theorists differed in their precise specifications of the developmental process and in the amount of influence upon it exerted by the environment, but *biological thinking*, as Morss (1990) terms it, is endemic among developmentalists.

What then is the implication of all this for the developmental psychology of female members of the human species? First, the biological emphasis implies that development is in important ways, in either sex, fixed and predictable. Such a theory places an inevitable restriction upon female capability and upon gender role expressions in both sexes. It suggests that those who are different are pathological and 'unnatural'. Although some variability is tolerated – indeed, strictly, is essential for evolution to occur – those deviations which are not functional are fated to die out. Evolutionary theorists locate their level of explanation in what they call the ultimate causes of behaviour as opposed to the proximate causes which may, they concede, be important determinants of the current behaviour of the individual. Ultimate causes, they argue, are those processes which shaped human genes and therefore determine our basic capabilities and proclivities. Behaviour tendencies are assumed to evolve and become established at the level of genes because they are functional – to understand the ultimate cause of behaviour it is necessary to understand the purposes which such behaviours served in the evolutionary history of the species. Adaptation is central to evolutionary thinking and is probably one of its most distinctive bequests to twentieth-century developmental psychology. At the individual level Piaget, for example, was obsessed with adaptation, a central impetus for growth and change in his model of the human organism.

Second, evolutionary theories have led to the emergence of specific sub-theories about the roles and proclivities of males and females. Darwin's own thinking, focusing on the greater mate selectivity and the supposedly associated less evolved status of females, has been summarized earlier. Well over a hundred years later, evolutionary theories about gender remain essentially unreconstructed. In his best-selling book *The Selfish Gene*, the second edition of which was published in 1989, Richard Dawkins asks, 'What is the essence of maleness? What at bottom defines a female?' (1989, p. 140). Dawkins promotes a view, often ascribed to Robert Trivers (1972), that the one fundamental feature of the sexes which distinguishes between male and female is the fact that the sex cells or gametes of males are smaller and more numerous than the gametes of females. As a consequence, it is argued, males and females adopt very different mating strategies. Males can afford to produce millions of sperm and are concerned to inseminate as many females as possible to increase the spread of their genes, whereas females have to concentrate upon ensuring the survival of a limited number of offspring. Males are designed to be polygamous and females monogamous. An inevitable struggle between the sexes arises because of the conflict between these different agendas, with females attempting to attract the sustained attention of the 'best' fathers for their few precious offspring. Such males will not only be those who are genetically fit but also those who are likely to make an investment in the rearing and ultimate survival of her offspring.

Aside from the adoption of different mating strategies by the two sexes a number of sociobiologists and evolutionary theorists have pronounced on the genetic origins of other sex differences in behaviour. According to Edward Wilson, 'in hunter-gatherer societies men hunt and women stay at home. This strong bias persists in most agricultural and industrial societies, and on that ground alone appears to have a genetic origin' (1978, p. 133). Alice Rossi argues that the capacity to mother is built into the female psyche (1977).

As I write, psychology is experiencing a resurgence of interest in evolution. Dawkins, a zoologist, is still producing books on this topic (e.g. Dawkins, 1998), but in many ways is identified with the 1970s sociobiology movement. Evolutionary psychology, which has a more explicit focus on humans and on the human mind, has produced from the ranks of psychologists its own stars, such as Barkow, Cosmides and Tooby (1992), and Pinker (1994, 1997). New works have emerged which discuss the evolutionary origins of sex differences in behaviour (e.g. Buss, 1994, 1995; Geary, 1998). Buss argues that men and women differ in some aspects of their physique, physiology and psychology because they 'have faced substantially different adaptive problems throughout human evolutionary history' (1995, p. 164). He claims that 'large sex differences appear reliably for precisely the aspects of sexuality and mating predicted by evolutionary theories of sexual strategies' (p. 166).

In response to the view that evolutionary theories about sex differences are conservative and prescriptive, Buss claims, 'the meta-theory of evolutionary psychology is descriptive not prescriptive – it carries no values in its teeth' (1995, p. 167). Of course, to the contrary, evolutionary psychology is not simply descriptive, since it promotes a theory about causation. It consists of a series of hypotheses which cannot be put to the test, since its arguments about origins relate to presumed behaviour patterns in our long-dead ancestors living tens of thousands of years ago. The evidence that evolutionary psychologists adduce is often current, but it is highly selected and tendentiously interpreted in order to fit the favoured theoretical framework. For example, Buss cites a study where 75 per cent of the men but 0 per cent of the women approached by an attractive stranger (of the opposite sex) consented to a request for sex (1995, p. 166). This finding is taken as evidence for the innate promiscuity of men. One might imagine many cultures and settings where nothing like this result would be obtained. Even where such results are found there are many possible alternative explanations other than those related to sexual selection processes that might have occurred at a much earlier point in evolution. According to evolutionary psychologists, current psychological sex differences in all their extraordinarily varied cultural forms are patterned in a manner that maps precisely on to the adaptive problems that men and women are assumed to have faced over evolutionary history.

The rise in evolutionary psychology and biological determinism which we have seen over the past decade has not escaped the critical notice of feminist psychologists, although there is perhaps less attention paid to the significance of the resurgence than one might expect. Lynne Segal is one psychologist who has clearly expressed her dismay at what she calls 'the renaissance of a Darwinian fundamentalism' (1999, p. 80). Segal points out that

> the claimed universality of sexually dimorphic behaviour patterns could as easily be seen as a cultural *effect*, rather than as an evolved adaptation operating as a *cause*, of the hitherto (though now often challenged) configuration of men's greater access to economic resources and social power and privilege compared to that of women.
>
> (Segal, 1999, p. 89)

From a developmental perspective, the primary concern is the consequence of adopting any theory of development which is at heart a promotion of genetic determinism, both in terms of its explanation of individual development and its assumptions about different developmental trajectories and end-points for males and females. There are various degrees of commitment to determinism among evolutionary theorists. Most would accept that because of their complex cultures humans can often override their genetically determined proclivities. However, it is the case that those who ally themselves with an evolutionary perspective also tend to see evolutionary adaptations as in some sense primary. They argue that we need to take on board and work with the *natural* behaviour patterns evolution has selected as most adaptive for the species.

There are reasons, both scientific and political, to be cautious about extreme genetic determinism, but at the same time genes and physiology cannot be disregarded; they are undoubtedly essential elements of the total picture. Issues to do with biology and the body and their place in a developmental psychology of women will be revisited in Chapter 5.

Behaviourism and social learning theory

Behaviourism, which was the dominant force within psychology for several decades in the mid-twentieth century, entailed a view of behaviour change as a function of reinforcement or punishment. Learning, whether taking place at age 2 or 22, was seen to involve identical mechanisms. Change was conceptualized quantitatively not qualitatively and was seen as prompted by external contingencies. Viewed in this light behaviourism was anti-developmental, although, taking a broad definition of development which does not tie it to unfolding or epigenetic processes, behaviourism did and does provide an explanation of behavioural change via learning mechanisms (Bijou and Baer, 1961). The major contribution, then, that behaviourists made to the developmental psychology of women was to provide an account of how sex roles were learned. Acquisition of sex-typed behaviour, it was argued, occurred in the same way as acquisition of any other behaviour, through a process of conditioning. Operant conditioning was the favoured mechanism to explain the acquisition of novel behaviours. By this process desirable behaviour appropriate to the sex of the child would be rewarded and undesirable behaviour punished. Theoretically such processes could continue throughout the life span, but most attention was paid to early childhood (Fagot, 1985).

Interestingly the strongest early statement of the importance of conditioning of gender roles came not from a behaviourist psychologist but from the anthropologist Margaret Mead (1935), who concluded after her study of the gender roles found among the Arapesh, the Mundugumor and the Tschambuli (all quite different from those typical of the USA at the time) that:

> We are forced to conclude that human nature is almost infinitely malleable . . . the differences between individuals who are members of different cultures, like the differences between individuals within a culture are almost entirely to be laid to differences in conditioning, especially during early childhood and the form of this conditioning is culturally determined.

> (Mead, 1935, p. 280)

As a historical aside, it is interesting that John B. Watson, the founding father of behaviourism in the USA, could not desist from making dogmatic statements about the role of women as mothers and on the likely developmental pathway of the average adult woman. In his 1925 text *Behaviorism,* he says, 'a female changes very slowly. . . . If you have an adequate picture of the individual at 30 you will have it with few changes for the rest of that individual's life – as most lives already are lived. A quacking, gossiping, neighbour-spying, disaster-enjoying woman of 30 will be, unless a miracle happens, the same at 40 and still the same at 60' (p. 278). Watson's low opinion of women as mothers is well documented and has been commented upon by such writers as Christina Hardyment (1983). His opinions on women had little to do with the tenets of behaviourism but were nonetheless influential among middle-class, progressive parents of the time.

Social learning theory, which was conceptually and historically an offshoot of behaviour theory, has been the basis of the most popular perspective on the acquisition of gender roles (Bandura, 1977). The central assumption for social learning theory is that behaviour appropriate to the sex of the child is learned largely through contact with others, who will act as models for sex-appropriate behaviour and will provide reinforcement for sex-appropriate behaviour. There is a certain amount of evidence for the proposition that parents selectively reinforce behaviours which are gender-typed. For example, early work by Beverley Fagot found that girls were encouraged to play games involving dolls and dressing up but boys were encouraged in rough play and in jumping and climbing (1978). In relation to observational learning the evidence is less than conclusive. Both boys and girls spend more time in early childhood in contact with women – their mothers, childminders and pre-school teachers – yet most children will acquire gender-role behaviours which are more or less in line with those expected of their sex.

The social learning and cognitive developmental perspectives have come closer together in recent years with Bandura's incorporation of cognition into his social learning perspective. What is interesting about both social learning perspectives and the cognitive developmental perspective, which will be discussed below, is that the focus is almost entirely on early childhood. Although in both these theories there is an acceptance that gender-typed behaviours and attitudes are acquired (i.e. are not natural or biologically given), there is an assumption that once you have got them you have got them for life and you don't lose them. These theories are, like many psychological theories, essentialist. The qualities and dispositions relating to gender are posited as inherent to the person in the same way as personality traits are thought to be inherent. The developmental story about the 'acquisition' of gender is all over by about the age of 5.

Cognitive developmental theory

Cognitive developmental theory, largely founded on the work of Jean Piaget, paid relatively little attention to sex or gender. It has been influential with reference to gender in two main ways: first, its explanation of how the young child comes to understand that they are a boy or a girl; and second, through its enshrining of logical thinking as the pinnacle of intellectual achievement.

Based on Piagetian constructs, Kohlberg (1966) proposed a theory of how children came to identify themselves as male or female and how their understanding of aspects of gender developed. His theory shares with learning theory a restricted concept of gender in that it entails an all-or-nothing typing as boy or girl, male or female. Kohlberg believed that understanding of gender proceeded in stages. The first step involved the child's observation that there are two categories of people in the world and that she belongs to just one of them. Thus by the age of 2 most children have this realization, which Kohlberg terms gender identity. However, the young child still does not appreciate that gender is constant throughout life and has a primitive and partial view of what gender identity entails. The arrival at an understanding of gender constancy, which for Kohlberg implies the understanding that gender is constant throughout life and cannot be changed by superficial adjustments to hair or clothing, takes a few years but is normally complete by the age of 5. It is tempting to suggest that the under-fives who see gender as flexible and inconstant are tuning into realities which Kohlberg was reluctant to admit.

This insistence on the part of cognitive developmental theorists that a major task for the young child is to recognize object constancy and permanency has been tellingly critiqued by Greenberg (1996) in relation to physical objects. This critique could be readily applied to children's understanding of personal identity and constancy as well. In fact, there is some evidence that children in middle childhood are aware of the existence of some flexibility in gender-role enactment and do not see infringement of strict gender-role boundaries as catastrophic (Serbin *et al.*, 1993).

Piaget's cognitive developmental theory also represents a vision of the intellectual progression of development which may be seen as gendered. His stages entail movement from sensory engagement with the world and direct action upon it to the hypothetico-deductive reasoning of his idealized adolescent. Like most intellectuals of his time Piaget saw the mastery of reason and logic as the height of human intellectual achievement. Valerie Walkerdine has written about the primacy of logic in Western discourse on intelligence and on the manner in which it permeates the educational system (1988). Piaget's theory did not create this emphasis on logical reasoning as the pinnacle of intellectual achievement, but it has certainly served to strengthen its hold on the imagination of psychologists and educators. Privileging reason above all other forms of intelligence has consequences for males as well as females. However, given the presumed conjunction of rationality and the masculine, there is a fundamental exclusion of all connected with the feminine – including a disregard for the actuality of being a girl or a woman – at the heart of this promotion of logic and reason. The popularity of the computational metaphor in cognitive psychology, and its undoubtedly useful applications in the commercial use and development of computers, have reinforced in recent years the already existing emphasis in cognitive and developmental psychology on the centrality of logical reasoning and the consequent neglect of forms of cognition associated with the feminine.

The cognitive developmental psychologist Gisela Labouvie-Vief has written a thought-provoking book *Psyche and Eros* on the gendering of intelligence and the development of intelligence across the life course (1994). Development, she argues, has been presented as the triumph of *logos*, reason and objectivity over *mythos*, the realm of imagination, emotion, unpredictability and the subjective. In the work of Piaget, rated by many as the most influential developmental psychologist of the twentieth century, one sees a clear instantiation of this progression. Labouvie-Vief sees the importance placed on Piaget's theory as reflecting both our culture's fear of the feminine and the irrational and also its fixation with youth. Older people she reports have a much deeper respect for the range and depth of potential expressions of intelligence and knowledge than do the young. She asks, '[Have] we in our own denial of aging and yearning for eternal youth perhaps scaled our models of human adaptation uniquely toward the young adult?' (1994, p. 5). I will return to Labouvie-Vief's work later, but in relation to cognitive developmental theory it presents, as does the work of Walkerdine, a challenge to the Western positioning of rationality as the pinnacle of development and also questions its youth-centred perspective.

Freud and orthodox psychoanalysis

Freud's views on the psychology of women have been widely discussed. His views are of particular interest since they represent a developmental account of the formation of female personality which has been extremely influential. Freud writes on this topic in several different papers, particularly, 'Femininity' (1933) and 'Some psychical consequences of the anatomical distinction between the sexes' (1925).

Freud's problem was to explain female psychosexual development and to give a credible account of female personality development. The solution to both problems centres on the concept of penis envy. As he states in 1925, first catching sight of the penis represents 'a momentary discovery which little girls are destined to make . . . they notice the penis of a brother or playmate, strikingly visible and of larger proportion and at once recognize it as the superior counterpart of their own small and inconspicuous organ and from that time forward fall a victim to envy for the penis'. He says, of the girl child, 'she makes her judgement and her decision in a flash. She has seen it and knows she is without it and wants to have it.'

Subsequent psychological development is dictated by the girl's envy of the penis and the conclusions she draws from her lack of penis about her status and the status of all other females According to Freud the girl is motivated to secure a penis for herself in a symbolic form. Freud describes what he sees to be the desirable pathway to womanhood and some pathological forms of dealing with penis envy. It is difficult from any contemporary perspective to see Freud's description of the normal pathway as anything but a prescription for psychopathology, but what it most closely represents is a description of the attitudes and lifestyle demanded of the middle-class women of his time.

Freud describes the chronological events as follows. At first, the girl, like her male counterparts, is closely attached to her mother. The boy must break this attachment to his mother and identify with his father, a process which is described as the resolution of the Oedipal complex. The girl has a different task. She must remain emotionally identified with her mother but must turn to her father as her love object. It is only through union with the male that the girl will ultimately, symbolically, regain the penis, first through sexual intercourse and then more satisfyingly through giving birth to a male child. Freud (1925) dates the girl's 'momentary discovery' to the phallic stage. She immediately feels inferior and to blame for having lost her penis or having allowed herself to be deprived of the penis. At this time she notices also that her mother has lost her penis. She blames and devalues her mother and all other women. Turning to her father, who alone possesses the penis and the power to rectify partially her loss, she must renounce clitoral sexuality for vaginal sexuality. Since the girl's identification is with her mother, she is by definition morally deficient. 'The foundation of the super-ego must suffer – it cannot attain the strength and independence which gives it its cultural significance.' And Freud notes, in a moment of insight in respect of women, 'feminists are not pleased when we point out to them the effects of this factor upon the female character'.

Envy and masochism are also seen by Freud as fundamental dispositional traits of women. He says, 'The fact that women must be regarded as having little sense of justice is no doubt related to the predominance of envy in their mental life' (1933, p. 134). Freud, utilizing the notion of penis envy, thus claims in one fell swoop to explain the genesis of the posited female personality configuration – feeling inferior, envious, passive and masochistic – of female heterosexual desires and of the female urge towards motherhood. Female moral deficiency is also accounted for, since women have been unable to resolve fully the Oedipal complex and thus establish a sturdy super-ego. In order to adopt the desirable passive-masochistic orientation girls must relinquish their active and aggressive tendencies. Not succumbing to this defeated role is seen as pathological. The masculinity complex results when the girl or woman refuses to accept the consequences of her lack of a penis and remains fixated on the clitoris. An alternate route leads to frigidity and a renunciation of sexual fulfilment.

Freud roots psychological development in, as he puts it, 'the anatomical distinction between the sexes'. It certainly did not take long before feminists, most famously one of his own disciples, Karen Horney (1926), pointed out that his focus was on *an* anatomical distinction, not by any means *the only* anatomical distinction. Freud's theory is developmental in the sense that it gives an account of the origins of personality structures and a description of typical developmental pathways. He accounts for adult personality but is not committed to the possibility of qualitative change or transformation after adolescence.

Freud's influence on theorizing about the psychological development of women is extensive and I will describe below the work of some of his followers, who vary considerably in the extent to which their thinking is in line with Freud's. Psychoanalytic concepts such as the unconscious, defence mechanisms, intrapsychic conflict, the role of the symbolic and of object relations and ultimately the constitutive role of language, as elaborated by writers such as Lacan, are all important influences on contemporary thinking about the psychological development of women which can be traced back to Freud.

In 1963, Betty Friedan accused Freudian theories of being 'an obstacle to truth for women in America today and a major cause of the pervasive problem that has no name' (1963, p. 96). The problem that has no name was the widespread level of depression and malaise detectable in American housewives and mothers in the 1950s. Women, she argued, were tied to a vision of femininity and the feminine role largely promulgated by Freud. She considered that Freudian theory was extremely influential in post-Second World War USA and Europe where 'Freudian and pseudo-Freudian ideas settled everywhere like fine volcanic ash' (1963, p. 115).

Some of Freud's followers continued to offer a view on the psychology of women which could be seen as within the tradition of the master in their adherence to anatomically based explanations and/or devaluation of the supposedly feminine personality characteristics. Feminist psychologists have reacted to Freud's work in a variety of different ways. Some see Freud's theory as hostile to women and unredeemable. A typical representative of that point of view would be Hannah Lerman whose book *A Mote in Freud's Eye: From Psychoanalysis to the Psychology of Women* appeared in 1986. She concludes that Freud's theory 'is so fundamentally flawed that it cannot be repaired, however extensive the tinkering with it. . . . Assumptions about the inherent inferiority of women are embedded in the very core of psychoanalytic theory' (p. 6).

However, other feminist writers on women's psychology have not arrived at the same conclusion. On the contrary, they have seen psychoanalytic theory as necessary to a full understanding of women's psychology, female subjectivity and its complexities, and the development of girls and women across the life course. Much of this writing is psychoanalytic without being faithful to Freud's specific formulations on women. Feminist psychoanalytic approaches to the psychology of women will be addressed in Chapter 4.

Erikson

Erik Erikson's extension of Freud's stage theory of psychosexual development to cover the entire life span has provided one of the most influential models of psychological development. As first presented, the essay 'Eight Ages of Man' was intended to describe the development of both males and females. It took some years for Erikson to make explicit his view that male and female development followed somewhat different pathways. In papers written in the 1940s, Erikson explored his thinking on the relationship between sex and psychic orientation. For example, in an essay in *Childhood and Society* (1950) he describes his observations on the different structures built by boys and girls in their play with blocks and other toys. Boys built towers and other tall structures and girls built enclosures, or so Erikson claimed.

In his paper 'Womanhood and the inner space' published in 1968 (a revision of a paper originally published in 1964), Erikson explores the implications for women's psyche of the existence of the inner space. He takes issue with Freud's view that female psychological development may be understood as a way of dealing with penis envy. He says, 'the existence of a productive inner-bodily space safely set in the centre of female form and carriage has, I would think, greater actuality than has the missing external organ' (1968, p. 267). In this paper, Erikson revisits his 'Eight Ages of Man' from the perspective of women's development and questions the appropriateness for girls and women of the ordering of his original stages. Women, unlike men, he now suggests, cannot establish identity until they have dealt with issues relating to intimacy. (In the original scheme the fifth stage, Identity vs. Role Confusion, precedes Intimacy vs. Isolation.) He says, 'something in the young woman's identity must keep itself open for the peculiarities of the young man to be joined' (p. 283), and then 'womanhood arrives when attractiveness and experience have succeeded in attracting what is to be admitted to the welcome of the inner space for keeps' (p. 283).

Erikson wrote in a manner which set out to gently extol the wonderful virtues of femininity, and he was apparently amazed when feminists of the time reacted negatively to his paper. His argument is clearly another variation on the 'anatomy is destiny' theme set out so cogently by Freud. Erikson asserts that 'the basic modalities of women's commitment and involvement normally also reflect the ground plan of her body' (1968, p. 285). He believed that, because in his paper he suggested that refined moral sensibility, creativity and artistic leanings were correlates of women's 'inwardness and sensitive indwelling', he would be seen as a champion of womanhood. Alongside his biological determinism he seemed totally unaware of his unthinking heterosexual bias. Women, in Erikson's life plan, are destined to be the sexual partners of men, finding fulfilment in the filling of the empty inner space through penetration by the penis and in pregnancy.

Despite the blatant limitations of Erikson's theory of female psychosexual development, his stage theory still stands as the most quoted life span theory of psychological development for both sexes. Every life span textbook destined for the undergraduate market includes extensive and often not very critical coverage of Erikson's 'Eight Ages of Man'.

Lacan

The work of Jacques Lacan (1977, 1978) is not easy to read or to summarize, but his work is important because of his influence on feminist theory which has been apparent for more than two decades and because he provides a (somewhat truncated) developmental perspective on female psychology. Although not explicitly postmodern in his orientation, Lacan may be seen as contributing to the 'turn to language' which marked post-Second World War scholarship (Bowie, 1991).

Lacan was a psychoanalyst but, unlike Freud, his primary emphasis was on the role of language and the *Symbolic Order* in regulating society and subjectivity, and he resisted vigorously any explanations which rested on biology. His developmental account of the first few years of life is a description of how each child comes to enter the Symbolic Order of signs, rules and rituals and incorporates these symbolic systems into his or her psyche. Lacan labels this system of rules 'The Law of the Father' and the primary signifier of this law is the phallus.

The first phase in his developmental sequence he describes as the *Imaginary* phase, coincident with infancy. The child at the beginning of this phase has no clear bodily or ego boundaries. The discovery of self occurs in the *Mirror* phase (1977). When the child is faced with an actual mirror, Lacan argues, he or she is forced to recognize that they have a self which can be represented in a way that is separate from their own bodily existence, i.e. that they are not an undifferentiated one but can be, in a sense, two via imagery and symbolic representation. The acquisition of language, the defining symbolic system, marks entry into the human race. As Malcolm Bowie points out, the 'specular moment' is both the moment of creation of the human subject and its fall (1991). For Lacan the ego is fated to be fragmented and besieged. The mirror image is in a sense a mirage and a fragile basis on which to construct a sense of self. Desire also comes into being at this point in the child's existence and it is a desire for wholeness, completion and satisfaction, which can never be fulfilled.

The next stage in Lacan's developmental sequence he labels *Oedipal*. By this time the child has become aware of the separation of his or her own body from that of the mother and also aware of the inability of the mother to meet his or her desires. Armed with this awareness the boy turns away from the mother to the father, who alone can rescue the child from its pre-Oedipal submersion in inchoate narcissism. The mother–child dyad is taken to lie outside both language and culture, and exists only in the realm of the *Imaginary*. The male child is able to identify with his father who represents social order and authority. Girls, who do not possess a penis and therefore cannot identify themselves as like the father, cannot internalize 'The Law of the Father' as their own but must survive as *the Other*, living in a society and using a language which is centred on the phallus. Desire for both sexes is constructed in terms of the phallus, its presence or absence. Desire being active is masculine.

In this way Lacan paints a very negative picture of the psychological development of girls and women. As with Freud, the normative developmental path is that of the male child. Basically the female child and women are excluded from the Symbolic Order as Lacan defines it. Lacan permits women the experience of sexual *jouissance*, but this is an experience which is in a space outside language and therefore outside expression and understanding. Lacan's representation of the feminine as *unrepresentable* is, as Judith Butler (1994) points out, a fundamental stumbling block to feminist discourse and activism. Despite Lacan's movement away from anatomical determinism he has arrived at a structural determinism in his insistence on the inevitability of phallic supremacy. Also from a developmental point of view, as Bowie points out, the Lacanian version of the Oedipal discovery of the phallus is one which 'the individual can never expect to outgrow' (1991, p. 127).

Jung

Jung's views on the psychology of women and the feminine have never achieved the currency and influence attained by Freud and his followers, but have nonetheless been influential in some academic and lay circles. They have also been explored from a feminist perspective in recent years, thus ensuring that Jung's work retains some contemporary significance. It is also the case that Jung had a life span developmental perspective on the person which has interesting aspects to it, although what he offers is undoubtedly a partial and not very well-elaborated developmental theory.

Jung was one of the few influential personality theorists of the twentieth century who placed gender explicitly as a central feature of personality development and functioning. He also formalized within psychology the distinction between the feminine principle and the psychology of women, although having done so he goes on to conflate them in some of his own writing. Jung saw every personality as having both feminine and masculine elements. Through the process of socialization, Jung argues, men come to accentuate their masculine side and women their feminine side, resulting in an intrinsic imbalance in the personality structure. For Jung, the masculine and the feminine represent complementary ways of relating to the world. The feminine principle centres on feeling, intuition, empathy for others and closeness to nature; the masculine principle represents logic, reason, objectivity and detachment. Clearly, Jung was tuning in to the long-standing gender dichotomy so evident in Western myth, philosophy and cultural tradition. He was also very aware of the Taoist doctrine of Yin and Yang.

Unlike many other psychologists of the early twentieth century, who simplistically identify being male with masculinity and being female with femininity, Jung saw both gender modes as persisting features of the personality structures of all individuals, and argued that it was psychologically healthy for the woman to access her masculine side and for the man to access his feminine side. The feminine principle is a broader concept than the anima, but in relation to personality structure the feminine in man is represented via his anima and the masculine in woman via her animus. The anima and the animus are only partly available to the conscious mind, and in their unconscious manifestations can make their presence known only in dreams and unguarded moments. Each sex must therefore come to terms with their 'contrasexual other'. It is this core feature of Jung's theorizing which has been taken up and employed by feminist Jungians. It must be said, however, that the orthodox Jungian account of gender is at heart totally conservative and Jung made some blatantly misogynistic statements on women.

In Jung's writings the feminine and the masculine are rigidly defined and essentialized. In addition, Jung's descriptions of the feminine are often patronizing at best and offensively derogatory at worst. Just as Erikson does, Jung characterizes women as empty. He says,

> finally it should be remarked that emptiness is a great feminine secret. It is something alien to men; the chasm, the unplumbed depths, the yin. The pitifulness of this vacuous nonentity goes to his heart (I speak here as a man) and one is tempted to say that this constitutes the whole 'mystery' of women.
>
> (Jung, 1954, p. 98)

Demaris Wehr comments that Jung 'projects his own anima willy nilly into the discussions of women's psychology' (1988, p. 104). In his own life, Jung surrounded himself with women supporters and acolytes, enacting his belief that women's main role in life was to bolster the self-worth of men (Anthony, 1990).

Jung's account of life span development centres on the process of individuation by which the person becomes a fully balanced and evolved self. Jung believed that in the first few years of life, the ego (the conscious, here-and-now self) has a conviction of being 'master in its house'. In the course of development, the person becomes aware that they are indeed not masters of their own fate but are influenced by forces beyond their control, including the personal and collective unconscious. It is necessary, Jung thought, to 'annihilate the ego'. As Demaris Wehr points out (1988), the language Jung adopts is masculine and there has to be a question mark over the advisability of exhorting women to annihilate the ego when for many women there are huge difficulties in ever establishing a strong ego and sense of mastery in the first place. Jung identifies the mid-point of life, which he locates as somewhere around the age of 35, as a major turning point in the life course. Whereas the focus of the first thirty-five years is on dealing with the demands of the outside world, Jung considers that the rewards of this kind of existence begin to fade and the person turns their attention to the need for balance and wholeness. From a gender perspective this is the time when the call of the contrasexual side of the self surfaces. In dreams and other manifestations of the unconscious, the person becomes increasingly aware of the unexpressed but crucial hidden facets of their personality. The woman begins to express more of her animus and the man his anima. Individuation is achievable only through this turning inward because it is built on fidelity to personal goals and meanings, not to the societal, conventional goals so dominant in the first half of life.

There is some evidence for the fading of sex-role typing in middle-aged and elderly people in Western societies. For example, Daniel Levinson, author of *The Seasons of a Man's Life* (1978) and *The Seasons of a Woman's Life* (1996), endorses Jung's perspective, stating that 'all of us at mid-life must come more fully to terms with the existence of masculine and feminine parts of the self. The splitting of masculine and feminine, so strong in childhood, cannot be overcome in early adulthood. It is a continuing task of middle and late adulthood' (1999, p. 33). Levinson (1996) claims that his two studies on men and women in mid-life provide evidence for this proposition. Gutmann also cites empirical evidence of what he labels 'the normal unisex of later life' (Gutmann, 1975).

Despite Jung's theoretical view that the individuated woman has to develop her animus side, in reality he had great difficulty in coping with women who were assertive or engaged in intellectual pursuits, as the following quotation attests:

> In intellectual women the animus encourages a critical disputatiousness and would-be highbrowism which however consists essentially in harping on some irrelevant weak point and nonsensically making it the main one. . . . Such women are solely intent upon exasperating the man and are in consequence the more completely at the mercy of the animus. 'Unfortunately I am always right' one of these creatures confessed to me.
>
> (Jung, 1954, p. 98)

It is difficult to read Jung on women and the feminine without concluding that he saw women as essentially inferior to men and incapable of full development as human beings.

Feminist appropriations

When considered as treatments of the psychological development of girls and women all the theories discussed in this chapter are, as I have argued, fundamentally flawed. Yet, for a number of reasons, they remain important. Many of these theoretical perspectives are still powerful and hold an influential position, either within academia, as is the case with cognitive and evolutionary psychology, or in therapeutic applications such as counselling, psychology and psychoanalysis.

In addition, as in all areas of scholarship, new theories do not emerge from a vacuum, they build on what was there before. Many of the woman-centred or feminist theories, which will be the focus of Chapter 4, have emerged from the theoretical traditions discussed above.

For example, the influence of psychoanalysis is evident in a number of theories capable of being filed under the feminist label. Karen Horney was very much a disciple of Freud, albeit a rebellious one. She was dismissed from the New York Psychoanalytic Institute in 1941 because of her lack of orthodoxy but still remained within the fold theoretically, founding her own psychoanalytic association, training institute and journal. Lacan, who differed from Freud in many ways but always identified with him, had a major influence on the emergence of psychoanalytic feminism (Tong, 1989). Thus the Lacanian emphasis on language and the symbolic has been a strong influence on the thinking of French feminist philosophers/psychoanalysts. Feminist theorists working in France such as Luce Irigaray (1985), Julia Kristeva (1981) and Hélène Cixous (1981) have in different ways responded to Jacques Lacan's theories. Luce Irigaray was actually a member of the Freudian School of Paris founded by Lacan.

Janet Sayers has described the life and work of four of Freud's female followers – Helene Deutsch, Karen Horney, Anna Freud and Melanie Klein – each of whom helped to set the scene for what Sayers sees as a revolution in psychoanalytic thinking. Writing in 1992, she says, 'Psychoanalysis has been turned upside down. Once patriarchal and phallocentric, it is now almost entirely mother-centred' (1992, p. 3). It is the case that, with the exception of Karen Horney, none of these women could be identified readily as feminists. However, by their focus on the mother and on pre-Oedipal development they have indeed paved the way for contemporary feminist developmental accounts, both within and outside of the psychoanalytic tradition, which focus on the importance of the mother–daughter relationship and of relationality in general. These women, Sayers claims, 'drew our attention to the interpersonal and maternal determinants of our personality so scandalously overlooked by Freud' (1992, p. 4).

The object relations framework pioneered by Melanie Klein (1937) and Donald Winnicott (1958), itself a development of Freudian theory, has been taken up by a range of developmentally oriented feminist psychologists – most famously Nancy Chodorow (1978). Chodorow's work on the reproduction of motherhood is basically a reworking of Freud's theory with an emphasis on the role of the mother as the first identification object for both boys and girls.

However, Chodorow locates the source of psychic gender differentiation in the nuclear family structure rather than in anatomy and is concerned to re-evaluate feminine qualities. Many of the writers who emphasize female embeddedness in relationships adhere to an object relations orientation tacitly or explicitly. Even Carol Gilligan, whose early work with Lawrence Kohlberg was very much within the cognitive developmental tradition, endorses Chodorow's suggestion that early identifications shape the female commitment to a voice of care and connection rather than a voice of justice and rights (Gilligan, 1982).

Some of the core principles of Jung's work have been found amenable to a feminist perspective by writers such as Polly Young-Eisendrath (1984) and Demaris Wehr (1988). Wehr considers that 'Divested of its sexism, Jung's psychology is invaluable for an adequate understanding, not only of ourselves but of the world' (p. xii). In order to adopt the stance of a feminist Jungian, one must find a way of accommodating to Jung's many misogynistic pronouncements, such as his statement that 'emptiness is a great feminine secret. . . . The pitiful-ness of this vacuous nonentity goes to his heart (and I speak here as a man)' and so on (1964, p. 133).

Gisela Labouvie-Vief, a noted neo-Piagetian, has produced an interesting fusion of work on gender, cognitive development and Jungian theory. She calls Jung's work 'the most significant attempt thus far to deal with development not as the single progression of one mode of knowing but rather as an interweaving of two modes . . . (bridging) multiple dualisms – subjective and objective, mind and body, reason and instinct, masculine and feminine' (1994, p. 9).

It is interesting that many of the above theorists who have an interest in female development have drawn upon psychoanalytic theory or depth psychology, broadly defined. This is the case despite the widespread disparagement of Freud's ideas on the formation of the female personality. Indeed, psychoanalysis has provided one of the most fertile and persisting theoretical frameworks for feminist theorists in general, and not only for those who might identify as psychologists. Both Lacanian and object relations theory have been the basis for influential analyses of the construction of female subjectivity. The continuing fascination, on the part of feminist theorists, with psychoanalytic theories of development has both negative and positive sides to it. On the negative side, psychoanalytic theories share a belief in the formative role of early experience which is a deter-minist, essentialist and thus conservative view of development On the positive side, psychoanalysis provides a way of accessing and theorizing the complex and contradictory nature of female subjectivities.

Attempts to construct a specifically woman-centred account of psychological development, both those that do and those that do not build directly on evolu-tionary, psychoanalytic, behaviourist or Piagetian theoretical foundations, will be discussed in more detail in Chapter 4.

4

WOMAN-CENTRED
DEVELOPMENTAL THEORIES

In Chapter 2 of this book I argued that a critical developmental perspective has much to offer as an approach to understanding the psychology of women. In Chapter 3 I outlined and critiqued what traditional developmental psychologists and personality theorists have had to say about women's psychological development. In this chapter I will describe some of the attempts to provide a woman-centred perspective on the psychological development of girls and women. Several of the writers whose work will be described adopt a specifically feminist stance, some do not. Most have made a strong contribution to an understanding of female psychology, one which does not suffer from being derived from male norms and values. Importantly, these writers have succeeded in revaluing the attributes often associated with the psychology of women and of the feminine. However, I will also outline some of the ways in which these authors fail – to a greater or lesser extent – to interrogate the foundational assumptions of their developmental thinking.

Karen Horney and early opposition to Freud

Karen Horney's work on the psychology of women dates from the time when Freud was developing his own ideas on this topic but as a body of work it was not widely recognized until the 1970s, after the publication of a collection of Horney's papers entitled *Feminine Psychology* (Horney, 1967). Before this discovery of her work on the psychology of women, any reference to Horney's work tended to emphasize her contributions to personality theory and the causes of neurosis.

Karen Horney suffered neglect and rejection for her views on the neurotic personality because they were not seen as acceptable to the Freudian establishment. She was accused of being superficial in her insistence that current social circumstances had an influence on the psyche. In relation to her views on women, Horney was forthright in her disagreement with Freud. Her keynote paper, 'The flight from womanhood', was originally published in 1926 but has a refreshing directness of tone which is surprising still. She starts by remarking that 'like all sciences and all valuations the psychology of women has hitherto been considered only from the point of view of men' (1967, p. 56), and she goes on to suggest that 'the psychology of women hitherto actually represents a deposit of the desires and disappointments of men' (p. 56).

Although I have not found evidence of Horney using the term 'womb envy' she clearly promotes this concept, wondering why the genital difference between the sexes is the one to be accentuated, not the other significant biological differences associated with the different parts played by men and women in the gestation and feeding of babies. She claims that there has been an underestimate of male 'envy of pregnancy, childbirth and motherhood as well as of the breasts and of the act of suckling' (pp. 60–1). For Horney the basic motivational force in male psychology is to be found in envy of women, a neat turning of the tables on Freud. She asks, 'Is not the tremendous strength in men of their impulse to creative work in every field precisely due to their playing a relatively small part in the creation of living beings which constantly impels them to over-compensation in achievement?' (p. 61). 'Men', she concludes 'are evidently under greater need to depreciate females than conversely' (p. 62).

Horney's courageous questioning of Freud can be seen throughout her work, not only in her classic paper, 'The flight from womanhood'. For example, in 'The problem of female masochism', which was published in 1933, one can see just how radical Horney was for her time. She rejects Freud's views on the normality of female masochism, arguing that 'the hypothesis that it is psychobiologically necessary in all women is unconvincing'. She demands evidence and asserts that 'the peculiar configuration denoted by the term Oedipus complex is probably non-existent under widely different cultural conditions' (p. 218). She continues, 'omission of these considerations (social and cultural factors) may lead to a false valuation of anatomical differences and their personal elaboration as causative factors for phenomena actually partially or wholly the result of social conditioning' (p. 224).

Despite her acknowledgement of socio-cultural influences, Horney's position is still very much that of a psychoanalyst. As Garrison (1981) suggests, she offers, in the end, 'a limited revisionism'. Her ideas on ontogenesis rely on the same kinds of principles as do Freud's, although her interpretations differ. Thus she concedes that women envy men, but sees it as based on envy of male status rather than their possession of the penis. She does not carry her political analysis much further than this. Certainly she differs from Freud in her valuations. She resists and resents Freud's devaluation of women and his neglect of their powers and capacities. She is prepared to find weakness and envy in the psychic dispositions of men, whereas Freud is blind to such possibilities. Nonetheless, like Freud, Horney sees anatomy as playing an important role in the production of gender difference. She says, for example, 'The girl's nature as biologically conditioned gives her the desire to receive, to take into herself' (p. 142). However, she does note that 'this should not be equated with passivity'.

At the same time, since Horney argues for a recognition that it is society's valuations which Freud mirrors in his theory, she is undoubtedly one of the first feminist voices in psychology. As a psychoanalytic developmental theorist, Horney offers an important counterbalance to Freud's views of the motivations fuelling early female development. Her commitment remains to what she describes as the 'far reaching consequences of early experience', the existence and significance of infantile sexuality and the psychic consequences of the configuration of the body. In this sense she is a psychoanalyst in the classical mode and suffers from some of the same failings as Freud.

Horney was not alone in questioning Freud's views on women. Clara Thompson, a younger friend and professional ally, shared Horney's view that culture and the social context were important determinants of personality differences. She shared also Horney's opinion that females envied male status rather than the penis itself. Thompson was sensitive, at a time when such thoughts were not very common, to the ways in which the restricted social roles available to women throughout the life course could lead to frustration and low self-esteem (Thompson, 1964). She discussed the consequences of women being used in the sexual act and the social and psychological barriers to women's sexual fulfilment (Thompson, 1950).

On the other hand, Helene Deutsch, another psychoanalytic writer on the psychology of women, offered a very orthodox reading of women's psychology, which did not challenge Freud's views of women as deficient beings. As Janet Sayers (1992) points out, Deutsch tends to be an object of scorn for feminists, but she can be credited with making some advances in the fledgling study of the psychology of women. Her book, *Psychoanalysis of the Sexual Function in Woman* (1925), was the first book devoted to a psychoanalytic study of women and she was a pioneer in focusing on the significance of the early mother–daughter relationship.

Nancy Chodorow and the object relations school

Nancy Chodorow's influential book, *The Reproduction of Mothering*, was published in 1978. In this book Chodorow asks how women come to be mothers, a question which she claims is rarely asked since motherhood is assumed to be natural for women. Chodorow's approach to answering this question is developmental since she sees the roots of women's desire and capacity to mother as being in the first relationship between the infant girl and her mother.

Nancy Chodorow would locate her work as in the tradition of the British object relations school, a neo-Freudian school associated with the work of Winnicott, Fairbairn and Klein. None of these early theorists would identify their work as feminist or as woman-centred, although some of Melanie Klein's work could be seen in this light. Klein intoduced a variation on Freud's thinking about female development by proposing that the girl child experiences envy of the mother, whom she assumes has consumed the penis, rather than the father and possessor of the penis himself. The child then equates the breast with the penis, both organs being the focus of resentment and desire. Resolution of conflict with the mother becomes the foundation of later psychological and sexual maturity. Sayers (1992) points out that Klein played a crucially important role in drawing attention to the importance of early mothering and to the complex of feelings both positive and negative generated in that first relationship.

The focus on the part of early object relations theorists on the role of the mother and on relationship has provided fruitful ground for later feminist accounts of development. Chodorow describes object relations feminists as those who 'put self–other relations and the development of the self (whether whole or fragmented, agentic or reactive) as it is constituted through its consciously and unconsciously experienced relations in the center of development' (1989, p. 184).

Chodorow rejects biological and conditioning explanations of women's interest in mothering. She says, 'The capacity and orientations I describe must be built into personality: they are not behavioral acquisitions' (p. 39). Like Freud, Chodorow sees personality structures as formed in the first few years of life and as built into the unconscious at an early stage. Unlike Freud she argues that personality formation, including the desires and capacities which ensure the reproduction of mothering, 'occur through socially structured, induced psychological processes' (p. 39). Personality is, then, neither a product of biology nor of intentional role training. The pattern of personality structures typical of males and of females is, Chodorow argues, a function of the family structure in which the mother is the primary caretaker for both boys and girls and the father is a more distant figure. Surprisingly, Chodorow does not see this as a Western phenomenon but talks about it as 'universal'.

Chodorow presents her account of female (and male) early development as a reinterpretation of Freud's theory. For girls, the urge to mother is 'built developmentally into the female psyche'. Chodorow is convinced that gender identity is firmly established in the first few years of life. Unlike boys, girls and women do not need to separate from their first love object. As they grow they remain in touch emotionally with their mothers and with the experience of being mothered. Boys, on the other hand, must move away from their mothers and identify with their fathers; in this process all that is feminine and nurturing is repressed and the memories of being mothered are put aside. Thus psychically men who have been reared in the traditional nuclear family are neither motivated to mother nor equipped to mother. Girls are motivated to seek to perpetuate the blissful symbiotic relationship which they experienced as infants with their mothers. Unlike Freud, Chodorow does not argue that this is the way it must be. She sees these psychic structures as a consequence of our dominant pattern of familial organization. She also advocates 'a fundamental reorganization of parenting' in order to liberate men and women from their current personality typing. According to Chodorow, 'our sexuality and engendering take a particular form because we grow up in families where women mother' (p. 9). Her core propositions are encapsulated in the following quotation from *The Reproduction of Mothering*:

Because women are themselves mothered by women they grow up with the relational capacities and needs and psychological definition of self–in relationship which commits them to mothering. Men because they are mothered by women do not. Women mother daughters who, when they become women, mother.

(Chodorow, 1978, p. 209)

Although Chodorow's theorizing focuses on explaining the cyclical reproduction of motherhood, it also stands as a developmental theory about the construction of the female personality. It has been widely taken up – by other object relations theorists and by Carol Gilligan, for example. Gilligan (1982) uses Chodorow's work to support her own argument that girls and women have a personality disposition which is oriented towards relationships with others and which permits a greater level of empathy than that found in males. Gilligan cites with approval Chodorow's descriptions of the different pathways followed by male and female children and also endorses Chodorow's view that as long as individuation is taken as definitive of psychological maturity, women are at risk of being found intrinsically lacking.

There are many features of Chodorow's work which are important and attractive. Along with Horney and Gilligan she refuses to accept the Freudian account of female development. Her emphasis on the positive feminine qualities which result from the mother–girl child bond has been echoed in the work of a number of other feminist writers (e.g. Eichenbaum and Orbach, 1983; Gilligan, 1982; Miller, 1976). She also points to the vulnerabilities which are a consequence of this bond with the devalued parent which include difficulties in asserting one's own worth and needs and difficulties in maintaining emotional boundaries.

However, there are problems with the credibility of Chodorow's analysis. What is the evidence for the proposition that female babies experience a deep and persistent psychic fusion with their mothers? Attachment theory would suggest that equal numbers of both boy and girl babies form deep attachments with their mothers and that these attachments, contrary to the predictions of Chodorow's theory, may change in form but not in depth or intensity over the childhood years (Ainsworth, 1989). Chodorow does not deal with the mothers who through personality problems or a fraught life situation may fail to provide a secure emotional foundation for their infant of either sex. Identification with the mother is by no means an easy achievement for all girls and women, and the desire and capacity to mother is not neatly built into the psyche of all young women. Her analysis is also determinedly heterosexist and allows very little space for family constellations which deviate from the classic nuclear family.

Object relations theorists have, in contrast to Freud and his orthodox followers, placed a great deal of emphasis on pre-Oedipal development and on the child's first relationship (which is assumed to be) with the mother. For feminist theorists, this has provided a theoretical foundation for exploration of the mother–daughter relationship and its place in the formation of the female personality (e.g.

Eichenbaum and Orbach, 1983; van Mens-Verhulst *et al.*, 1993). As a theoretical model it is at heart committed to a deterministic, early formation view of personality development which is not that much different in its assumptions from Freudian theory. Both empirically and theoretically the credibility of such theories of human development has been radically undermined in the past two decades, as argued in Chapter 2. It is striking that such theoretical advances have failed to percolate through to the work of feminist scholars both within and outside psychology.

Carol Gilligan and other relational theorists

In 1979, Carol Gilligan published an influential essay titled 'Woman's place in man's life cycle', which was later to become a chapter in her book *In a Different Voice; Psychological Theory and Women's Development* (1982). In this essay, Gilligan discussed developmental theories and argued that 'Implicitly adopting the male life as the norm they have tried to fashion women out of a masculine cloth' (1979, p. 6). Carol Gilligan is the writer most strongly associated with the attempt to forge a new developmental psychology of women, and she deserves much credit for her critique of the male bias evident in developmental theorizing up to the late 1970s. She noted the tendency of male developmental theorists, such as Freud, Erikson and Piaget, to base their theorizing about female psychological development on the development of boys and men or to use only males in their empirical work, as Kohlberg did in his work on moral development.

Gilligan comments on the promotion of developmental goals such as separation, autonomy, rationality and competitiveness, all traditionally associated with masculinity rather than femininity. She noted also the tendency evident in developmental theorizing to devalue the experiences of women and to see women and girls as developmentally inadequate in comparison to males whether it be because they lagged behind or because they appeared to be heading in a different and, by reference to male goals, wrong direction. As she stated in the introduction to *In a Different Voice*, 'The disparity between women's experience and the representation of human development, noted throughout the psychological literature, has generally been taken to signify a problem in women's development' (1982, p. 2). She suggests that 'when one begins instead with women and derives developmental constructs from their lives, then a different conception of development emerges' (p. 441). This is a statement which sets an agenda and it is an agenda which could theoretically result in a number of different outcomes. For Gilligan, the agenda calls for the examination of women's lives with the aim of discovering the goals which shape their development, 'to expand the understanding of human development by using the group left out in the construction of theory to call attention to what is missing in its account' (p. 4). She says, 'The elusive mystery of women's development lies in its recognition of the continuing importance of attachment in the human lifecycle' (p. 445). It is the elaboration of this hypothesis which occupies much of her book *In a Different Voice*.

Gilligan's assumption is that one can rectify the problems which she has clearly identified in developmental theories by developing a parallel theory focused on the development of girls and women. In this way Gilligan's challenge to developmental psychology is important but incomplete. She is not questioning the dominant developmental model; she is asking that it be expanded to include the experience of women and that it examine its values with a view to incorporating and respecting the goals which women value. Her call for a woman-centred developmental theory is radical, as is her insistence on using methods which permit women and girls to speak with their own voice. However, in terms of developmental theory Gilligan's model of development is a traditional one.

Gilligan's conservatism has left her open to attack from colleagues, who accuse her of essentialist thinking. Critics argue that she is concerned to discover and understand the basic difference/s between men and women and sees these differences as definitive and fundamental to the psychology of the two sexes. The commitment to the idea of the 'real difference' signals Gilligan's positivistic orientation. Statements, then, such as that 'the elusive mystery of women's development lies in its recognition of the continuing importance of attachment in the human lifecycle' tell us that all women are alike in this way and are different from men in this way. It is implied that the importance women place on attachment applies to all women in all places and at all times. Although Gilligan's thinking is open to charges of essentialism, it should be noted that she is not a biological essentialist like Freud. Her explanation for the origins of women's caring orientation resides solidly in the area of early experience. Indeed, she endorses Nancy Chodorow's social-psychoanalytic theory about the divergent developmental pathways of boys and girls.

Gilligan herself would refute the charge of essentialism. She says that the different voice is empirically rather than essentially related to gender. This is a starting point which has implications that are not explored fully in her work. It may have led to an exploration of the conditions associated with the empirical finding of a different voice instead of further elaboration of the quality of the different voice as heard in the interviews with women and girls. Gilligan does suggest, however, that the suppression of the authentic voice of adolescent girls is a response to patriarchy. From this point of view it seems unfair to accuse her of a total neglect of political and cultural context as some of her critics have done, including Helen Haste (1994), who says that 'the main criticism is that Gilligan ignores culture' (p. 402).

Another way in which Gilligan's writing has essentialist overtones is in relation to her theorizing about the authenticity of self. She takes the view that we all possess in some way a real or authentic self which is being denied or repressed by patriarchy. Such a notion is fundamentally questionable for social constructionist feminists, who see the self as a construction, a social process which is neither real, nor unitary nor fixed nor knowable. Thus it makes no sense to talk about giving voice to the authentic self. Even if one were to accept the utility and phenomenal reality of the idea of self, a topic which will be explored further in

Chapter 6, the idea of a 'real' or 'authentic' self is a reification which must be suspect.

As developmental theorists, Gilligan and her colleagues have made an important contribution to mapping out the issues which arise in relation to the transition from girlhood to womanhood. This work has resulted in several publications associated with the Harvard Project on Women's Psychology and Girls' Development, most notably *Making Connections; The Relational Worlds of Adolescent Girls at Emma Willard School* (Gilligan *et al.*, 1990), and *Meeting at the Crossroads: Women's Psychology and Girls' Development* (Brown and Gilligan, 1992).

In *Meeting at the Crossroads,* Brown and Gilligan describe a crucial developmental transition which occurs as girls move from the freedom of early childhood into adolescence and their first encounter with the demands of a patriarchal society. They say that 'adolescence is a time of disconnection, sometimes of dissociation or repression in women's lives'. In a later summary of their views, Brown states: 'our research suggests that girls are rewarded for adopting narrow conventions of femininity that require them to bury much of what they know' (Brown, 1994, p. 383).

There has been much debate, including a special feature series in *Feminism and Psychology* (1994, Volume 4, Number 3), about whether or not adolescence is a time of silencing for girls, and whether or not relationships are central to the lives of girls in a way that they are not for boys, and whether it is helpful to talk about the repression of the authentic voice and real self of girls. At the start of *Meeting at the Crossroads,* Brown and Gilligan claimed that they were setting out 'to explore hitherto uncharted territory in women's psychology, this land between childhood and adolescence'. They must be given credit for turning attention to this long-ignored stage in female development. Certainly there was very little work indeed on the lives of young girls and adolescents until this time and there has been comparatively more since. Prior to the 1980s there was some work on the psychological impact of puberty and on eating disorders in adolescent girls but little else. Gilligan and her colleagues have also pioneered the use of methods for enquiry into girls' perspectives on their own lives such as the Listeners' Guide (Brown and Gilligan, 1992) and interpretive poetics (Rogers, in press).

There are several other groups of theorists who, although quite distinctive in their contributions, share Gilligan and her colleagues' emphasis on the importance of connection and relationship in the lives of girls and women. Much of the work of the group of women working at the Stone Center, located in Wellesley College, Boston, seems to have been inspired by Jean Baker Miller's book *Toward a New Psychology of Women* which was published in 1976. The ensuing articles and papers from Miller and her colleagues form what has been termed 'The Feminist Interpersonal School', and have much in common with the work produced not far away in Harvard by Gilligan and her co-workers. The work of Miller and her colleagues appears to have grown more directly from an interest in psychoanalysis and psychotherapy, whereas Gilligan's work on women's psychology, initially at least, grew from her empirical research in moral development. However, despite working independently and from different premises, these two groups arrived at some highly compatible conclusions about women's development.

Two books, *Women's Growth in Connection* (1991) which was edited by Judith Jordan, Alexandra Caplan, Jean Baker Miller, Irene Stiver and Janet Surrey and *Women's Growth in Diversity* (1997) edited by Judith Jordan, have elaborated the Stone Center model of women's development. This model aims to 'articulate a perspective on women's development that more accurately reflects women's experience' in opposition to 'models of development inspired by a male culture' (Jordan *et al.*, 1991, p. v). In the Introduction to *Women's Growth in Connection*, the editors note the similarity between their work and that of Gilligan and her colleagues, and both bodies of work, they suggest, could be labelled as 'relational' in focus.

The central principles of the Stone Center model are that girls and women are socialized differently to boys and men in Western societies. Women are socialized to be relational beings, concerned about their relationships with others and more equipped than males to respond empathically and caringly to other people. The male developmental route is towards individuation, autonomy and mastery, and these accomplishments are valued more than the relational path of girls and women. In fact, as Jean Baker Miller argued in 1976, the empathic skills and interpersonal orientation of girls and women are in many ways more valuable to humankind and should be fostered in the development of both men and women. Women, it is argued, are less competitive and more motivated to foster growth in others.

Once again, as with Gilligan, the writers turn to Chodorow for a developmental explanation of the different developmental histories of girls and women. Jordan adds to Chodorow's account the view that 'boys are actively socialized towards a power-dominance experience of selfhood while girls are socialized towards a love-empathy mode of being in the world' (1997, p. 18).

The work of the Stone Center, found not only in books and articles but in a long series of working papers, stands as a very important exploration of the meaning of relationships to women and the central place of relationships in their lives. The perspective is captured in the following statement: 'the Stone Center relational model emphasizes the centrality of connection in women's lives. Disconnection is viewed as the source of most human suffering' (1997, p. 3).

As an alternative theory of development to male-centred theories it presents some difficulties. First, there is not much attention to the question Why? Why do women invest so much in connection, connectedness and relationships? As has been pointed out, such attention and sensitivity to the needs of others is a feature of those without power, but the Stone Center model fails to address this or any other alternate explanation. The model is also tainted by its explicit prescriptiveness. For example, Jordan says, 'In the ideal pattern of development we move toward participation in relational growth rather than toward simple attainment of personal gratification' (1997, p. 31).

The year 1986 saw the publication of *Women's Ways of Knowing: The Development of Self, Voice and Mind*, co-authored by Mary Field Belenky, Blythe McVicker Clinchy, Nancy Rule Goldberger and Jill Mattuck Tarule. They take a similar starting point to other relational feminists, but their focus is on intellectual rather than moral or socio-emotional development. At the same time, they take as a starting point the view that a woman's emotional and moral orientation is part of the fabric of her intellectual orientation towards the world, an orientation they refer to as 'connected knowing'. This form of knowing, they claim, is traditionally undervalued and under-researched. They state that 'nowhere is the pattern of using male experience to define the human experience seen more clearly than in models of intellectual development' (1986, p. 7).

Influenced by Gilligan and by William Perry's work (1968) on intellectual and ethical development in college students, they interviewed 135 women for two to five hours each on a range of topics concerning what they knew about life and how they knew it. From these interviews, examples are given that provide convincing evidence for the proposition that 'too often in American families, girls and women are socialized to be seen, not heard' (Goldberger, 1996, p. 257). They found that women repeatedly used the metaphor of voice to depict their intellectual and ethical development and their struggle to know and to be heard. Some women were capable of or had been enabled to find their voice and some had achieved 'constructed knowing'. Constructed knowing implies an integration of 'separate knowing', the traditionally valued (in the Western academy) objective stance towards knowledge, and 'connected knowing' which they see as a distinctively feminine orientation towards knowledge of the world. Belenky *et al.*'s (1986) work is interesting in that it draws attention to undervalued but valuable forms of knowledge but again raises questions about why 'connected knowing' should be associated with women, questions which can be addressed only by taking into account the social and political location of women in late twentieth-century America.

In fact 'connected knowing' is a feature of the approach to knowledge adopted by many oppressed groups and cultures working outside those systems which prioritize detachment, objectivity and logical reasoning. It is also the case that work on cognitive development in adulthood carried out over the past thirty years has drawn attention to the neglect of the everyday knowledge of adults living their daily lives. Theorists like Gisela Labouvie-Vief and Michael Chandler (1978) were pioneers in critiquing the dominance of Piagetian, child-centred models of cognitive development and their inapplicability to the contextualized, relativistic thinking of the (male or female) adult actively engaged in his or her working or domestic life. Women's ways of knowing may not be specific to women but rather may be ways of knowing that psychology has in the past been inclined to ignore.

In a later study carried out by Helen Haste and colleagues in the UK, interview data collected from adolescents of both sexes indicated greater evidence of connected knowing in contrast to separate knowing among girls, but the girls were prone to using both styles. Haste argues that the importance of work on the feminine form of knowing is that it is 'making explicit, rediscovering and validating an existing cultural alternative which the culture has attempted to deny, hide and denigrate by labeling it feminine' (Haste, 1993, p. 218).

Similar conclusions have been arrived at by Gisela Labouvie-Vief in her exploration of gender and mind, *Psyche and Eros: Mind and Gender in the Life Course*, published in 1994. Labouvie-Vief contrasts rationality with imagination, rationality being masculine and imagination feminine. Her perspective is developmental in that she sees the story of development as one where the imagination and associated modes of relating to the world are to be subjugated in the course of development to permit the triumph of reason and the rational. Both Haste and Labouvie-Vief make use of the idea of *the feminine* which is perhaps a more productive way to think about gender dualisms than relating them to female persons (Greene, 1997b). *The feminine* is instantiated in socio-political discourse and deeply embedded in our culture's myths and stories. It acts as a template for the construction of female subjectivity in girls and women as they encounter the cultural world.

Levinson's *Seasons of a Woman's Life* and the analysis of biographies

One of the most widely cited studies of adult psychological development has been Daniel Levinson's book *Seasons of a Man's Life*, which was published in 1978. In the life span texts of the 1990s, Levinson's work is almost invariably discussed at length and with respect (see e.g. Santrock, 1992, 1999). As mentioned in Chapter 3, Levinson reported the results of interviews with forty middle-aged men. On the basis of the interviews and other biographical and literary sources, he expanded his theory that developmental change during adulthood could best be conceptualized in terms of seasons. Seasons follow each other but are not organized in a hierarchical progression. Winter is not better or more advanced than spring, it is just different. According to Levinson, the movement from one 'season' to the next is a time of transition and instability. As the man settles into early, middle or late adulthood he experiences periods of stability. In the later years of early adulthood most men, Levinson claims, enter the phase called Becoming One's Own Man (BOOM), an achievement which should characterize the man of 40. Levinson's empirical work involved only men, and the issues addressed and terminology used are totally male-centred. But, rather astonishingly, he asserted that his seasons, transitions and crises could all be found in women's lives.

Shortly before his death, in 1994, Levinson completed the work for *Seasons of a Woman's Life* which was published in 1996. In the Preface he states, 'In *Seasons of a Man's Life* it was difficult to say which aspects of the theory and findings were true of human development generally and which held for men only. The present study provided the opportunity (and indeed the necessity) of arriving at a clearer distinction' (p. x). In this new study, Levinson reports the results of intensive interviews conducted with forty-five women between 1980 and 1982. He states his primary aim as learning 'about the life course and development of women from the late teens to the mid forties' (p. 4). To this end he uses a method he calls *Intensive Biographical Interviewing*.

The women studied were aged between 35 and 45 at the time of interview. Fifteen were classified as homemakers, fifteen were academics and fifteen were employed in corporate financial organizations. Levinson draws a number of conclusions from his study about the nature of adult development, and most of these conclusions seem to be very much in line with his thinking as recorded previously in *Seasons of a Man's Life*. He considers that he has evidence that 'the course of life is not a simple continuous process, there are qualitatively different phases or seasons' (p. 14). Nine different phases encompassing ages 17 to 65 are described, and these are seen to be 'standard', i.e. typical of the life course of all adults, men and women (p. 27), and 'applicable to individuals of all classes, cultures and genders' (p. 36).

Levinson remarks: 'I must admit that I am surprised and even somewhat embarrassed by the order and elegant simplicity of this sequence' (p. 28). However, he does concede that '*Within the general framework of human life structure development*, the genders differ greatly in life circumstance, in life course, in ways of going through each developmental period' (p. 36). In his descriptions of the lives of the women who participated in his study, Levinson shows that he does not consider that the character of women's lives is fixed by their gender. He is aware that gendered aspects of lives are mutable, saying, for example, 'Humanity is now in the early phases of transformation in the meanings of gender and the place of women and men in every society' (p. 414). However, in the end the differences between men and women are relegated to matters of detail, and he remains firmly attached to the notion of a fixed life structure, with standard issues arising in a predictable sequence.

On finishing *Seasons of a Woman's Life*, it is difficult not to conclude that Levinson had a pre-existing framework into which he was inevitably going to fit the lives of the forty-five women interviewed. Very few of the women appeared to follow pathways similar to those of the men in the 1978 study, but Levinson manages to convince himself that the same structure and developmental issues underpin the women's development. For example, the novice phase in early adulthood is the time when men are expected to form their Dream of Adult Achievement, find a mentor and 'the special woman' who will help in the realization of the Dream. Aside from the heterosexual assumptions, few of Levinson's women interviewees seem to fit such a pattern. Levinson does identify some common gendered themes in the lives of his interviewees as, for example, the homemakers' struggle for their sense of identity at a time in history when their traditional role is less supported than it was. But there is no attempt to theorize gender in relation to power differentials or to examine the constraints on women's aspirations, the meaning of gender and femininity in their lives and the way they think these meanings may have changed as they have aged.

Levinson offers a normalized view of the life cycle. The basic structure, consisting of eras, transitions and crises, is claimed as universal. The theory is an organismic theory since the origin of change is internal, part of the developmental process that will inevitably unfold. Such a theory acts potentially like a strait-jacket for both sexes; it dictates the appropriate timing and sequencing of experiences in the adult life course with a relative lack of awareness of their historical and cultural specificity. If such patterns and timing are found to be usual in North American society, we are learning more about that society than about the supposed universals of human development.

George Vaillant is another researcher who is well known for his work on adult psychological development. The Grant Study, which was a longitudinal study of 204 men first contacted when they were Harvard undergraduates, has been widely cited and is seen as providing empirical support for Erikson's later developmental stages. In 1977 Vaillant said, 'The absence of women in the Grant Study was an unforgivable omission, an omission that will require another study to correct' (1977, p. 13). The manner in which Vaillant expresses this regret is telling. He, like Gilligan and Levinson, believes that the way to arrive at a complete account of adult development is to include women. The questionable assumption is that there can be such a thing as a complete account of human psychological development. From this point of view it is entirely acceptable for a researcher to embark on a study of the adult development of 204 white male Harvard students, if they understand that this is precisely what their study is about – the development of a 1930s cohort of white male Harvard students. In and of itself such a study has interest; the problem arises when the study is seen to carry more meaning and relevance than it actually has. Of course, this problem of over-generalization and universalization is one that is entirely typical of the use of psychological studies throughout the twentieth century; it is not specific to developmental psychology.

The biographical interview has formed the basis for a number of studies of women's psychological development. In recent years much of this work is affiliated in approach if not by explicit declaration with a school of psychology centred on the idea of narrative and the exploration of its powerful role in the construction of people's individual life stories and identity (Sarbin, 1986; Freeman, 1993). In relation to the study of women's lives, one of the most prominent examples is the series *The Narrative Study of Lives* edited by Ruthellen Josselson and Amia Lieblich, the first volume of which appeared in 1993. The stories of men are not excluded from this series, but the editors note that their method and orientation is one which draws from ideas central to feminist research and its critique of positivism. Thus they assert the value of single case studies, qualitative data and of reflexivity on the part of the researcher. There is a long history of single case studies in psychology, but the approach of narrative psychology is different in that the emphasis is on the ways in which people construct meaningful lives and the ways in which researchers interpret and can come to know or not know the lives of others. Carol Franz and Abigail Stewart (1994) also argue for the sustained biographical study of diverse women engaged in living their lives. Their edited book *Women Creating Lives: Identities Resilience and Resistance* contains accounts of women's lives gained mainly by means of interviews.

There is no doubt that much of this work on life story and narrative qualifies as developmental in that it deals with change in women's lives over time. The strengths of this kind of work are that it is sensitive to context, both cultural and historical, and to diversity. It also deals with the whole woman and her meaningful lived life, not some abstraction of woman. Abigail Stewart (1994) articulates an explicitly feminist approach to the study of women's lives, arguing that by choosing to highlight lives which are regarded by male authorities as not important, the realities of women's lives may become central rather than peripheral. She also focuses on the role of power and social position in women's lives in a way that traditional biographers would not. She makes the case for identifying ways in which women's lives are constrained and marked by oppression but also ways in which women resist and are agents in the making of their own life stories. Interestingly Stewart also confronts the temptation which is at the heart of the construction of story and the biographical process itself – that is, making coherent that which is probably not coherent. She also includes a troubled section on the place of reflexivity in the interpretation of the story of another, noting that identification with the subject of the life history can make one blind to issues about which one is motivated to remain blind but acutely sensitive to issues which one has addressed and recognized as significant in one's own life story.

The interest in narrative is part of the exploration of alternative ways of seeking psychological knowledge which, as mentioned in Chapter 1, has been eloquently outlined by Jerome Bruner (1990). The active meaning-making of the human subject is at the centre of this perspective. As an approach it is to an extent compatible with a social constructionist perspective as typified in the work of Kenneth Gergen (1985) and Mary Gergen (2001), although the use of narrative also sits comfortably with a feminist standpoint. From a rather simplistic 'listening to the voices of the marginalized' perspective, women are taken to be in possession of the truth about their own lives and are in many ways, as an oppressed minority, also in possession of greater insights about human life than are dominant males. Women's stories are taken as direct reflections of their experience, and the job of the researcher is to listen to and bring out into the open their hidden and marginalized voices. By contrast, the social constructionist approach to narrative is to see the narrative as text which is open to deconstruction and interpretation. From this theoretical perspective, personal narratives are never merely that. They are the result of the multiple discourses to which that individual has been exposed and the individual's subjectivity is itself a social construct which can be understood as a shifting, elusive text. Mary Gergen's recent book,

Feminist Reconstructions in Psychology: Narrative, Gender and Performance (2001), adopts a specifically social constructionist perspective. Gergen emphasizes the interest among social constructionists in understanding how people create meaning together through discourse. She comments that 'the stories women tell of their lives are ventriloquated through the narratives that culture has made available to them' (2001, p. 39).

Neither the cultural feminist/feminist standpoint nor the social constructionist perspective on narrative seems to be adequate. On the one hand, we have a view of narrative as a way of accessing women's life stories and getting closer to their true selves, and on the other hand, the woman telling her life story is positioned as if she were a ventriloquist's dummy.

In Chapter 6, I will return to the topic of narrative and life stories as they relate to the construction of self. At this point, suffice to say that narratives and biographies are a promising method of understanding women's psychological development which has been used by feminists working from very different theoretical perspectives.

Contemporary woman-centred psychoanalytic theory

It is interesting that many of the above theorists, who have an interest in female development, have drawn upon psychoanalytic theory or depth psychology, broadly defined. As Miller and Scholnick comment, 'Feminist scholars rarely mention major developmental theories other than older psychoanalytic ones' (2000, p. 241). In some ways the alliance of feminism with psychoanalytic theory is surprising since psychoanalytic theories speak of determinism and the dictates of the past, not about the future and the possibility for transformation which, one might imagine, would be a more useful underpinning to any liberation movement. Although there are many contemporary reworkings of psychoanalytic theory, it is the case that psychoanalytic theory of one kind or another is the developmental perspective most familiar to feminist theorists inside and outside psychology. Both Lacanian and object relations theory have been the basis for influential analyses of the construction of female subjectivity. From a developmental perspective, for example, Gilligan was strongly influenced by Chodorow who in turn is writing in an object relations framework with her emphasis on the pre-Oedipal attachment to the mother – the first love 'object'. Many of the writers, who emphasize the female embeddedness in relationships, adhere to an object relations orientation either explicitly or tacitly.

The Lacanian emphasis on language and the symbolic has been a strong influence on the thinking of French feminist philosophers/psychoanalysts. French feminist theorists such as Luce Irigaray and Julia Kristeva have in different ways responded to Jacques Lacan's theories which present a view of women as always and inevitably *the other*, condemned to exist outside the symbolic order. Rather than accept the Lacanian negative valuation of the feminine, they have explored its positive character and powers. Irigaray focuses on 'the female imaginary' which is based on the biology and sexuality of the female. For example, she claims that the two lips of the vagina produce a sexuality which is about duality and an ongoing self-sustained sensuality (Irigaray, 1985). The most intense self-expression and pleasure are to be found in reconnecting with the experiences of infancy before entry into language and its patriarchal modes of thought and restrictions on female desire and pleasure. Both Irigaray and Kristeva have explored the idea of a female language rooted in pre-Oedipal experience.

Jane Flax notes, 'for all its shortcomings psychoanalysis represents the best and most promising theory of how a self, that is simultaneously embodied, social, "fictional" and real, comes to be, changes and persists over time' (1990, p. 16). Flax's point of view is very interesting but to my mind this is an overstatement. There are other ways of theorizing how the self comes into being, changes and persists over time. This book elaborates on some of them.

Nonetheless, it may be the case that feminist psychology still needs psycho-analysis as it provides the fullest account we have of the complex and contradic-tory nature of subjectivities formed in part through desire and identification. Where the psychoanalytic perspective casts light and other perspectives do not mostly relates to the perhaps unknowable ways in which the unconscious and the irrational intrude upon the person's thoughts and impulses. Such thoughts and impulses are however only a part of the picture. There is a fundamental problem in the adoption of psychoanalytic theories as the only basis for a feminist devel-opmental psychology. Essentialist and fatalistic principles lie at the heart of both Lacanian and object relations feminism. They require either a backward view of what constitutes the person, insisting that who she is is largely dictated by her first relationships with her father and/or mother, or that her life amounts to a perennial struggle with pervasive and immutable symbols of phallic ascendancy.

Conclusion

In an important paper titled 'Finished at 40: women's development in the patri-archy' Mary Gergen argues that most life span developmental theory offers a limited and limiting understanding of women's development. She suggests that 'By treating theories as literary works such as plays or stories new understanding can be created' (1990, p. 476). The life story which she discerns in developmen-tal theories is focused on marriage and childbearing. Gergen offers a graph of 'women's life narrative' which shows a progressive buildup to the early twenties when the woman is assumed to find her male partner and the father of her children, a plateau where nothing much changes until about age 40 and a decline from 40 onwards. Gergen critiques the work of Freud, Erikson and Levinson but also points out that similar stories are repeated in the psychology of women textbooks available at the time when Gergen was writing her paper (the latest textbook was from 1987).

More than ten years later, the picture has changed little. As mentioned in Chapter 1, the treatment of life span issues is often under-theorized and where developmental theories are referenced they are typically those which derive from psychoanalysis in its various guises. Even explicitly woman-centred or feminist accounts of women's life span development, as discussed above, fail to capture the diversity, multi-directionality and open-endedness of women's lives. They also fail to offer an account which can provide the basis for change or transformation of women's lives, which is surely at the heart of feminism. It is the thesis of this book that this failure results from a very limited perspective on the range of possibilities that is open to women and the extent of the potential for change across the entire life course.

Failure also results from lack of attention to the regulating discourses, about time and ageing and proper behaviour related to age, which confront and constrain women and men. What is of interest here is how the construction of age, ageing and development shapes the life trajectories of women and girls. Thus from the above review we are left with avowedly feminist accounts of women's development which promote heterosexism (Chodorow), which construct girls and women's lives only in terms of relationships and connection (Gilligan, Baker Miller, etc.), which pinpoint mothers as the people most responsible for their daughters' psychological well-being (Chodorow again), which reinforce the otherness of women and their inevitable debarment from power within the patriarchy (Irigaray), which see women's development as formed by the dynamics of their early relationships (Chodorow again).

In this chapter I have outlined a number of developmental theories which are widely cited both in psychology of women texts and in the general feminist literature. The limitations of these theories are worrying in that despite their avowedly woman-centred perspective, they continue in many ways to perpetuate an extremely restricted version of women's lives, focused on heterosexuality, reproduction and relationships.

5

BIOLOGY AND THE CHANGING BODY

The extent to which biological factors influence female psychology is a deeply contentious question. Much of the work of feminist psychologists writing in the twentieth century may be seen as a refutation of Freud's dictum that 'anatomy is destiny'. The contrary view that such gendered psychological differences that do exist are a consequence of social determinants has become a central tenet of equality feminism and social constructionist feminism alike.

The debate has not been helped by a persisting dualistic conceptualization of the biological and the social by psychologists who favour either a biological or a social determinist perspective. In recent years, numerous calls have been made for the dismantling of the old *biological vs. social* or *nature vs. nurture* polarity. Certainly there are very few psychologists who would disregard totally the proposition that both so-called forces play a part in shaping the person.

In relation to the *biological vs. social* dichotomy, it is the case that theoretical perspectives which emphasize almost totally the biological *or* the social are not in step with contemporary thinking on the relationship between the biological body and its context. Even within the science of biology, biologists are to be found who emphasize most strongly the complete dependence of the organism on its context.

Of course, one might say that this interdependence has been recognized for a long time, but when one examines, for example, the thinking behind the work of sociobiologists and neo-Darwinists one finds a very strong commitment to biological determinism. This may be seen in Richard Dawkins' representation of genes as the programmers of the organism. Dawkins argues that genes 'are in you and me: they created us, body and mind; and their preservation is the ultimate rationale for our existence' (1989, p. 20). Or again, he states that 'Living bodies are machines programmed by genes' (p. 98). Some psychologists adopt a similar position. Thus the developmental psychologists Sandra Scarr and Robert McCartney (1983, p. 443) state, 'We are products of the cooperative effects of the nature/nurture team, directed by the genetic quarterback'. As noted in Chapter 3, evolutionary psychology is gaining ground as one of the most powerful paradigms in contemporary mainstream psychology, alongside cognitive neuroscience.

In response to neo-Darwinism, the biologist and neuroscientist Steven Rose presents an alternative vision of the nature of the organism/environment interaction. He says, 'The phenomena of life are always and inexorably simultaneously about nature *and* nurture and the phenomena of human existence are always simultaneously biological *and* social' (Rose, 1997, p. 279). Some psychologists are also beginning to lose patience with the constant relapse into polarizing the biological and the social. It is clear that we need a new vocabulary which would allow us more easily to think about and write about the total interdependence of the human body, mind and culture. Richard Lerner, a developmental psychologist, asserts that 'it is counterfactual to contend that nature is separable from nurture' (1993, p. 122), and he continues, 'the concept of developmental systems, and not genetic reductionism is the (only) valid conception of the role of biology in human development' (p. 123).

There is a further major problem in relation to both social determinism and biological determinism. They create very little space for a view of the person as agentic and as a contributor to her own development. From this point of view they both present a reductionist view of the person which fails to take on board the evidence for person-generated activity, novelty and unpredictability. For reductionist theorists the psychological is to be understood as secondary to the biological or the social in terms of causation. From a scientific perspective such theories represent a failure to address the psychological in its own terms. And from a moral perspective such theoretical perspectives often fail to value the personhood of the individual, seeing her as a product rather than as a unique agent. Susan Oyama considers that the persisting adherence to the nature–nurture dichotomy in developmental thinking makes it easier 'to see people as objects formed and moved by causes rather than experiencing subjects who may act for reasons – that is as persons' (1993, p. 471).

In this chapter and in those which follow I will, in a sense, be perpetuating those divisions by dividing my examination of the different perspectives on the person into the biological, intrapersonal, social and historical. However, I do so with the ultimate goal of presenting a less fragmented and more complete picture of the quality of individual life span change as it applies to the female life course. In each chapter an attempt will be made to locate each level of analysis as an element in a complex system. In the following chapters the overarching, organizing construct will be *time*. Therefore, special attention will be paid to how *time*, as it is variously expressed and understood, is associated with psychological change and development in the lives of girls and women.

Biological inevitabilities?

Because of the very understandable suspicion of psychological theorizing which locates women's motivation and personality in her biology, many contemporary feminist theories about the psychology of women ignore the body or locate it in the realm of discourse and text. However, the material reality of the body is ungainsayable and must be taken into account, as many contemporary feminist theorists would recognize (Ussher, 1997).

One of the defining facts of our status as living creatures is our finite life span. Even so, within the discipline of psychology there is comparatively little focus on how the reality of our limited existence in time affects our psychology. As we travel through the life course our bodies are transformed from their baby shape to that of the old person, should we live that long. Our allotted time is predictably restricted to a maximum of about eighty or ninety years – although we are now in the midst of discussions about a possible substantial extension of the average life span. Our mortality and our biological ageing and vulnerability are so obvious that they seem to require little comment from psychologists.

On the other hand, finitude is so fundamental to the character of our existence that it must be examined and taken into account. One of the few schools of psychology that has taken the human relationship to time and mortality seriously is the existential school, largely disregarded by mainstream psychology. Existentialists such as Rollo May have argued that we cannot live life to the full without acute awareness of its finitude and without coming to terms with our own mortality. The fact that we have a limited duration as a living creature is arguably the most defining of the biological constraints on our psychology. But, as Ernst Becker argued in his (1970) book *Denial of Death*, we are, on the whole, expert at living without full recognition of our own transience.

Our embodiment is also an incontrovertible fact of our existence. After years in which feminism more or less ignored the body it has over the past twenty years become a focus of renewed interest on the part of a number of feminist scholars. The body at the centre of this recent wave of feminist scholarship is the thought body or, as Gatens calls it, 'the imaginary body' (Gatens, 1983). From this perspective the body is analysed as a social construction or as a text. The experience of embodiment is seen as historically and socially specific, and to a great extent a function of prevalent discourses on the meaning and uses of the body. Undoubtedly there is much to be gained in an analysis of the effect of discourse on the meaning and experience of the body and its functions but, if one takes such theorizing to its logical conclusion, there is little room left for the reality of the biological body.

To argue, as I am doing, for a recognition of the existence of the biological body – the embodied body rather than the thought body – should not be seen as a rejection of the view that how bodies are construed for us and how we construe our bodies are essential aspects of our lives. These construals affect us profoundly both as flesh-and-blood creatures and persons and the meanings we ascribe to the body will always influence our relationship to it. In relation to the passage of time and ageing the relevant discourse on these themes plays a central role in mediating between our biological and psychological selves. Recognition of the reality of the material body and the events which impinge upon it does not imply a collapse into a positivist biological determinism. It must be possible to take into account both the centrality of discourse to the meaning of our bodies and the material fact of our embodiment. Such a resolution has been adopted by Jane Ussher, for example, in her exploration of a material-discursive approach to health issues (Ussher, 1997). Ussher defines this approach as 'The view that we need to move away from the binary divide between material and discursive analyses of the body, towards a position which allows us to recognize the interaction and inter-relationship between the two' (1997, p. 1). As Corrinne Squire notes, 'the material is discursive; equally the discursive is material' (1997 p. 51).

The female relationship to nature

From this position one turns to the analysis of the psychological significance of the developing body, the changing and mortal body which is both home to the psyche and is intimately involved in making it what it is. The context in which the female body grows and changes is both a psychological and a social context, replete with meaning and consequences.

Women have been seen in centuries of Western writing as the sex which is psychologically closest to nature. Indeed, nature 'herself' has often been personified as a female person, often as 'Mother Nature', depicted variously as benign or threatening. Milton in *Paradise Lost* says, 'Earth felt the wound and Nature from *her* seat, sighing through all *her* works, gave signs of woe that all was lost.' If personified, nature is rarely if ever personified as male. God, on the other hand, in monotheistic religions has almost always been male.

Scientific discourse quickly adopted the metaphor of nature as female person. Scientists were motivated by the goal of subduing and controlling the mysteries of unruly nature. Francis Bacon spoke of nature as female and exhorted his fellow scientists to 'bind her to your service and make her your slave' (Farrington, 1951, p. 197). In this same tradition women are seen as rooted in their bodies, incapable of the transcendence of the biological which makes man 'noble in reason' (Tuana, 1993). The inferior intellect and moral sense of women and their malleability, all features of most accounts of the nature of women since Aristotle, were, Lorraine Daston argues, 'corporeally grounded, largely determined by women's allegedly cold, moist bodily complexion. Sensory impressions, stamped upon the brain as a seal upon wax, therefore adhered more easily, distinctly and durably in the soft, humid, female matter than in that of the hot dry male' (Daston, 1996, p. 171). These notions about female moistness and coldness, Daston argues, were prevalent well into the eighteenth century.

Other theories about the basis for female bodily and mental weakness persisted for longer, but were based on equally dubious 'science'. Most of these theories confirmed women's destiny as mother, homemaker and nurturer, forever tied to the fulfilment of her body's design and its needs. As Rousseau firmly asserted in 1762, 'The male is only a male now and again, the female is always a female at least in her youth; everything reminds her of her sex: the performance of her functions requires a special constitution' (1974, p. 324).

In general, women have been identified as biological creatures to a greater extent than men and more of their behaviour has been seen to be explicable in terms of their bodies. This placing of women as closer to nature than men and more influenced by their biology is current in contemporary thought. Hormones are the modern version of floating wombs or cold, moist complexions. 'Raging' hormones or depleted hormones are common explanations of pre-menopausal women's mood changes and the supposed irascibility and depression of women at and after menopause. As Linda Gannon comments, 'men are above their biology, they are objective, while women are controlled by their biology, they are emotional and illogical' (1994, p. 110). As I discussed in chapters 3 and 4, the biologizing of the female life course patterns it in time, imposing upon it a structure which is largely dictated by the reproductive cycle.

Women's bodies and time

The first question to ask is to what extent girls and women have a distinctive relationship to time and whether any such relationship which may be found relates to the body. The assumed nature and functions of the female body and the assumed female closeness to nature have resulted in some speculation about the female relationship to time. This may be seen, for example, in the Greek myth of Demeter, the goddess of corn and harvests, and her daughter Persephone (Proserpine), which 'explains' the origin of the seasons. Proserpine was abducted by Pluto and, so the story goes, while Demeter demented by grief sought high and low for her daughter, the cultivation of the earth was neglected and the ground became barren, as in winter.

However, the female relationship to time is not a topic which has received much attention from contemporary psychologists, but there are a few exceptions. Helen Haste (1994), for example, suggests that women experience the cyclicity of time more strongly than do men. As the myth of Demeter and Persephone (Proserpine) would suggest, the association between the female and cyclicity has a long history and such an association is not surprising when one focuses upon the menstrual cycle or upon the regularity and repetition of domestic life. Haste notes,

> Women's lives are experienced in so many areas in terms of cycles –
> physical and biological cycles, diurnal cycles of nurturance and prepa-
> ration of food, cycles of caring, cleansing and the annual cycles of
> family life.
>
> (Haste, 1994, p. 6)

Julia Kristeva has written a paper entitled 'Women's time' which is very much of a piece with her views on the importance of the body in shaping women's experience. She says, 'When evoking the name and destiny of women, one thinks more of the *space* generating and forming the human species than of *time*, becoming, or history' (1981, p. 15). She continues,

77

> As for time, female subjectivity would seem to provide a specific measure that essentially retains *repetition* and *eternity* from among the multiple modalities of time known through the history of civilizations. On the one hand, there are cycles, gestation, the eternal recurrence of a biological rhythm which conforms to that of nature and imposes a temporality, whose stereotyping may shock.
>
> (Kristeva, 1981, p. 16)

Female subjectivity, Kristeva claims, is also related to both cyclical (repetitive) and eternal or monumental time. It is, however, out of sync with linear time, communicated via language that relies on a linear form of expressing relationship ('noun + verb; topic – comment; beginning–ending'). According to Kristeva, linear time is patriarchal time. She appears to be tying women to conceptions of time which are indeed shocking in their degree of stereotyping. It is the frequency with which Kristeva makes such statements that makes one question her frequent categorization as a 'postmodernist' feminist.

Nonetheless, it seems interesting to me to ask whether or not there is a *woman's time*. Does the existence of the monthly period or her engagement in tasks to do with feeding and nurturing result in increased feeling for the cyclicities in life? There does not appear to be any conclusive answer to this question. Perhaps some women feel this way. However, it would appear that most Western women are inevitably caught up in linear time and that notions of women being more in tune (than men) with the rhythms of nature and of their own bodies hark back to a mythic past. In this mythic past neither the clock nor notions about linear progression as the model of life course change played a role in structuring the lives of either men or women. Both Haste and Kristeva are teetering on the edge of the old equation of woman with the natural, and in reference to time, with natural cycles to do with menstruation, the moon and tides, the turning of the earth, the seasons and so on.

Reproduction

A dominant theme in centuries of discourse on the nature and therefore proper status of women has been her role in reproduction. The so-called reproductive cycle is one which acts potentially as a frame for the life of women, dictating the use of her time and its patterning. Typical of this view of woman is the statement by a nineteenth-century author: 'Be it pleasant or unpleasant, it is none the less an absolute truth – the raison d'etre of a woman is maternity' (Linton (1891) cited by Walker, 1998). Simone de Beauvoir quotes the Latin saying, *Tota mulier in utero* which she translates as 'Woman is a womb' (1997, p. 13).

Anne Fausto-Sterling cites this word picture of a woman's life course as seen by the President of the American Gynaecological Association a hundred years ago:

Many a young life is battered and forever crippled in the breakers of puberty: if it crosses these unharmed and is not dashed to pieces on the rock of childbirth it may still ground on the ever-recurring *shallows* of menstruation and lastly upon the final bar of the menopause ere protection is found in the unruffled waters of the harbor beyond the reach of the sexual storms.

(Fausto-Sterling, 1985, p. 90)

As one examines the history of the life span developmental accounts of women's psychology written in the twentieth century, the extent to which the female life course is seen as being shaped by her reproductive cycle is remarkable. The use of the term 'cycle' is interesting in itself. It is as though women are caught up in a repetitive non-progressive sequence of events which returns them to where they began. There is no doubt that developmental psychology played its part in what Mary Gergen has called 'the biologizing of the woman's life course' (Gergen, 1990).

As outlined in chapters 3 and 4, in life span developmental theory there has been a strong tendency to define woman's life cycle in terms of her role in reproduction. Thus the major events and turning points of women's lives have been seen in terms of her arrival at womanhood, at menarche, her becoming a mother and the cessation of menstruation at menopause – not so different from the perspective of the eminent gynaecologist quoted above. These, the three Ms – Menarche, Motherhood and Menopause – are often presented as the major markers and defining moments of a woman's development. Far less attention therefore is given to her finding her own identity, or, to paraphrase Levinson, becoming her own woman, finding a job or retiring. Yet all these events and processes are widely discussed as important life events for men. Perhaps most tellingly, biological events do not figure in or structure the life course of men. Levinson's *Seasons of a Man's Life* tells a story centred firmly on achievement and identity in the public arena and the world of work.

The changing body and the personal meaning of that change

In her exploration of the differences between the published autobiographies of men and women, Mary Gergen (2001) comments on the constant reference to the body on the part of women and its absence in the life stories of men. Where the body is mentioned by men it is as a well-oiled machine which has typically assisted them in achieving athletic glory or feats of tremendous stamina or, at the end of the life course, as a machine which has either let them down or is standing the test of time remarkably well. Women, on the other hand, in accounts of all life stages, talk about how they feel about their appearance and their bodies and very often about their feelings of bodily inadequacy.

From a life span perspective we do not have a very satisfactory account of the significance to women of the changes that take place in their body over the life course. We have interesting studies of parts of the life course which when put together may form the basis for a life course approach. Clearly it cannot be possible to provide a description which is applicable to all women at all times. But I consider it necessary to theorize the significance of inhabiting a changing body to the psyche of women. A similar analysis could be offered for men. The meaning of the changing and ageing body for women will be highly influenced by the meaning of that change in her culture. We need culture- and time-specific analyses of what current discourses on women's ageing bodies are doing to women psychologically and how women actively negotiate the significance of age and the passage of time.

Childhood

Focusing first on childhood, it is difficult to find studies of the young girl's relationship to her body. Very little attention has been given to how girls relate to their bodies and to how they change over time. Are little girls confident in their bodies and daring in their physical activities? Because of a lack of empirical research we simply do not know. On the other hand, most research on sex-role typing in childhood indicates that, as babies, girls are better coordinated neurologically and physically than boys (Vasta *et al.*, 1999). Boys are given more physical stimulation and more encouragement to crawl and walk, although girls tend to crawl and walk a little earlier (Beal, 1994). In contemporary Western societies, girl babies are still seen as more delicate physically than boy babies, notwithstanding the fact that medical statistics in affluent countries would indicate more vulnerability to infant mortality and illness in boys rather than girls.

Katherine Karraker and her colleagues (1995), in a US-based study, found that parents of boy and girl newborn babies matched as to size and health were more likely to rate boys as strong and hardy and girls as weak and delicate. Fathers play more boisterously with their boy infants than with their girl infants. To what extent being treated as more delicate inculcates a sense of caution in girls concerning the use of their body is difficult to assess. In the absence of relevant empirical research, one can only speculate about what purpose is served by construing sturdy little girl babies and toddlers as dainty and delicate, especially when it is known that cross-sex-typed behaviour in girls is more tolerated than cross-sex-typed behaviour in boys (Turner *et al.*, 1993).

Physical attractiveness is a more salient facet of women's lives than men's and this phenomenon seems to have its beginnings in the childhood years in our culture. A study conducted in the USA found that pre-school girls rated as attractive by college students were recipients of more pro-social behaviour than those seen as unattractive (Smith, 1985). 'Unattractive' girls were more likely to be kicked and hit. The same correlation did not hold for boys.

One can only conjecture that key lessons about the body are being learned from these early potentially traumatic experiences since there is typically little effort to access children's own thoughts and feelings on these matters. Work on little girls' perceptions and feelings about their own bodies is very scarce, and what research there is on the topic tends to be psychoanalytic in orientation and tends to focus on girls' relationship to their genitalia. Lisa Cross has reviewed some of the work in this area in her paper on body and self in female development (1993). She reports that girl toddlers have more difficulty in naming their genitalia than do boys and that little girls masturbate less frequently than boys. Presumably these findings relate to children born in the USA where Cross is based, but the more hidden nature of the female genitalia is a universal reality. Germaine Greer has challenged the idea that little girls typically are unaware of their vaginas, citing the frequency with which adults have to 'fish out beads and coins which the little girl has secreted in her vagina' (1999, p. 360). The hiddenness, she suggests, is an imposed 'forgetting'.

Some of the recent work on body image has included girls as young as 8 years of age and there is evidence from a number of different Western societies that girls of this age are beginning to adopt a negative attitude to body weight and fatness (Hill and Robinson, 1991). In the USA boy and girl children as young as 6 have been found to demonstrate an active dislike of obese body builds and seem to have taken up the prevalent adult criteria for judging attractiveness (Feldman *et al.*, 1988). The strange proportions of the Barbie doll form one potent image of the adult body. Greer (1999) reports that the average little girl, in the USA and the UK respectively, owns eight and six Barbie dolls.

Early experience of physical or sexual abuse will very often have an impact on the girl's sense of her body and how she perceives it. Persistence of negative or positive appraisals of the body and views of the body as ally or enemy may be rooted in traumatic early experiences or in negative commentaries on the body and its functions as somehow dirty or unsafe. The self-silencing which Gilligan and her colleagues at the Harvard project on girls' psychology and women's development have noted as normal in girls as they move from girlhood to adulthood is even more acute for the girl who has experienced physical or sexual abuse. Based on her clinical work with girls, Annie Rogers has described the frequent occurrence of dissociation as a strategy for dealing with trauma and how in some girls 'writing on the body' by means of delicate self-mutilation may substitute for speaking the unspeakable, which has been lost to conscious memory (Rogers, 1994, in press).

Adolescence

By contrast to the lack of attention to the pre-pubertal girl there are numerous studies of the changing body of the adolescent girl, most of which describe the typical changes that occur during puberty. They note that puberty is more readily marked in girls than in boys and that its onset is earlier. In addition, the age at menarche has dropped over the course of the twentieth century in developed countries – although it appears to have stabilized recently – thus shortening the amount of time girls spend as a pre-pubertal child. Some of these studies examine the meaning of such changes to the girls themselves. There is a small number of studies which explore girls' reactions to their first period or to periods in general, and these are very valuable in terms of the kinds of insight they offer. The meaning of menarche varies widely. Some girls are delighted by it, some neutral, some dismayed, and no doubt for many there is a mixture of reactions and feelings. Exactly what determines the quality of their response seems to be difficult to pinpoint. Studies by Brooks-Gunn and Ruble (1983) indicate that those girls who expect pain and discomfort during periods prior to reaching menarche are more likely to experience pain than girls who have a more positive attitude.

Another well-researched aspect of adolescent girls' bodily changes is their weight. In Western culture being heavier than the ideal is typical but is nonetheless disdained. Anorexia and bulimia appear to have increased significantly in the past fifty years. The culturally specific nature of these syndromes is indicated by their rarity in other cultures. For example, Pakistani girls in the UK are thirteen times more likely to be diagnosed with anorexia nervosa than girls in Pakistan (Mumford *et al.*, 1990). This finding does not appear to be a function of economic development or sophisticated diagnostic practices since anorexia nervosa is extremely rare in affluent Japan. Genuine obesity is also increasingly widespread among girls and women in the West. The topic of eating disorders will be revisited later in this chapter but at the very least it is obvious that puberty brings dramatic and involuntary change in the body, all of this change having major implications for the girl's sexual and social role in life. For one thing, sexual intercourse and pregnancy rather suddenly become relatively high-risk sequelae of pubertal change.

Lisa Cross finds explanations of eating disorders focused on the contemporary demand for thinness unsatisfactory since they do not take account of the long history – going back to holy women of medieval Europe – of female self-starvation and self-mutilation. She argues that there is 'a cause more profound than cultural factors at work, a cause rooted in the psychological consequence of biological realities' (1993, p. 52). She argues further that the 'sudden transformations, dilemmas and ambiguities of female anatomy and function across the developmental span' are at the heart of these disorders (p. 54).

Kestenberg (1975) considers that women are more prone to difficulties in 'localizing, identifying and soothing sexual feelings in particular because of their partially internalized genitalia and the unlocalized nature of their sexual sensations'. In a similar psychoanalytic vein, Cross refers to the evidence that an early history of child abuse or trauma is a common feature of the histories of young women who go on to suffer from eating disorders. She claims that these women have early difficulties with identifying, verbally expressing and regulating *all* forms of physical tension. Thus tensions build up which cannot be vented or expressed except through their bodies.

Dusty Miller quotes a client who said, 'I never thought I could stand the pain I felt when I quit cutting myself' (1994, p. 237). The sensation of detachment from the pain and distress they are inflicting on themselves is often reported by women who starve themselves or who are engaged in self-mutilation, particularly the considered and careful acts of cutting, burning or piercing customarily labelled delicate self-mutilation. According to Cross, the woman may seek out physical pain because it is 'a more clear-cut controllable experience' than sexual tension or psychic pain.

Fewer studies examine other less obviously sexual aspects of bodily change. After all, during puberty girls become taller, they acquire hair in places where there was previously no hair, their breasts grow and their hips typically become fatter and their waist relatively thinner. The boys around them are changing in different ways, becoming even taller, more muscular, and all these changes high-lighting sexual differences which are there between the bodies of pre-pubertal boys and girls but to a far less marked extent. What meanings are attached to all these changes in girls' bodies? Of course that depends to a great extent on the valuation of these changes in the girl's cultural or social group. Girls appear to react negatively to bodily changes which they perceive to be in a direction that is socially undesirable. Thus they dislike accumulating body fat and having breasts which they see as too small or too large.

Magnusson's work in Sweden shows just how much depends on the social consequences of a biological event such as puberty. As part of the Swedish Individual Development and Adjustment Longitudinal Study (Magnusson *et al.*, 1986), he identified girls who experienced an early menarche and followed them up until adulthood. Girls who had an early onset of periods (menarche under the age of 11) were more likely to have dropped out of school and to indulge in a range of norm- and law-breaking behaviour in adolescence. By adulthood these women were more likely to be married, not working and to have had significantly more children than their later maturing counterparts. The increased level of prob-lematic outcomes was directly related to whether or not the early maturing girl had mixed with older teenagers on a regular basis. Some of the early maturing girls who had not mixed with older teenagers had more positive outcomes. Thus, as Rutter (1989) comments, although the stimulus was physiological, the mecha-nism was social.

One study which addresses the meaning of bodily change and the transition to adolescence for young women themselves was published by Anne Woollett and Hariette Marshall in 1996. In this study teenaged women were asked to talk about their social and sexual lives and their relationships. The authors conclude that for the adolescents in their sample, being able to carry one's body where one wishes is taken as signifying maturity. The young women asserted very clearly that 'one's body is one's own'. At the same time, the young women were aware that there were constraints on this independence which were specific to their sex. Woollett and Marshall infer that 'the possibility of rape is seen as shaping the differential reading of the vulnerability of young women's bodies' (p. 203). The findings question the assumption that the central task for all adolescents is the achievement of independence since the respondents were very accepting of their relative dependence and the need to protect themselves. In addition, because the group interviewed included young women who were black, white and Asian, differences in attitude were apparent. For example, the young Asian women were much more likely than the other ethnic groups to see preservation of virginity prior to marriage as important.

There are suggestions, then, that the need to protect themselves from rape or other unwanted sexual contact is a widespread preoccupation for women which has its onset in puberty. The meaning of menstruation and the management of her own menstrual cycle will also be a matter of some significance to all women. The average Western woman spends six years of her life menstruating (Ussher, 1989), but, hopefully, not six years of her life in constant awareness of her menstruating. I say 'of some significance' in that no matter how untroubling or psychically peripheral the menstrual cycle may be to a woman who menstruates, the reality of menstruation still has to be managed. It is important to note that even when considering a phenomenon as all but universal in women's lives as menstruation, cross-cultural and individual differences ensure that the meaning of menstruation will vary dramatically even in relation to the amount of time spent menstruating. As Anne Walker (1998) points out, in less economically developed societies, women reach menarche later and spend longer pregnant and breastfeeding, thus ensuring that the number of menstrual periods is considerably less than that of the average Western woman.

Because of an understandable resistance to the view of the woman as a poor thing in the grip of her 'raging hormones', many feminist writers have promoted a minimalist view of the impact of menstruation on a woman's life. Empirical studies of women's performance on cognitive and other tasks have reinforced the view that women are not, contrary to the old stereotype, less capable of functioning efficiently when menstruating (Parlee, 1973). Anne Walker in her book *The Menstrual Cycle* (1998) labels the promotion of the view that menstruation has little significance in women's lives and certainly no impact on their competence as a liberal feminist perspective. She says, liberal feminists 'are keen to demonstrate that the menstrual cycle is not a liability for women' (p. 193). A more recent and alternative perspective, which is identified by Anne Walker as 'postmodern' and which corresponds with a social constructionist perspective, examines public and personal discourses surrounding menstruation and how they influence women's experience of menstruation. The myths, beliefs and practices specific to her culture will be assimilated by the young girl to a greater or lesser extent: some form of assimilation of prevalent attitudes will be unavoidable. At the same time each person's attitudes and feelings will be shaped by her contact with her mother, sisters and other important women and men around her. Her own personality adds to the unpredictability of the picture. It is likely that most women will have a complex of attitudes and experiences of menstruation, their own and others, which make this biological phenomenon a matter of some psychological significance to their lives.

It must be remembered that some women suffer disabling pain and other uncomfortable symptoms associated with menstrual periods. It is not helpful to them in their distress to argue that their discomfort is a social construction or that it is 'all in the mind'. Anne Walker points out that there is a need for a biopsychosocial perspective on pre-menstrual syndrome (PMS), an approach which recognizes the biological reality of menstruation and the possibility that for some women cyclical changes in the hormones and in bodily functioning may produce bodily changes which are experienced as uncomfortable and distressing. The experience of menstruation for some women, it should be borne in mind, may be happy, reassuring or even joyful (Angier, 1999). At the same time there is enough evidence about cross-cultural and inter-individual differences in the interpretation of menstrual symptoms to necessitate taking into account psychological and social factors which influence the perception and expression of distress.

Eating disorders and self-mutilation may both be construed as extreme behaviours by which women are attempting to harm their own bodies. Susie Orbach (1986) interprets young women's self-starvation as being akin to a 'hunger strike'. Just as a prisoner might resort to hunger strike because it is the only way in which he or she can demonstrate resistance or exert control, the young woman, experiencing herself as trapped by patriarchy and, in a political sense, powerless to resist, exerts control over her own body. In tandem with this interpretation is the view that anorexia represents a refusal to be female, since femaleness has so many potential negative consequences. Thus the effect of starvation is to minimize the young woman's newly acquired secondary sexual characteristics (Bruch, 1973). Favazza and Conterio surveyed 240 women who self-mutilated and reported that 58% of them 'hated' their periods, 34% hated their breasts and 19% indicated they would be better off without a vagina (cited in Farazza, 1996).

Such levels of self-loathing and body dissatisfaction in physically healthy and intact young women are deeply disturbing. Few women, it would appear, have a contented relationship with their body. It is important to remember that the impossible quest for bodily perfection has profound implications for girls and women who are disabled. Lisa Cross (1993) concludes that 'partially internal genitalia, menstruation, relatively abrupt changes in body contours at puberty and pregnancy all contribute to an ambiguous, paradoxical and discontinuous experience of the body for women'.

The onset of puberty marks a transition from childhood to adulthood or, at least, to adulthood's anteroom, adolescence. In the West, we have marked out adolescence as a separate period of the life course with its own features and demands. As a girl's body turns into that of a woman she confronts the meaning of what it is to be an adult woman in her culture. Theorists like Bruch (1973) and Brown and Gilligan (1992) have argued that this realization constitutes a crisis for many young women, expressed in eating disorders or a loss of confidence and voice. Simone de Beauvoir saw the changes wrought by puberty as cataclysmic for the girl of her time:

she feels in these changes a presentiment of a finality which sweeps her away from selfhood: she sees herself thrown into a vital cycle that overflows the course of her private existence, she divines a dependence that dooms her to man, to children and to death.

(de Beauvoir, 1997, p. 333)

Mature sexuality

A simplistic view of the origin of female sexuality sees it as being a straightforward function of membership of the female sex. In fact female sexuality takes numerous different forms and is a complex consequence of individual experience and exposure to particular socialization practices and local discourses. Sexuality is not fundamentally biological in its origins and expression, but the bodily experiences of sexual desire and its expression and bodily encounters involved in sex with another are an obviously important part of most girls' and women's lives. From a developmental point of view, it is also important to note the extent to which sexual desire and the object of that desire change across the life course.

Despite the 'sexual revolution' in the 1960s where women were supposed to have attained sexual freedom, there is still a remarkable agreement about what constitutes mature female sexuality in Western societies. Young women are expected to desire men and to desire sexual intercourse with men, but not to a point where they abandon all vestiges of traditional modesty. The woman is expected to make herself desirable to men and ultimately to one man who will be the father of her children. In sexual intercourse they are expected to be responsive and to reach orgasm via vaginal penetration by their male partner. The recognition of female desire as normal and the expectation of orgasm as equally normal are probably the two main additions to the picture of normative female sexuality since the turn of the twentieth century.

Despite the assumption of heterosexuality as the normal pathway, or even, as Adrienne Rich (1976) asserts, as 'compulsory', a substantial minority of women will have homosexual experiences during their lifetime. The exact number of women who are lesbian or bisexual is impossible to calculate since the definition of either is fraught, and much of the research evidence indicates that sexual orientation is not something that is fixed at an early stage of the life course never to change again. Christine Dancey reports that in one of her samples of lesbian women (1990), 35% said that in the past they had been 'in love with' a man. The route towards a clear lesbian identification is often one which has been taken in some period of heterosexual identification and activity. For some women these experiences have been negative and for some acceptable or pleasurable. It would also seem to be the case that for many women the choice to be a lesbian is not based on the grounds of sexual desire but on those of the emotional closeness and other psychological attractions of female-to-female intimacy.

Of course, such a progression, from heterosexual to homosexual, is to be expected where heterosexuality is, as Christine Dancey puts it, 'the default position', and the costs and difficulties of coming out as a lesbian remain high.

Movement from identification as a lesbian back to being heterosexual appears to be uncommon but does occur. There is also a small minority of women who identify themselves as bisexual. Sexual attraction of women to women would appear to be far more widespread than the number of women who identify themselves as lesbian might suggest. Again, social disapproval of lesbianism may account for some women's hesitancy about enacting their desires, but such data also reinforce the argument made by Rich that lesbianism exists on a continuum.

The first sexual experiences of young women are surprisingly under-researched. Most women seem to have felt ill-prepared for these experiences and the vagueness of sex education on the subject of desire and sexual response as opposed to the mechanics of intercourse and reproduction seems to be widespread. Erin McNeill (1994) comments that girls are exposed to 'a systematic dissociation of their biological and sexual selves' (p. 70). Deborah Tolman notes that

> despite the sexual revolution of the 1960s, society's conception of sexuality for adolescent girls who want to be considered good, normal and accepted remains constrained. Good girls are still supposed to 'just say no', not supposed to feel intense sexual desire and remain responsible for the sexual desire of boys and for protecting themselves from harm.
>
> (Tolman, 2000, p. 94)

Such constraints create difficulties for girls as they negotiate their first sexual experiences and as they attempt to discover the nature of their own sexuality. Adolescents who identify as lesbian may become distressed and socially isolated as they confront the pressures to involve themselves in heterosexual activity (Mooney-Somers and Ussher, 2000).

The constraining assumptions about how women should express their sexuality do not cease to be important as the woman matures. Being a 'good, normal and acceptable' woman from a sexual point of view may entail a restricted and conflicted expression of sexuality which persists across the life course.

Pregnancy

Feminist writers have adopted very ambivalent attitudes towards their bodies and their bodies' demands, particularly in relation to reproduction. A negative view of the way women's bodies function to constrain their lives is typical of a number of feminist writers. Simone de Beauvoir is positively vituperative about pregnancy:

> Ensnared by nature the pregnant woman is plant and animal. A stock pile of colloids, an incubator, an egg; she scares children proud of their young straight bodies and makes young people titter contemptuously

because she is a human being, a conscious and free individual who has become life's passing instrument.

(de Beauvoir, 1997, p. 553)

Other feminist writers have glorified maternity and seen it as the basis of a superior psychological orientation towards the world (Ruddick, 1989). Women, they argue, are more loving, concerned and nurturant than men. Chodorow's work on the reproduction of mothering and the supposed capacity of girl children to mother is often cited as the basis of the argument that a maternal, nurturant stance is built into the psyche of women in our culture in contrast to the emotional detachment and individualism of men. Such arguments, as discussed in Chapter 4, leave very little room for the many incontrovertible exceptions to this theory's predictions or for the proper acknowledgement of the ongoing cultural and psychological constraints on women as potential or actual mothers.

After adolescence the next time when many women will experience a period of rapid body change will be in pregnancy. Women seem to vary considerably in how they perceive and cope with these changes. Since pregnancy extends over nine months there is plenty of opportunity for women to have different reactions at different stages of pregnancy. For some, the physical symptoms of nausea and fatigue may be dominant in the first trimester of pregnancy and fade in the second trimester. Some women cope well until their body's changing shape becomes very evident to them and to others. Studies by Lederman (1996) and Ramona Mercer (1995) in the USA indicate that many women feel unattractive while pregnant, complaining of being fat and ugly. In a society which values thinness, putting on weight even for the gestation of a baby may be hard to tolerate for some women. The animal physicality of pregnancy, as colourfully described by Simone de Beauvoir, may be a source of some ambivalence in a Western society preoccupied by the intellectual distance from and control of the animal side of self.

Occupation of the body by another human being is an experience as yet confined to women. Studies have shown that many women have difficulty connecting psychologically with the growing foetus. Ultrasound can serve as a potentiator of the bond felt by a woman towards her child, serving to make the baby more real. As Greer comments (1999), it is ironic that only on a TV screen will the baby seem to be 'real' to some modern mothers. Sbisa (1996) discusses the way pregnancy is represented in popular books designed to help women through pregnancy and childbirth and the kind of discourse produced in pregnancy and childbirth by women themselves. The books, she concluded, 'convey to varying degrees some of the classic stereotypes of femininity: weakness, fragility, unreliability, passivity, self-sacrificing motherly love' (p. 366). The picture of the body as weak and unreliable is alarming when one considers that this is a survey conducted in the 1990s. In her interviews with twenty women, Sbisa found evidence of the incorporation of this negative discourse and its unflattering stereotypes about the pregnant body. Many of the women used impersonal constructions and constructed their role in events as passive. Five of the women, however, resisted this passive role and were able to present themselves as active agents and subjects of their own birthing labour.

If a woman lives long enough she will very probably experience menarche, motherhood and menopause. The majority of women become mothers but a sufficiently large percentage do not, enough to question the frequent assumption that motherhood is a normative experience in the life of all women. What is highly probable is that all women will in some way have to come to terms with the meaning of becoming or not becoming a mother because of the importance of that role in almost all societies.

Changes in the body wrought by pregnancy, delivery and breastfeeding are unlikely to be forgotten or to leave no mark on the body itself. Many women after pregnancy will have a stomach and breasts traced by stretch marks. They may struggle for years to lose the weight they gained and will rarely regain the same youthful shape and tone. Women have a different experience to men in relation to their bodily fluids. The female body is simply more leaky. Men do experience the involuntary release of bodily fluids in ways which are specific to men – nocturnal emissions, premature ejaculation – and in ways which are common to both men and women, such as bleeding from injury and vomiting. But vaginal bleeding, breaking of waters prior to delivery and low-level leakage of other vaginal secretions are a more persistent feature of women's lives which it could be argued call attention to the permeability and openness of the female body. Pregnancy entails the occupancy of the female body by another human being, an experience denied to men (at this point in time). During the course of pregnancy dramatic changes take place in the appearance and functioning of the body. Some women welcome these changes and some find them distressing. Women who have struggled for years to be slim find themselves in a body which is bulky, with ballooning breasts and stomach.

Menopause

Until very recently a relentlessly negative picture of menopausal and post-menopausal woman has been commonplace in the West. The excesses to which gynaecologists went to persuade women of the benefits of oestrogen replacement therapy and the necessity for psychiatric intervention for their involutional melancholia and empty nest syndrome have been well documented by writers such as Germaine Greer and Anne Fausto-Sterling. The work of Robert and Thelma Wilson is quoted by both Greer (1999) and Fausto-Sterling (1985). An example from the Wilsons' (1963) book refers to:

> Unfortunate women abounding in the streets walking in twos and threes, seeing little and observing less. . . . The world appears to them as through a grey veil and they live as docile, harmless creatures missing most of life's values.

However, some of these wraiths turn bad and 'the untold misery of alcoholism, divorce and broken homes caused by these unstable estrogen-starved women cannot be presented in statistical form'. It was not only physicians who promoted this pathological view of women in middle age. The psychoanalyst Helene Deutsch wrote that at menopause 'woman has ended her existence as a bearer of future life and has reached her natural end – her partial death – as a servant of the species' (Deutsch, 1944). Interestingly, contemporary anthropologists have proposed that far from being of no use to the species post-menopausal women have a major role in gathering food and supporting young mothers in hunter-gatherer societies (Angier, 1999).

Since the 1960s there has been a backlash against extreme medical and psychological views about the disastrous physical and psychological consequences of menopause. For example, a paper by Rosalind Barnett and Grace Baruch (1978) carefully appraised the evidence for widespread disturbance and distress in menopausal and post-menopausal women and found that it was lacking. Work which has examined the actual lived experience of women in their forties and fifties has established that most women resist the negative expectations of this time of life and do not experience their middle age as a time of misery and decline (Neugarten, 1977; Gergen, 1992). So, far from the fifties being a time of misery and decline, many women experience this age as one of new freedom and renewed energy. Whether this has anything to do with age as such or is a function of the structure of the life course for women in the West is an open question. Menopause often coincides with the departure of children and the freedom that can bring. However, despite the reality that many women are enjoying life post-menopause, negative discourses on menopause and on middle-aged women persist and the rehabilitation of the image of menopausal woman is still incomplete.

The de-sexing of the middle-aged woman is a process which is not apparent in the life of her male age-peer. Although few would endorse the Wilsons' view that 'all post menopausal women are castrates', middle-aged women are rarely presented as sexually attractive and desirable in the media. Staying young is a goal which preoccupies the majority of Western women, not just those who are approaching middle age or who are middle-aged, but also women in their twenties and thirties. The focus of most of this activity is the body, which must remain taut and fat-free, and the face, which must not sag or have wrinkles. Thus middle-aged women aspire to have the body of a teenaged girl, to stop or turn back the clock. Even for those who manage a reasonably successful holding operation the reality is that the clock cannot be stopped and that the body is making its inevitable way towards decline. However, if people focused more readily on the health side of ageing rather than on appearance, they would become aware that the news in terms of the possibility of retaining strength and vigour into old age is in fact good.

Lock's work on menopause in Japanese and North American women (1993) shows that Japanese women do not complain about hot flushes (or hot flashes as they are called in the USA) or depression associated with menopause. Different meanings of menopause may account in part for the differing experience of bodily change in Japanese and European and Northern American women, but some of the difference may be due to a very direct effect of diet on bodily function. The lack of dairy products and the increased consumption of soy products may make negative symptoms of menopause less likely in Japan. These may, Lock argues, be examples of a 'local biology'.

In recent years there has been a discussion about the significance of menopause to the psychology of the middle-aged woman to the exclusion of the consideration of other aspects of ageing. Margaret Matlin (2000) reports that when she carried out a computer search of psychology listings since 1990 under the topic of women and retirement she found 116 articles and books, whereas a search under the topic of menopause generated 21,405 citations for the same period. Menopause has certainly provided a focus for those who wish to explain women's psychology as being rooted in their biology and for those who wish to portray the female life cycle as punctuated by biological events linked to her procreative role. From this perspective the woman who is facing menopause is also facing the end of her useful years.

For Linda Gannon, 'the most salient consequence of biological determinism for ageing women is the labeling of menopause as a disease' (Gannon, 1999, p. 8). In fact even in societies where this medical discourse is very prevalent, many women seem to be able to avoid the personal labelling of their own menopause as a disease and see it as a 'natural' stage, and one which is not very difficult to navigate at that. The danger of the feminist countermanding of the pathologizing of menopause is that, as with menstrual pain, it comes to be seen as unacceptable to have troubling menopausal symptoms at all. After all, if these are social constructions, one should be able to think one's way out of them. Unfortunately for a number of women, whether they are succumbing to powerful medical discourse, stress or unhelpful dietary practices, or the direct effects of normal change, their daily reality involves having to cope with distressing hot flushes, lack of sleep and fatigue.

Beyenne's study of rural women in the Yucatan and in Greece indicates that, in societies where older women are given high social status, menopause is less troublesome. The two cultures varied nonetheless in that the Mayan women, who have typically not used contraception and had many children, reported no symptoms of menopause, whereas the Greek women, who had limited their families using modern methods of contraception, had symptoms but viewed them as passing and normal (Beyenne, 1992). Even in countries which are menopause obsessed, there are many women who barely notice their own menopause and the vast majority find other issues to be more troubling (Friedan, 1993).

Although the general perception of the middle-aged or menopausal woman is negative, women's actual experience of this stage of life can be positive. Valory Mitchell and Ravenna Helson (1990) argue that in their sample of US college graduates aged 26 to 80, women in their early fifties were the most satisfied with life. They had often happily waved goodbye to their adult children, had good income levels and were, despite the menopause, in good health. The authors argue for the utility of the notion of 'the prime of life' and that for women, the fifties might be it. These women rated themselves as healthier than both younger midlife women and older women. At the same time a study by Alice Rossi (1980) revealed that most middle-aged women in her sample wanted to be ten years younger.

Ageing

Physical vulnerability is a feature of our life as mortal beings. We are prone to accidents, illnesses, disability and we will all eventually die. Our bodies can let us down and can cause us pain and distress. From that point of view they are unreliable. Nonetheless, healthy, fit people can amaze us by their confidence in their bodies and in their capacity to exert control over their bodies. Athletes and dancers, of both sexes, are admired in part because of the discipline they exert over their bodies. We admire bodies which are brought under control to a point where they are more powerful, more graceful, more refined than those of the average man and woman. Part of the pain of ageing is in the failure of the body to behave, to respond as it should, or as it once did. Physical disability is feared and those with disabilities widely stigmatized.

In the West, we live in an age-fearing society. The aged are in general the target of negative stereotyping. A study conducted in the USA in 1985 showed that young people feel that a person's social status declines linearly from the age of 30 to the mid-eighties and there is little reason to believe that such findings would not be replicated elsewhere in the developed world today.

Ageing of the body proceeds at different rates depending on which aspect of bodily function is involved. For example, the elasticity of the lens of the eye begins to diminish in the twenties. Physical signs of ageing begin to become more apparent in the forties, although a severe diminution in capacities is not usual until the seventies and eighties and, even then, half of those aged 85 and over in North America and Europe are capable of living and managing on their own.

The meaning of ageing seems to be distinctively different for men and women in Western culture. The so-called double standard for ageing men and women is widely accepted and empirically supported (Wilcox, 1998). In a study conducted by Kogan in 1979, in which adults in the USA were asked to classify photographs as 'young', 'middle-aged' and 'elderly', women were placed in the middle-aged and old categories at a much younger age than were the men. Middle-aged women are rated as less attractive and are seen to have more undesirable characteristics than men of the same age.

Women, not surprisingly, given the negative stereotyping of old or ageing women, are more negative than men about growing old. How do old women think and feel about their aged bodies? We don't know. Neugarten reported in 1968 that women seem to be less threatened than men by loss of physical prowess and the threat of illness, but I have not come across any comparable recent studies.

Recent research on brain function in the elderly indicates that improvements in learning and memory capabilities are possible well into old age (Gould *et al.*, 2000). In the light of such findings, common beliefs such as those concerning the forgetfulness of the old or their inability to learn ('You can't teach an old dog new tricks') have to be reviewed as damaging self-fulfilling prophecies. Neurobiologists Lawrence Katz and Manning Rubin comment that 'the mental decline most people experience is not due to the death of cells'. Rather, they claim, "it is due to atrophy of connections between cells brought about by an over-reliance on routinised behaviours which demand little effort from the brain' (1999). Physical activity is also proven to have a positive effect on brain function in the elderly. Thus it seems that both mental and physical activity are important in maintaining a high level of functioning. Women are in the majority in the elderly population and also may be more likely to lead lives dominated by routine and lack of daily challenge. According to US-based studies women are also very likely to be physically inactive. There is a sharp decline in physical activity after age 39 (Dan *et al.*, 1990). Many of the negative changes associated with age are avoidable. To make this statement is not a denial of the realities of ageing, decline and mortality, but a recognition that neglect of the health of the body and the mind has a major impact on the quality of life of the ageing woman.

Negative ageing may be a function of the social circumstances which the woman faces. Poverty and stress militate against good mental and physical health. Active engagement with people and issues is also associated with health and well-being in the elderly. Many old women are impoverished and live alone. Many find it increasingly difficult in a world where retirement by age 60 or 65 is commonplace and community activities are diminishing to maintain an active and rewarding social life.

By the time we reach retirement many of us will have been well primed to accept the reality of decremental ageing (Coupland *et al.*, 1991, p. 104). We are playing a part in the construction of decline in the aged and ultimately our own decline by propagating negative perceptions of the old. The findings of psychologists on the actual competencies of the aged and the conditions under which positive ageing can be supported should be a matter of concern to feminist psychologists but are not widely discussed. For example, feminist journals, such as *Feminism and Psychology*, rarely publish articles on older women.

Conclusion

There is reason to be concerned about the way girls and women in the West are being encouraged to think and behave towards their bodies. Although the promotion of the idea of the body as text seems to be confined largely to obscure areas of feminist theory, there is a sense in which young women and older women are increasingly behaving towards their own bodies as though they are indeed texts or slates or personal/public material to be moulded, carved or etched. How far removed are the highly theorized actions of Orlan and her 'carnal art' (one of Orlan's latest 'performances' consisted in having bony devil horns grafted on to her forehead) from the actions of the 16-year-old getting her tongue pierced in her local high street or the 46-year-old undergoing liposuction?

Of course, such an orientation to the body as a site for alteration and ornamentation has been with us since the beginning of human culture, but the early twenty-first-century context may be different in important ways. Medical technology and antisepsis permit extraordinary interventions in relation to surgery at a level of safety previously unattainable. We may also be on the brink of an era of genetic manipulations of the body, creating possibilities presently in the realm of science fiction. Women, even very young women, are opting for plastic surgery in ever larger numbers (Greer, 1999). A major goal for these interventions is the maintenance of the appearance of youth. Several multi-million-dollar industries (cosmetics, cosmetic surgery, alternative medicines, fitness classes) are fuelled by the female terror of ageing.

In 1976 Adrienne Rich said, 'women are controlled by lashing us to our bodies' (p. 13). Has feminism succeeded in untying the ropes that bind women to their bodies and cause them discomfort and distress from childhood to old age? The answer is almost certainly no. Two issues need to be addressed in this conclusion. The first is to what extent it is at all possible for women to escape from being *lashed to our bodies*. The second issue concerns the mapping of the manner in which women are in actuality *lashed to their bodies*.

I am arguing that we must confront the reality of the biological body, its strength and resilience as well as its finitude and vulnerability. Work such as that by Lackoff and Johnson (1999) has demonstrated the extent to which our mental processes are formed by the structures and movements of our body. Lackoff and Johnson's focus was not specifically on gender. However, just as our upright posture and positioning of our eyes influence the metaphors we use to locate ourselves mentally in the world, so too might the femaleness of the female body play a role in shaping woman's orientation to the world. This is not a collapse into Eriksonian determinism, the view that 'the basic modalities of women's commitment and involvement also reflect the ground plan of her body'. On the contrary, the constructions, which we build around our sensory and bodily experience, are multiple, and are never uninfluenced by our own interpretations and those discourses which encircle us.

Some contemporary theorists suggest that girls and women are increasingly able to 'perform' gender in a self-conscious manner. Accepting Judith Butler's view that gender is to a great extent enacted or performed, there is a possibility that, in the relative freedom of the postmodern world and armed with a postmodern consciousness, women will be able to variously accept, subvert or resist the normative enactment of the feminine. Jane Ussher believes that 'at an individual level, women and girls negotiate the scripts of femininity in order to take up or resist the position of "woman"'. In her book *Fantasies of Femininity* (1997), she describes four possible ways of relating to the notion of 'girl' ('girl' being the archetype of perfect femininity). Women, she suggests, have the option of being, doing, resisting and subverting 'girl'. Her main point is that women are not passive recipients of messages about how to be feminine; they can sometimes renegotiate and even subvert the demands that are made on them to conform. Undoubtedly this is the case. But what is depressing, after years of attempts to liberate women from oppressive models of their psychological ties to their reproductive and sexual function and from the tyranny of keeping up a youthful and conventionally pretty appearance, is that so many women, from childhood to old age, are in thrall to these restrictive images of what it means to be a woman.

Foucault perhaps more than any other recent theorist has assisted us to appreciate the extent to which the body is and probably always has been a site of social control. As he elaborates in his analysis of punishment, *Discipline and Punish* (1975), what we see in modern times is a shift from direct control and punishment of the body to control via discourse. For Foucault, the body is still the focus of control in any society, but the methods by which control is exerted can change. The subjugation of the body in the twentieth (and twenty-first) century is now typically achieved via the soul or psyche. Foucault notes, 'in thinking of the mechanisms of power, I am thinking rather of its capillary forms of existence, the point where power reaches into the very grain of individuals, touches their bodies and inserts itself into their actions and attitudes, their discourses, learning processes and everyday lives' (1980, p. 36).

Foucault does not locate the source of power in one institution or structure. Power relationships pervade social life, but they move and re-form continuously. Traditionally the institution which oppresses women is taken to be patriarchy. But women are also oppressed in terms of their class, race, sexuality, age and looks. Consumerism colludes with remnants of traditional patriarchy to produce and then feed off the need women experience to be 'attractive'. Women typically wish to be sexually desirable to men, envied by other women, young and fecund, and so find themselves constantly struggling with and dissatisfied with their appearance. From girlhood to old age, women feel obliged to work on their bodies; from girlhood to old age, women generally feel more connected than men to bodily functions, especially those related to their reproductive role.

Developmental psychology has reinforced this tyranny. It has (in its multiple variants) colluded in the regulation of women's bodies and in women's definition in terms of biology and reproduction. Developmental psychology is but one form of discourse on women's life course and it is by no means the case that it exists independently of those in the non-academic realm. Indeed, as historical and political analyses of developmental psychology (Sears, 1975; Burman, 1994) have shown, it both reflects and helps form popular forms of discourse.

Ideas about women's life course trajectory, the periodization of the female life course, the valuation put upon one stage of life versus another, all function as regulatory discourses in the lives of girls and women. Women's time is very much not their own. We need to understand more fully the role played by biology in psychological change across the life course and we need to further deconstruct current conceptions and discourses which dictate – in ways that limit and constrain – the meaning of the female body and how it changes and ages.

There is no doubt that psychological theories of women's development need to get away from the traditional focus on women's biological role in life and the neglect of other important aspects of her life as a rounded woman and human being. As Mary Gergen (1990) expresses it, we need 'a richer theoretical framework for studying women's lives emphasizing political, economic, moral and aesthetic forms' of life not solely the biological (p. 480). It is centrally important to theorize the meaning of the body from a life course perspective, seeing it as an intrinsic part of women's life but not its defining centre.

6

THE MAKING OF THE FEMALE SELF

In this chapter I will deal with issues which relate to the self, identity, personhood and subjectivity. Some of these issues are extremely vexed in that they generate a confusing plethora of definitions and theoretical explanations. By contrast, the traditional developmental perspective, coloured by a modernist conception of self, promotes the deceptively straightforward point of view that every person has an identity and a self. However, troubling questions immediately arise about the meaning of words like self and identity. The assumptions underpinning any statement about self and identity are open to severe challenge. The very concept of self is under siege from postmodernist writers inside and outside psychology. For example, some theorists (e.g. Gergen, 1988) have suggested that the notion of the individual self is just a misleading and spurious construction – a reference without a referent. Others (e.g. Markus and Nurius, 1986) question whether there is one self or many co-existing selves.

However, from a person-centred feminist perspective, it is necessary to take on board the experience of self and selfhood as central to each woman's lived psychology. We need to understand how people come to see themselves and are seen by others as persons, and how their self-conscious sense of themselves and their relationship to the world is shaped and changed as they travel through the life course. The extent to which the person's identity, self and subjectivity are gendered is a central issue.

Definitions of self and identity

The definitions of self and identity employed by different authors tend to reflect their theoretical standpoint, and therefore it is somewhat artificial to separate definition and theory. Dictionary definitions of *self* and *identity* also tend to enshrine traditional conceptions of these terms. As Morny Joy says, 'such terms as self and identity . . . come loaded with Enlightenment baggage' (1993, p. 277). Even so, on examination it is clear that many definitions of self and identity are essentially indistinguishable or substantially overlapping. For example, Rama *et al.* (1987) define *identity* as 'the symbolic structure that permits a personality system to insure continuity and consistency under changing biographical conditions and different positions in the social space'. This could stand equally well as a definition of *self*.

The dictionary definition (*Shorter Oxford English Dictionary*) of *identity* tells us that the root meaning is probably the Latin *idem*, 'the same', or possibly the Latin *idetitem*, which translates as 'repeatedly'. Contemporary meanings are given as 'the quality or condition of being the same, absolute or essential sameness, oneness' or 'individuality, personality'. *Identity* is thus not a property associated solely with persons: one may discover identity between two apparently separate substances or between the beliefs of two different people or between a belief expressed at one time and a belief expressed by the same person at a later date. But the key insight is that *identity* is a janus word conveying two related but almost opposed meanings, that of sameness and that of distinctiveness.

In relation to human psychology both the first and second meanings may apply. Thus *identity* implies both sameness over time and the distinctiveness of those features which define the person's individuality. *Identity* is about continuity and distinctiveness, recognizable by self and others. Furthermore, often, in describing the identity of self or others, the emphasis is not on individuality but on commonality with a group or category of others. In this way, a person's *identity* as a woman may be both distinctive and, in some sense, identical to that of other women through shared membership of the category 'woman'.

The word *self* also has the meaning of same – as in a flower which is self-coloured, implying that it is the same colour throughout – and in the phrase 'self-same'. But the *Shorter Oxford English Dictionary* also provides more psychological definitions of *self* such as the following:

- 'that which in a person is really and intrinsically he (in contradistinction to what is adventitious)';
- 'the ego';
- 'a permanent subject of successive and varying states of consciousness';
- 'what one is at a particular time or in a particular aspect or relation';
- 'one's nature, character (sometimes), physical constitution or appearance considered as different at different times'.

Clearly this is a concept with multiple connotations which vary significantly depending on who is viewing the self; that is, whether the viewpoint is internal or external.

Richard Stevens (1996) draws an important distinction between personal identity and social identity. Personal identity, he suggests, 'arises from experiences specific to us and our private reflection on these', whereas social identity constitutes 'the characteristics and roles which tend to be attributed to us by others'. Personal identity is a function of self-awareness or the capacity for reflexiveness. Social identity does not depend on or require the existence of personal identity. For example, a newborn baby may be said to have a social but not a personal identity. On the other hand, although the key element of personal identity is self-reflection, social identity precedes and is centrally involved in the construction and maintenance of personal identity. Thus Dan McAdams is referring to personal identity not social identity when he defines identity as 'a life story – an internalized narrative integration of past, present and anticipated future which provides lives with a sense of unity and purpose' (1990, p. 161).

In what sense is personal identity distinguishable from the self? The self is perhaps a more inclusive term, encompassing all that one experiences as a person, whereas personal identity is that which is seen as distinctive and/or enduring about the self. The self may thus be equated with the embodied locus of individual experience both conscious and unconscious. The self may participate in experiences which are transient and not definitional of the self's identity even though they may have an influence upon it. Thus the self may have an identity but the identity does not have a self. In relation to identity it is the case that most people's identities are multiple and complex, so that a person may 'identify' herself, for example, as Irish, as middle-class and as a woman. Some might argue that the self may also be multiple but the self or selves are not coterminous with the woman's range of identities. The self or selves refer to the woman's ways of defining her multifaceted relationship to her world and her own experience.

The concept of personal identity and the clearly very similar but somewhat broader concept of selfhood are of particular interest to this book's project. This is because these concepts refer to powerful modes used by the individual to organize her experience in time and to position herself in the life course.

Subjectivity

Subjectivity, self-awareness and reflexiveness are all terms which describe the capacity of most human beings to reflect on and be aware of their own perceptions, experiences and thought processes. They are both properties of and enabling conditions for the self-phenomenon. These processes are not essential to the arrival at a social identity but they are involved in the self's construction of a personal identity.

The capacities essential to a sense of self are also those which enable each person to locate herself in time. Humans are capable of reflecting on their past and their future, reworking memories, constructing plans and dreams of the future. As Martin and Sugarman note, 'memory and imagination become the gates that open to the wealth of accumulated past experience in one direction and to the call of future possibility in the other' (1999, p. 27). Although each and every person is in her objective existence firmly fixed in space and time, in her subjective world, events actual and imagined in time, past and anticipated events, and images belonging to the future are fundamental elements of each person's experience of being in the world. Being in time and engaging with the experience of relationship with the parameters of both public and subjective time is foundational to the construction and experience of self.

From a developmental perspective, subjectivity is an emergent property of the complex competencies of the human person actively engaged with her world. Subjectivity is both constrained and open, contingent and unpredictable. It is the product of physical, socio-cultural and discursive events but also the origin of its own realities which play a part in determining the ongoing form and content of the person's experience and behaviour.

Personhood

Developmental psychology, hand in hand with mainstream positivist psychology, has tended to adopt a reductionist view of the person. In fact the quest for determinants of human behaviour can readily leave human personhood out of account altogether. As Susan Oyama argues, 'our conception of development makes it easier to see people as objects formed and moved by causes rather than experiencing subjects who may act for reasons – that is as persons' (1993, p. 471).

The feminist project involves a basic commitment to ensuring that all girls and women are valued as persons, in the context of placing value on the lives of all humans, male and female. This is not necessarily a perspective which all feminists would endorse. In vocabulary it belongs to a liberal, modernist or even romantic tradition, and one must be careful about the affiliations and comparisons one invites. However, there are potentially unhelpful consequences for women in the fact that both contemporary positivist psychology and its main opposition, social constructionism, disdain and discount a psychology which insists on the primacy of the person. The doctrine of the primacy of the person, as I understand it, does not imply a theory about origins but does demand a central place for the idea of the person and for the individual's experience of being a person in the ordering of values and commitments within the discipline of psychology.

Theoretical approaches to the self

To give a complete account of the multiplicity of theoretical approaches to the self would be beyond the scope of this book and not necessary to the book's thesis. It is useful, however, before proceeding to examine gender issues to look at some current accounts of the role of the self-construct and the development of the self.

It has been argued quite convincingly that psychology for most of the twentieth century accepted and promoted a view of the self as a self-contained, unitary and stable property of the person (Sampson, 1985). Psychology's view of the self did not arise in a vacuum or through a process of discovery but reflected the Western model of man which has been dominant since the Enlightenment. Kenneth Gergen (1991) is one of a number of psychologists and philosophers who has written on this topic (see also Charles Taylor, 1989) and for the sake of brevity I will employ his taxonomy of models of the self. Gergen argues that we can distinguish three different theories of the self which succeeded each other historically but which now co-exist and may be found in various manifestations within psychology as a discipline.

The first is the romantic view of the self which was at its strongest in the nineteenth century. According to Gergen, 'it is a perspective that lays central stress on unseen, even sacred forces that dwell deep within the person, forces that give life and relationships their significance'. The languages of love, passion and commitment are fundamentally romantic as is the notion of the person as unique, special and irreplaceable. On the other hand, in the modernist view of self, Gergen argues, 'reason and observation are the central ingredients of human functioning' (1991, p. 19). The achievements of the natural sciences arise from a modernist conception of the universe as knowable through the application of reason and scientific method. The self is, likewise, knowable, measurable and to be subjected to regulation by reason, its own regulation or that of others. The romantic and the modern views of the self both assert the importance of the unitary (albeit multifaceted) and autonomous self. Over a number of decades both conceptions of personhood have come to be threatened as a consequence of social and technological change. Particularly in the Western world, people are bombarded with information and experiences which invite them to rethink and refashion their lives. The self, Gergen proposes, becomes over-populated, saturated with 'multiple and disparate potentials for being' (ibid., p. 69). He argues that 'the technologies of social saturation are central to the contemporary erasure of individual self' (ibid., p. 49). In such an environment, 'committed identity becomes an increasingly arduous achievement' (ibid., p. 73) and the person finds herself in 'a multiphrenic condition in which one begins to experience the vertigo of unlimited multiplicity'. Thus Gergen labels the third model 'the saturated self'.

All three models of the self are seen to be culturally and historically generated. Gergen, as befits a social constructionist, is not arguing that his model of the saturated self is a more satisfactory theory of the nature of self than the romantic or modernist conceptions of self, although he is saying that it may be a more accurate reflection of the self-experience in the postmodern Western world. The major thrust of Gergen's analysis is not so much the threefold categorization – theoretically there could be many more versions of self – but the thesis that culture formulates our conception and our experience of the self. The self, in this view, is not a natural given.

Gergen's proposal that the postmodern self is saturated with alternative meanings and possibilities may be seen to harmonize with a number of similar recent reconceptualizations of the self. Part of the impetus for this reconceptualization came from the work of anthropologists like Clifford Geertz (1973) and from cross-cultural psychologists (e.g. Triandis, 1989; Guisinger and Blatt, 1994). As Brewster Smith stated in 1994, 'It is now well established that the Euro-American sense of strong individuality that we take for granted is a historical emergent and that more collectivist orientations remain the norm elsewhere' (p. 406). Some would argue that the Western self, particularly the female self, has always been more collectivist than received psychological theory would suggest, but Western philosophy, psychology and economics have shaped a common understanding and discourse of the self which posits it as natural, distinctive, unitary and independent. Postmodern and even anthropological discussions of relational and collectivist selves are therefore alien to Western minds reared on the Enlightenment model of self.

Traditional developmental psychology and the self

Developmental psychology has strongly promoted an account of the self-concept and the development of identity, which combines the romantic and the modern in Gergen's terms.

From a developmental perspective psychologists have seen the goals of self-development as becoming more aware of the self as an independent entity and attaining an increased capacity to self-regulate. Current developmental textbooks adopt this perspective. For example, John Santrock's book *Life-span Development* introduces the self-concept in a chapter on social development in early infancy. He states, 'Children begin to develop a sense of self by learning to distinguish themselves from others' (1992, p. 203). Subsequent themes, emphasized in relation to the self, focus on the child's growing independence. Theories brought to bear are Margaret Mahler's work exploring themes of separation and individuation, and Erikson's stage theory in which 'autonomy' is an important stepping stone towards psychological maturity. Santrock comments, 'The development of autonomy during the toddler years gives adolescents the courage to be independent individuals who can choose and guide their own future' (1992, p. 204).

The view that the goal of development should be achievements, categorized in terms of mastery, independence, autonomy, individuation and so on, has been criticized as reflecting both cultural bias and gender bias, an issue which will be explored further in the next chapter.

Relocating the self

None of the three conceptions of self described by Gergen is adequate. There is, however, a more satisfactory alternative to the determined essentialist self of modernism than the postmodernist saturated self. This is the idea of the self as a phenomenologically real mode of organizing experience that both derives from and makes possible self-awareness of existence in the world and continuity in time. This view places reflexivity at the centre of the theory of selfhood, personal identity and human personhood. Reflexivity generates the self and is the foundation for self and identity, but reflexivity can itself be sustained only by an enduring subjectivity; that is, by an enduring sense of self and personal identity.

However, this self is constantly under construction not just by the push of biology and of the socio-cultural context but also by the active process of self-construction. If we take on board the view of person as an active agent, undoubtedly shaped by genes and environment, but also capable of behaving so as to create her own inputs into a dynamic system, we have a view of self which fits neither the modern nor the postmodern nor the romantic categories posited by Gergen. However, it is a conception of self that shares the so-called romantic perception of the person as 'unique, special and irreplaceable'.

In a recent article, Jack Martin and Jeff Sugarman (2001) argue that it is not necessary to choose between the traditional fixed and bounded self of modernism and the demolition of centred personhood, which seems to be the inevitable consequence of the adoption of a postmodern perspective. They propose that there are dangers in moving too far in the postmodernist direction, despite the accuracy of the critique it offers of modernism. They comment, 'without psychological agents who develop, learn and change in ways that can be understood, at least in part, psychology and education are not only problematized, they are liquidated!' (p. 399). One could add to this sentiment the view that the negation of psychological agency threatens to undermine all social action, including transformative social movements such as feminism.

The ambition of Gergen and like-minded theorists is the ultimate achievement of 'a de-psychologized account of human action' where explanation for '"psychological predicates" will reside in socio-cultural processes'. For Gergen, 'word and mind' are 'entries in the discursive practices of the culture' (1991, p. 103). Martin and Sugarman argue instead for a 'conception of human being and understanding as dynamic, constrained and highly contingent processes that nonetheless may be constructed as real and as possessing epistemic and moral significance'. It is this middle ground which I also occupy and it is a middle ground which is supported by a number of current models of the developing person, including Charles Taylor's influential theory of the self.

The self at the phenomenal level consists of the subjective awareness of personal embodiment and psychological continuity. Charles Taylor would argue, however, that the self can exist only within what he terms 'webs of interlocution' and this is a view which is hard to contradict (Taylor, 1989). The self comes into being and has meaning through our relationship with others, and through the capacity for extended and extensive self-reflection granted to us through language. A conception such as this provides a possible foundation for a feminist conceptualization of the *self-in-time*, which reveals both the nature of constraint and the potential for change in each woman's life story.

Seyla Benhabib (1999) suggests that if 'we think of the identity of the self not in terms of a strong set of evaluative commitments but rather in terms of an ability to make sense, to render coherent, meaningful and viable for oneself one's shifting commitments as well as changing attachments then the post-modernist objection loses its target'. The self is a product then of that effort after meaning and continuity which seems to be a consequence of human self-consciousness, cognitive and linguistic competence, and motivation to engage in and survive in the world. The experience of selfhood is imbued with cultural meanings as well as the meanings accumulated by the person herself. Thus we have the sometimes remarkable variability in the understanding of self that is evident from cross-cultural and historical comparisons.

The feminine self?

Gender identity is clearly but one aspect of identity and it is also likely to vary considerably in salience from person to person and also from time to time in the same person. The questions which immediately arise are to what extent girls and women have a feminine or female subjectivity and to what extent the qualities of female selves are distinctive in their femaleness or in their (varied) instantiations of the feminine.

The modernist view of the self, many feminists have argued, does not acknowledge the female experience of self. For example, Jordan et al. assert that 'As we have inherited it, the notion of a "self" does not appear to fit women's experience' (1991, p. 11). This is an extreme statement but is made as prelude to the development of a thesis which posits the existence of a female relational self as opposed to the individualized, autonomous self of the male. Assertions such as Jordan's can be seen as arising from an essentialist conception of women's personality as discussed in Chapter 4. Women are assumed to share a fundamental disposition towards relating to others and to find their central meaning in life through relationships.

One might choose to argue that the self or selves of women are to a greater or lesser extent gendered and that, given the configurations of contemporary Western society and the construction of gender difference within it, many women will, in comparison to men, place more emphasis on relationship and connection. Such features of the gendering of female subjectivities have been well described in the work of Carol Gilligan and other relational theorists. However, by talking about the gendered self one is adopting a modernist position, albeit modified. The idea of a relational self, originating in early childhood experience, derives from the modernist conception of self as unitary and fixed, and fails to recognize the ongoing responsiveness to context and experience which characterizes the self system.

A social constructionist perspective on the gendered self is not the answer, however, since, as argued earlier, it insists on the obliteration of the psychological. If the word 'self' is used by social constructionissts, it is as the intersection of discourses, a 'site of subjectivity' which has no identity (Joy, 1993). As Patricia Waugh comments, 'Despite common concerns the post-modern deconstruction of subjectivity is as much a problem for women as the liberal construction of self' (1989, p. 16).

The most obvious problem presented to feminism by the postmodern view of the distributed or otherwise multiple, fugitive and obliterated self, located in the social, is the political and moral consequence of adopting such a view. Politically, feminism depends on a shared identity (i.e. the feminist identity) which does not and should not imply the neglect of other crucial differences between feminists.

There can be no politically astute and meaningful collective action without individual action and reflection. Morally there are dangers from a basic human rights perspective in any model of humankind which removes the uniqueness and importance of the person (every person) from central consideration. The dismantling of the psychological subject also invites a new form of reductionism in psychology, the reduction of the psychological to the social, to accompany the already rampant tendency within the discipline to reduce the psychological to the biological.

Morny Joy wrote an article in 1993 called 'Feminism and the self' in which she asks which theory of self is most helpful to feminists and warns against the dangers of rushing to embrace postmodernist conceptions of the self. She notes that 'it is not a question of women advocating a reappropriation of a pristine and unified notion of the self' (p. 277). Instead she advocates a hermeneutic approach to understanding the self, based on the work of Paul Ricoeur (1991). Interestingly, as mentioned in Chapter 1, recent work by Martin and Sugarman also converges on the hermeneutic perspective as one which offers a more hopeful and productive understanding of the self (Martin and Sugarman, 2001). A hermeneutic perspective on the self entails 'the interpretation of the self against the wider social backdrop' (Joy, 1993, p. 291). Joy cites Ricoeur's conception of the narrative form of identity, where neither the self nor the world is taken as a timeless ontological entity. Any interpretation is open to revision, as the self is open to revision. Such a conception of self allows a recovery of identity in the sense of a core identity, a distinctive self, but in a form which is perpetually developing and changing as a function of the person's ongoing efforts to interpret and understand their engagement with the world. This perspective on self avoids the dangers inherent in theories which posit a naturalized feminine self or which, like social constructionism, call for the obliteration of self.

Those who are immersed in feminist literature, which is very focused on the postmodern, tend to overlook the persistent dominance of the model of the natural and essential self which is embedded in Western culture and thought. The whole edifice of psychotherapy, for example, is premised on this modernist view of self, largely unperturbed by postmodern challenges (Cushman, 1990). The decontextualized view of self pre-empts a political analysis of the conditions which compromise personal growth and fixes the potential of each individual. Neither consequence is helpful to women.

Time and the self

A key implication of the conceptualization of self as the function of an emergent process rather than as a fixed entity is that it changes over time. Benhabib suggests that personal identity resides in the capacity of the self to generate meaning over time, 'so as to hold past and future together' (1999, p. 353). The philosopher Galen Strawson, on the other hand, thoroughly disagrees on the basis of his account of his personal introspection. He says that he has no personal sense of diachronic unity and sees his life in terms of a string of unconnected events, can make little sense of the connection between past events and has great difficulty in imagining himself engaged in any future events. He claims to have no sense of his life as an ongoing narrative (Strawson, 1996). It is likely that the sense of self and its existence in time is a very variable one. Some people may have a strong sense of location in time, reflecting constantly on their past and their future, and others may live largely for and in the present.

In the West we are time-conscious to an extent not found in all cultures and in all periods of history. The social construction of time will be discussed in Chapter 7 and, in the final chapter, I will discuss the manner in which psychoanalysis and developmental psychology have served to accentuate the importance of the past for our ideas about who we are as persons and how we come to be the people we now are.

The determinist models of psychological causation adopted and promoted by mainstream psychology have encouraged us to see our fate as determined, an inevitable unfolding of our genetic make-up or the consequences of our experiences in our formative years. Our orientation towards the future is fostered by the industrial society's need for citizens, who plan ahead, who have goals and who make their decisions with an eye to their long-term best interests. The good citizen reflects on the past and plans for the future. For many of us 'the self reaches from the current situation into the past and the future, unifying perceptions of "what currently is" with those of "what once was" and those of "what one day might be"' (Cross and Markus, 1991, p. 231). We make sense of ourselves in terms of what we once were or what we once did and where we one day will be or what we one day will do.

The manner in which we locate ourselves in time is not a natural given but, since it is a strong feature of our culture and the enculturation of its members, it needs to be part of our analysis of psychological functioning. Bernice Neugarten asserts the importance of taking the person's time perspective into account, when she urges psychologists to attend to 'what the person selects as important in his past and in his present and what he hopes to do in the future, what he hopes will occur, what strategies he elects and what meanings he attaches to times, life and death' (1977, p. 639).

Not only is it important to recognize the extent to which location in time is a feature of self-configuration, it is also important to recognize the extent to which people make value judgements about themselves, using across-time comparisons. Ryff (1985, 1991) comments on the manner in which we are encouraged to believe that our lives should be getting better all the time. This ideology is probably the popular counterpart of the progressive model of human development, which has been at the centre of twentieth-century developmental psychology (Kessen, 1990). As a result people commonly make comparisons between how they were and how they are now and how they hope to be in the future.

More nuanced contemporary life span perspectives can incorporate the idea of development entailing both gain and loss, but it might be argued that the popular view is that one should be aiming to remain young (i.e. with potential and capable of growth) and at the same time should be aiming towards the perfectibility of body and soul. The message of many books in the 'Mind, Body, Spirit' sections of bookshops is that perfection should be your goal, and whatever you are at the moment you could be better. You could love yourself more, for example!

Life span change in the gendered self

Most conventional accounts of the development of the female self are couched in terms of the acquisition of the female gender role and a female identity. These accounts are typically derived from Freudian, social learning or cognitive theories. For example, Santrock's text states that gender identity is the sense of being male or female which most children acquire by the time they are 3 years old (Santrock, 1992, p. 281). The gender role, on the other hand, is defined as 'the set of expectations that prescribe how males and females should think, act and feel' (ibid.).

Lawrence Kohlberg (1976) describes the girl's arrival at the understanding that she is a girl as follows. By the age of around 2 children are capable of correctly labelling themselves and others as either girl or boy, man or woman. However, their understanding of what it means to be a girl, Kohlberg suggests, is incomplete. Children of this age still do not understand that girl and boy are not arbitrary or mutable categories, i.e. that a little girl cannot grow up to be a man or that a little boy cannot be a mummy. They think people can change their gender by changing their hairstyle or clothes. Gender constancy is achieved by the age of about 6 when children come to understand that a boy remains a boy whether or not he wears a bow in his hair. Some might say that the pre-schooler has a rather sophisticated postmodern appreciation of the fluidity of gender, singularly unappreciated by Kohlberg.

By the age of 6 or 7 girls are motivated to behave according to the prevalent models of feminine behaviour. Their thinking follows the following logic: 'I am a girl, therefore I do girl things.' Behaviour and attitudes accrue which are congruent with the person's early identification of self as belonging to one or other sex. Gender schema theory, as elaborated by Sandra Bem, reverses the sequence described by Kohlberg. For Bem (1993) the motivation to conform to gendered rules and roles comes first. Later the child will build gender schemas through which to process incoming information. Thus Bem's gender schema theory combines both social learning and cognitive approaches.

Theories which emphasize the acquisition of gender in early childhood subscribe to the view that once established, gender role identity is very unlikely to change. Such theories, however, clearly belong to the essentialist view of gender which sees gender as a fixed characteristic of the individual, a neat social overlay on the foundation of biological sex. The social constructionist perspective on the other hand sees gender as the property of social engagements, not as a trait. As West and Zimmerman (1987) stated succinctly, gender is something

107

people do, not something people have. People do gender differently according to the social context. Interestingly, there is very little discussion in social constructionist texts about the beginnings of this gendering activity for the young child. The gendering of the girl in the sense of actions towards her, which engage her in feminine activity, must begin typically at birth. Although the baby is not subjectively aware of being gendered, she is caught up in this process from the first moments after her arrival outside the womb. In these days of ultrasound, the process has begun in the minds and actions of her parents even before her birth.

As argued earlier, a satisfactory theory of self should account for both the ongoing transactional nature of psychological change and a located phenomenal self. Therefore in terms of early development, we need to look to the nature of the gendering process which is enacted in discourse and in relationships, and in the sense of self as an interpreter of this experience. Both discourse analytic and intrapsychic theorizing are required.

As Margaret Wetherell notes, 'Gender is not a matter of consistent unitary single identities . . . but develops from contradictory and frequently fragmentary pieces of discourse, repertoires and accounting systems available to individuals to make sense of their position and which historically and contingently have come to be marked as feminine or masculine responses' (1986, p. 77). This process of making sense begins early and reflects, in all probability, features of Bem's gender schema theory which gives a credible socio-cognitive account of the psychological processes entailed in the genesis of gendered thought and behaviour.

The fragmentary pieces from which little girls construct their ideas about gender and their ideas about themselves as gendered will also include ideas about how to 'do masculine'. The phenomenon of the tomboy is a good illustration of how easy it is for girls to be involved in gender shifting. By the same token, it is far more difficult in most Western societies for little boys to 'do feminine', even today. In certain contexts, masculine behaviour by girls is tolerated or even indulged. Girls may enact a masculine, boyish role for years without any untoward comment or sanctions. Then, at or around puberty the masculine behaviour becomes unacceptable and will typically cease. I have not been able to source any empirical work on the phenomenon of the tomboy from the girl's perspective, although there is an interesting early paper on the phenomenon *per se* by Janet Hyde *et al.* (1977). Hyde *et al.* report that 63% of the US teenagers they surveyed said they were or had been tomboys. What is going on subjectively in the mind of the girl who dresses and acts like a boy? There will be a small number of girls who have a strong sense of gender dysphoria and who will want desperately to be a boy, but for most tomboys both masculine and feminine elements would appear to co-exist without too much conflict. Such flexibility in the gendering of self becomes increasingly difficult but it is not at all unusual at later stages in the life course. People may change their level of adherence to expected gender scripts from context to context, from time to time and from age to age. Thus we find examples of women who hold positions of power showing behaviours, including language behaviours, which are traditionally identified as 'masculine' (Henley, 1977) or men acting like mothers when minding small children (Risman, 1987).

This variability lends weight to a social constructionist view of gender. For example, Janis Bohan (1993) concludes: 'none of us is feminine or is masculine or fails to be either of those. In particular contexts people do feminine; in others they do masculine.' This may well be true of people's behaviour in contexts where cross-sex behaviour is supported or strongly rewarded. One wonders, at the same time, whether the power-dressing, power-wielding female executive necessarily has a masculine sense of self while acting 'masculine' or whether the nappy-changing father has a feminine sense of self while acting 'feminine'.

As children become older, they become more capable of locating themselves in time. As far as we can judge, the temporal perspective of the pre-schooler is restricted largely to the here and now. However, there are various factors which contribute to the extension of their temporal range, primarily the acquisition of language and the development of memory and imagination. As Martin and Sugarman state, it is memory and imagination which open the doors to 'spatiotemporal fluidity' (1999, p. 26). Spatiotemporal fluidity is the capacity to move mentally into the past or the future, thus enabling the human mind to escape from the strictures of existence in the immediate context. In terms of the young child's sense of self these new skills open the door to memories of the self in the past and imaginings of the self in the future.

The focus of most of the work on children's subjectivities is couched in terms of their developing understanding of self. For example, work focuses on how children describe themselves (Harter, 1999) or on their understanding of the interiority of their own minds and those of others (Astington, 1993). There is not much work on how they see themselves in time.

However, one useful perspective on how children come to locate themselves in time is provided by work on young children's use of narrative. Katherine Nelson (1993) and Susan Engel (in press) are among those who have explored young children's beginning use of narrative. It would appear that much of the conversation between parents and children is involved with the telling of a story, however brief. Some of these stories are about others or even about the misdeeds of the family cat. Some are about the child herself. Children soon become active participants in this story-telling and in the process of telling a story learn to organize events in time. Stories have a beginning, a middle and an end – they entail duration. They are often located in the past or in the future. In terms of her own life story, the child begins to piece together an autobiography out of fragments – anecdotes about what she did when she was 1, the time she spilled her orange juice over granny, her hopes to visit the new zoo when it opens, her expectation of going to 'big school' in the autumn. In this way the child learns to see herself as having a location in time, in her own history and in her own future.

Undoubtedly this process is a function of instruction, supported by the child's cognitive capacities for memory and imagination. Observations of parents in conversation with young children suggest that the construction of autobiography is carried out in collaboration with adults in a manner which conforms to a Vygotskian interpretation. Parents play a very active role in prompting personal memories and in asking the child to project into the future. The kinds of events which are selected for telling and retelling and the kind of future which is anticipated by parents may be an early and important mechanism by which the child's sense of self and her story is gendered. Children soon become active participants in this gendering of their own stories, selectively ignoring events and opportunities which do not fit with their gender schema (Bem, 1993). As the child's social circle expands and as she begins to be exposed to other stories in the media and in books about girls and the desirable image of how their life stories should unfold, the gendering process continues (Walkerdine, 1991).

There are multiple sources for changes in self-perception and in subjectivity over the life course. As stated above, the gendering of subjectivity is liable to wax and wane according to the salience of gender in any particular context and at any particular time. For example, early adolescence has been identified in US culture as a time of 'gender intensification', implying increased gender stereotyping of behaviour (Galambos et al., 1990). One would predict that being a girl and being feminine form central preoccupations for the adolescent female. As noted in Chapter 5, the preoccupations of girls and women very often centre on their appearance and on their sexual relationships. However, to see this as the end of the story would be a serious disservice to the complexity of the lives of teenage girls. The gendering of subjectivity at this age does not only relate to the girls' biological role in life. Future careers, school performance and friendships will often be more important to some girls at certain times and to some girls at all times (see Johnson et al., 1999).

Achievement issues may, for example, be highly coloured by gender in terms of ambivalence about or ambition for success, restrictions on opportunities for achievement, competition with males and so on. Other issues around difference, such as social class or race, may at times be centre-stage, and gender may recede. Gender may interact with other distinctions and discourses. Age and gender may combine to create a new and powerful discourse and a new, defining way of seeing the self. Thus for a woman to become, in her own eyes, 'an old woman' has a whole set of implications in terms of how others might behave, how the person behaves and how she thinks about herself. The meaning of 'old woman' is, then, different to being old and to being a woman – it has its own set of distinct meanings (many of them negative in Western society).

Gender intensification may be a feature of other parts of the female life course other than adolescence. The time around the arrival of the first child, when those who have had a reasonably egalitarian relationship with their male partner may suddenly find themselves conforming to the traditional female role as mother and housekeeper, is another example (Croghan, 1991). Middle age has, on the contrary, been identified as a time when women may become more independent and assertive, and generally 'masculine' in behaviour and outlook (Gutmann,

1987). In general, the demands on a woman differ, depending markedly on her age. Along with these differing demands come quite profound, concomitant effects on her thoughts and feelings about herself.

The work of Carol Ryff is relatively unusual in the context of life span developmental psychology. She has explicitly adopted a focus on what she terms 'the "inner side" of life-span development' (1985, p. 97). Ryff sees the individual's own understanding and interpretation of her development as a key to understanding stability and change. Her distinction between the 'inside' and the 'outside' of development is perhaps questionable in terms of contemporary models of the self which take account of the interpenetration of the psychological and the social, but there is validity and utility in her emphasis on the subjective perspective on experience. In two studies of elderly women, Ryff seemed to have evidence for a self-perceived change in values from instrumental to terminal between middle and old age. Instrumental values are centred on achievement and how one is judged in the eyes of others, whereas terminal values are to do with desirable end states of existence such as having a sense of freedom or happiness. However, further studies involving elderly men established a similar recollection of the same transition occurring, if anything, earlier than in women. Her work with middle-aged women and men led her to conclude that 'the processes of subjective change appeared to be ordered around life stage rather than sex' (1985, p. 107).

Ryff points out that often in life there is lack of congruence between change in terms of life events and the subjective sense of change. Thus a person may find a new job or a new partner and feel subjectively unchanged, but, in the middle of a period of apparent stability, she may undergo a revolution in terms of values and commitments that is not obviously related to external demands. Where do such subjective shifts in commitment or self-perception come from? Ryff points out that the novelist is typically better than the psychologist at describing such processes and making them accessible to our understanding.

Ryff's comparative studies of young adults, middle-aged adults and old adults found that older adults recalled levels of personal growth in the past that were significantly higher than their personal growth in the present. This finding was particularly marked in women but both older women and men expected a marked decrease in personal growth in the future (Ryff, 1991). The young adults and middle-aged adults, men and women, both saw themselves as improving on all aspects of psychological functioning. Older people presented a picture of stability on some measures, progress on others and decrement in yet others. Older women, she found, claimed an improvement in environmental mastery and in relationships with others. These studies were carried out in the 1980s in the USA with mainly middle-class participants. Valuations and perspectives are likely to be different in other samples. What is interesting in a general sense is that many adults, up to old age, saw themselves as on an upward trajectory psychologically and thus seemed to have internalized the ideal of progression, which, formally and informally, is a pervasive model of development in Western culture.

Neugarten has called attention to the importance of our positioning of ourselves in the life course. She suggests that in middle age our time perspective typically shifts from thinking of our place in the life course from 'years since birth to time left to live' (Neugarten, 1968). For women, this new consciousness of the limitation in time left to live may coincide with the message that they have little left to offer now that their youthful attractiveness has waned and their childbearing and rearing years are over. Coming to terms with death and finitude may be a cause of distress, the kind of distress that is often difficult to articulate. Given this accumulation of potentially negative features, it is reassuring that so many older women rate their quality of life as high and seem to relish the freedom offered to them as they escape from the constraints of the traditional female sex role.

The Irish artist, Pauline Bewick, commented on what her age meant to her in these words:

> Stuff in me is coming up now because I'm 63 and I haven't got that many years to live. So I'm grinding away at it. It's like when I was pregnant; you're going to have it and you're going to be in pain so you work away at it psychologically, toward the time of having it. When you become 63, you're grinding away at death because you know it's inevitable.

Death themes had recently become apparent in her paintings for the first time.

Conclusion

Challenges to the notion of the fixed and unitary self have resulted in an understanding of personal identity and selfhood as processes which are always under way, never achieved. The feminine self or the sense of self experienced by the girl and woman as she moves through her life course is moving and changing in time. The sense of self preserves continuity within the normal dynamic flux of experience, mainly by dint of the active interpretation of experience and its meaning in place and time. Each woman's particular experience of gender is a product of complex social and psychological processes, which cannot be seen as a *fixed attribute* of self but is an important aspect of the *enactment* of self.

Most individuals identify as male or female at an early stage in life and are identified publicly as such. They will be treated differently and be subject to different regulating discourses and social encounters according to their sex. Sex and age intersect in important ways to shape the person's gender role-related feelings and behaviours throughout the life course. From situation to situation the salience of gender may vary, resulting in a discontinuity and fluidity in the expression of gender. Cultural and historical circumstances also conspire to ensure that the meaning of being female, girl or woman is constantly subject to change and revision.

At a subjective level, conscious activity may be more or less gendered, depending both on the individual (Bem, 1993) and on her current preoccupations and engagements. The salience of gender and the activation of gender-related schemas vary from situation to situation. The current social and political context in which a girl or woman lives her life will influence her current expression of gender. Unconscious and inarticulate activity at the level of mental processes will ensure that the significance of gender and its associated meanings and experiences will never be fully knowable or understandable. As Iris Murdoch said in *The Sea, The Sea*, 'We are such inward secret creatures, that inwardness is the most amazing thing about us, even more amazing than our reason'. The inwardness of the human person makes each person unfathomable to the other and in the end unfathomable to herself.

7

SOCIAL CHANGE AND SOCIAL CLOCKS

The changing context and its influence on development

Developmental psychologists have often presented a view of the child or the adult as *timeless*, in the sense of being unlocated in historical time. In recent years, awareness of the need to locate people in their cultural and historical context has certainly grown, more demonstrably in social and developmental psychology perhaps than in other areas of psychology. If one takes a historical perspective on the psychology of girls and women, what is readily evident is that the description of the features of normal or typical development and the criteria by which normal or typical development may be judged have changed dramatically over time. Just as a cross-cultural perspective enlightens us about the range and potential of human behaviour so too does a historical perspective.

Any perspective one cares to adopt on the historical context of individual development is perforce a cultural perspective, since at no time does any person exist in a cultural vacuum. It is the culture which changes as we examine context from a historical vantage point.

As argued in the previous chapters of this book, a developmental perspective on the person is one which should locate the person in her cultural and historical context. Theorists have been attempting in recent years to come to terms with and articulate a vision of the person as inextricably embedded in their context. Furthermore this context must be understood as something which both shapes development and is shaped by the actions and choices of the developing person.

In this chapter, I will examine ways in which changing historical events and accompanying norms and expectations about the structure and content of women's lives have resulted in different 'developmental' pathways and relationships with time. I will also explore the meaning of time in contemporary society and how social norms in relation to time and timing influence the female life course.

Personality development, social events and social change

It is extraordinary that as late as 1995 Urie Bronfenbrenner, the leading developmental psychologist, could write: 'Considerations of time and timing as they

114

relate to features of the environment as opposed to characteristics of the person have only recently begun to receive systematic attention in developmental research' (p. 641). He credits sociologists such as Glen Elder for having made greater advances in this regard, and cites Elder's studies of the impact of the Great Depression and military service on individual lives as examples of such work (Elder, 1974, 1986). Elder himself (1998) identifies his theoretical approach as 'life course theory'. His approach entails a selection of key features of the changing socio-historical environment and then an examination of how these social events change the behaviour and experience of the individual. Elder describes his four central principles along the following lines:

1   The life course of individuals is embedded in and shaped by the historical times and places they experience over their lifetime.
2   The developmental impact of a succession of life transitions or events is contingent on when they occur in a person's life.
3   Lives are lived interdependently, and social and historical influences are expressed through this network of shared relationships.
4   Individuals construct their own life course through the choices and actions they take, within the opportunities and constraints of history and social circumstances (Elder, 1998).

In many ways these principles would seem to be obvious, but they have not always been obvious to developmental psychologists or, for that matter, to psychoanalysts. Many of the theories discussed earlier in this book disregard such principles.

Elder gives examples from his book, *Children of the Great Depression* (1974), to illustrate each principle. In this study he analysed longitudinal data from the Berkeley Institute of Human Development collected originally on children who were born in the 1920s and who lived through the economic crash of the 1930s. In general, the participants who were children at the time of the Great Depression were negatively affected by the Depression, which caused considerable stress at societal and familial levels, a finding which is taken as an endorsement of Elder's first principle. In relation to the second principle of timing, the comparison with other cohorts was very telling. Those who were children and young adolescents during the Great Depression showed many more negative effects than the members of an earlier cohort who had enjoyed a secure childhood. Elder concludes that childhood is a time of particular vulnerability to family stress. The importance of the links between lives (the third principle) was shown in the negative impact on the children, particularly boys, of paternal stress and depression due to unemployment. Some parents and children coped better than others, for example, by showing great ingenuity and persistence in finding work or ways of earning money. This highlights the relevance of individual differences in coping and resilience (the fourth principle).

Elder did not focus on gender issues or on the lives of women. However, a certain amount of life course research, explicitly connecting personality change to social change, has been carried out on girls and women. An influential example of this kind of work is that of Abigail Stewart and her colleagues, based in the USA. Their focus is very much on women's personality development and its relationship to changing social norms and historical events.

In 1989 Abigail Stewart and Joseph Healy proposed a model for understanding how social events influence development. The first assumption they made is that the age of the individual is an important factor in determining the meaning an individual assigns to a social event. A further important factor is the extent to which a person is identified with a specific cohort or generational unit such as being part of the 'baby boom generation'. They propose that events influence development in different ways depending on the age of the individual when the events occur. Thus fundamental values and expectations which they see as being formed in childhood are more readily open to influence at that stage, whereas vocational preferences and choices are more readily open to influence at the time they are being formulated, in adolescence. In an echo of Elder's work on the Great Depression, they argue that children born in times of stability and plenty should have greater levels of optimism and trust in social institutions compared to children who have experienced social and economic instability and hardship. Those raised in poverty, they suggest, may come to value self-reliance whereas those raised in plenty may value self development. Events which coincide with a person's late adolescence might not shake their basic values and orientation to the world but may have a major impression on their identity. They take as an example the Vietnam War and how it shaped the consciousness and identity of a cohort of young Americans, whether they were veterans or protesters. Social events occurring in mature adulthood may, they propose, affect options, and restrict or enable certain behaviours but do not affect foundational values and identity. They present an example taken from Chafe (1972) concerning middle-class mothers in the USA, who returned to work in the 1950s and 1960s. These women had married and had children after the Second World War when working outside the home was unacceptable and their role in life was to have children and look after them and their husbands. According to Chafe, returning to work did not unsettle or change their value-system but was seen as a further step in providing for the family, not a step taken for their own fulfilment or career advancement. For some women the return to work was motivated by a desire to have money of their own. I recall that an expression in common use at that time was 'pin-money' – pocket money for grown-women, and of no real account. Stewart and Healy recognize the period of later adulthood as a time when individuals do experience radical reappraisal and revision of their beliefs. They say that such upheavals may occur either because of the 'accumulation of life experiences that cannot be accommodated by earlier experiences or identities' or because of 'internal developmental processes that we do not fully understand'.

Stewart and her colleagues have attempted to explore the postulates outlined in the 1989 Stewart and Healy paper by means of analysis of a number of different longitudinal datasets. I will look at their own study on Radcliffe graduates first (Stewart, 1994). Abigail Stewart has conducted a longitudinal study following up a sample of women who graduated from the prestigious Radcliffe College in 1964. The women were born during the Second World War and left the college just after the assassination of President John F. Kennedy, at a time when the civil rights movement was in full sway and just before the women's movement got under way (Betty Friedan's *The Feminine Mystique* was published in 1963). At a follow-up in 1986, the women were asked to rate a series of twenty-six public events in terms of the 'personal meaning' they had in their lives. Sixty-one of the total sample of ninety-one selected one event as particularly meaningful. Seventy-two per cent of the singularly significant events selected had occurred in late adolescence or early adulthood. This, of course, is the time Stewart and Healy had identified as the identity formation period.

Thirty per cent of these women chose the women's movement as the event which was the most personally meaningful to them. Out of the twenty-six events they were asked to rate, the women's movement was rated by the ninety-one women in the total sample as the event that meant the most to them. Other events included the Vietnam War, the Kennedy presidency, the civil rights movement and so on. Those women who rated the women's movement as particularly significant were more likely to have combined work with marriage and child-rearing and to have pursued a non-traditional career in the traditional male pattern, i.e. one of continuous employment and career advancement.

Interviews conducted with several of the women, who rated the women's movement as very important to them, served to raise serious questions about Stewart and Healy's original assumption that late adolescence/early adulthood is the peak time for identity-shaping choices. Some of the women who had not identified with the women's movement at the time when it was in full swing did so later, due to disillusionment with the traditional female role or as the result of a period of reflection and reappraisal in early middle age. These findings sit more comfortably with the view, which I advocate in this book, of development as responsive to changed circumstances and as potentially open-ended. Faced with results that somewhat disconfirm her thesis on the timing of the identity process, Stewart (1994) argues that perhaps the women's movement was meeting different developmental needs for the women in the sample who embraced it at different ages. Thus she suggests that it provided for validation of identity at adolescence, connection to community in early adulthood and the need for a renewal of meaning in middle age. Stewart is making a valiant effort to fit her data into a normative developmental framework. Nevertheless, what the data appear to suggest is that women can be open to transformative experiences at any age.

Abigail Stewart and Joan Ostrove published a paper in 1998 which reviewed a number of different longitudinal studies of women graduates, including the Radcliffe sample. They hypothesized, in line with the theoretical assumptions spelled out by Stewart and Healy in 1989, that 'there is a special importance to events that coincide with the identity-forming adolescent years because once identities are formed they are posited to have persistent effects' (1998, p. 1186). They hypothesized also that gender issues would have particular salience to 'baby boomers' who grew up at a time when there were dramatic changes in women's access to third-level education, employment and sport, and a new demand for equality, sexually, domestically and in the world of work. Most of their findings confirm that the women who identified with the women's movement as teenagers or young adults benefited in middle age from a strong sense of identity and confidence in their political and interpersonal orientation. However, many women who had followed a traditional path on graduation and had not identified with the women's movement until much later also achieved a confident and contented middle age. The only women who were psychologically not doing well were those who had a lot of regrets but felt unable to do anything about them. Women generally expressed a sense of freedom and mastery in middle age, which they had not experienced earlier.

In their interpretation of these findings, Stewart and Ostrove seem to be caught between a desire to generalize from their findings and an awareness that these findings may be very class and generation specific. In terms of their view that adolescence sets the tone for later life in relation to identity, the data are in part supportive but also in part disconfirming. It is not surprising, given the linkages and the logic of connections between life choices and life situations at an early stage of life and later consequences, that for some women a strong identification with feminism remained with them, and was confirmed and carried forward into later life. However, Stewart's data, reported in both the 1994 and the 1998 papers, describe a large number of women who discover a new and meaningful identification with the woman's movement in later adulthood.

From a life span theory perspective the longitudinal studies conducted by Stewart and other similar studies on women (e.g. Helson and Moane, 1987; Tangri and Jenkins, 1993) are very interesting. They confirm the importance of age and generation in shaping women's lives. They assert the historical variability in women's lives and, as a consequence, in their psychology. Social change can take place very quickly. One of the cohort comparisons which Stewart and Ostrove describe involves a sample of women who graduated from Radcliffe in 1964 and a sample of women who graduated in 1975. When the women from the class of 1975 were 24 years old, 13% were married and none was a mother. Eighty per cent were pursuing a career and 58% were in graduate school. At the same age, two-thirds of the women in the class of 1963 were married, 16% were mothers, and relatively few were established in careers or in graduate school.

Nearly all the US studies focus on women graduates, almost by definition a mainly middle-class group. For a change of culture and class I will mention briefly two UK studies. Jane Pilcher's study of three generations of women who grew up in twentieth-century Wales (Pilcher, 1998) enquired into their views on a wide range of issues including feminism and gender roles. She found that age (or more specifically generation) was a major source of difference in attitude and experience. The oldest group (aged between 62 and 87) were, not surprisingly, more conservative than the other two groups. Aside from attitude differences, Pilcher points out an interesting disparity in the vocabulary which each group used. For example, it was the middle group alone who adopted the vocabulary of feminism (these women would have been in their teens and twenties when the second-wave feminist movement was at its strongest). Nonetheless the younger groups had attitudes which could only be described as feminist while avoiding the vocabulary. Pilcher concludes that 'Age needs to be recognised to be a fundamental source of diversity and difference among women alongside class and ethnicity' (p. 138).

Sue Sharpe has carried out two studies of English teenagers which she has reported in her book *Just Like a Girl* (1994). The first study was carried out in 1972 and focused on 249 secondary school girls living in London: 149 from white families, fifty-one from West Indian families and forty-nine from Asian families. The girls were aged between 14 and 15 and most of them were from working-class families. In 1991, she went back to the same schools in London and gathered a sample of 232 girls with backgrounds similar to the girls in the earlier sample. Sharpe found that the girls she interviewed in the 1970s were beginning to question the traditional roles taken on by their mothers and were also beginning to question some of the inequalities between their opportunities and those open to young men. They planned to combine working with having a family, but most still endorsed traditional values and adopted traditional goals. They were aware of the women's movement but generally rejected it as not for them.

When comparing the 1990s sample with the 1970s sample, Sharpe found a mixture of similarities and differences. The girls in the later sample were 'more assertive and confident' and took it for granted that women would be independent and equal to men. At the same time they rejected feminism as not relevant to them since equality had been achieved (Sharpe, 2001). As Sharpe comments, the girls endorse the goals of feminism but refuse to identify as feminists. The girls in 1972 felt generally positive about marriage but the later sample was 'far more cynical and rejecting of marriage' (2001, p. 178). The 1990s girls expected equality and sharing of tasks, if and when they married. Neither sample of girls anticipated difficulties in finding affordable and good-quality childcare.

In her (1994) book Sharpe describes the changes in the lives of working-class girls in Britain over the twentieth century. Her survey indicates just how important class differences are. For example, the working-class girl at the turn of the twentieth century did not in any way face the life of leisure and idleness that was often the destiny of her middle-class counterpart. As in the American situation, significant changes can take place over a very much shorter span of history. Less than twenty years separated Sharpe's two samples, but clear changes were evident at a psychological level in terms of confidence, independence and life expectations.

To summarize, the work on the connection between social change and personal

119

change demonstrates that people who belong to different generations are exposed to different social contexts and that these contexts influence their lives in important ways. As Bronfenbrenner concludes, a basic principle underpinning developmental research should be that 'the individual's own developmental life course is seen as embedded in and powerfully shaped by conditions and events occurring during the historical period through which the person lives' (1995, p. 641). This unsurprising conclusion is sometimes labelled as 'cohort particularity'. This principle casts doubt on any over-generalized statement about women's psychology and the course of women's development. As well as knowing about women's social location, we must locate them in historical time. History does not stand still, so what we know about a particular woman or group of women can only be helpful to our understanding of women in the future if we take into account the new location in historical time.

Social changes, events and movements do not have the same effect on all those who are exposed to them. In any society, exposure to and awareness of social changes will vary, depending on the person's place within that society and the nature of the events and processes involved. For example, most but not all of the working-class girls in Sharpe's (1972) sample had heard of the women's movement, but what they were exposed to was 'its misrepresentation in the media'. As a result, they thought members of such a movement must be 'ridiculous or freaky' (Sharpe, 1994, p. 283). Despite this, the effects of the women's movement might be influencing their lives via equal pay and anti-discrimination legislation.

Duane Alwin (1995) refers to variability in the impact of social change as the principle of intracohort variability. Some of the research in this area is very unclear about making distinctions between different kinds of social events and processes. For example, in Stewart's research on Radcliffe graduates, events such as the assassination of Kennedy were listed with the civil rights movement, one being a one-off event (albeit with long-lasting repercussions) and one being a year-long, complex and multifaceted social process. Growing up in a time of unemployment and insecurity cannot be equated, as a socio-historical process, with the first moon shot.

The other source of heterogeneity is at the level of the individual person in terms of her personal resources and coping strategies. Rutter has pointed out, for example, how important self-esteem and a capacity to plan for the future can be in allowing the individual to escape the worst effects of adversity (1989). Different historical periods bring different discourses about how girls should behave, what women should expect. All these discourses and their accompanying restraints and opportunities will be filtered through the interpretive lens of the individual girl or woman.

From the perspective of age rather than generation the possibility that the timing of exposure to social and historical events has developmental significance should be taken on board. At the moment the evidence for the thesis developed by Stewart about the importance of the timing of certain events in relation to the developmental stage of the girl or woman concerned seems to be equivocal.

Undoubtedly, decisions and pressures which place the girl on a particular trajectory at any early stage may well have a lasting significance. Recent research in this area reminds us that both chance events and reappraisals on the part of the individual can cause them to move in another direction, thus confounding attempts at prediction (Clarke and Clarke, 1984; Rutter, 1989).

Deterministic developmental theories may be part of a set of popular and academic discourses which serve to pre-empt change at the individual level. For example, a belief that childhood experiences mark you for life can condemn a person to a neurotic preoccupation with her past and a conviction that she cannot change. A belief that women are psychologically disposed from early childhood to be maternal can cause distress and bewilderment to a woman who does not feel that way.

When examining the impact of socio-historical change on individual lives it should not be forgotten that society consists of people, and for the most part it is people who make events happen. As Klaus Riegel (1977) summarizes, 'through their activities individuals change the socio-historical conditions which at the same time change the individuals' (p. 16). Developmental psychologists are only beginning to theorize the ways in which historical societal change produces developmental change at the level of the individual. It is obvious that the matter is complex and that it operates via a number of different mechanisms which connect social change at the macro level with the lives of individuals who are themselves growing and changing.

As well as noting the importance of studies which link historical change with personal change, Bronfenbrenner notes the importance of the 'timing of biological and social transitions as they relate to the culturally defined age, role expectations, and opportunities occurring throughout the life course' (1995, p. 641). It is to this aspect of timing that I turn next.

Time and the social construction of life span change

Kohli is associated with the coining of the term 'chronologization' to refer to the temporal structuring of the life course (Kohli, 1986). In 1986, Martin Kohli and John Meyer made the statement 'Among the social sciences, there is no longer any dissent about the social construction of life stages' (p. 145). By the social construction of the life course they mean 'the patterned set of rules and mechanisms which regulate a key dimension of life, namely its temporal extension'. They do not specify to which social sciences they are referring, but I would suggest that such concepts have not penetrated very far into the thinking of many psychologists, even developmental psychologists and specialists in the psychology of women.

Modern society and time

Some kind of temporal organization is an inevitable feature of any social group-
ing. A number of authors have argued that time has very different meanings in
industrialized societies than it held in those same societies prior to industrialization. The requirements of rural, agrarian societies were very different and much
more linked to seasonality and to biological and natural cycles. Richard Lichtman
has argued that within the West 'capitalism has profoundly altered the nature and
meaning of *time, passage, growing up, growing old, aging* and *dying* itself'
(1987, p. 129).

In his paper on this theme, Lichtman quotes Thomas Hardy in *Tess of the
D'Urbervilles.*

> Tess started on her way up the dark and crooked lane or street not made
> for hasty progress, a street laid out before inches of land had value and
> when one handed clocks sufficiently subdivided the day.

He takes this quotation as an illustration of the key features of an era in history
when the clock was not the measure of time and when speed and progress were
not the primary goals. Lichtman (1987, p. 130) notes,

> Time and value are inseparable. In systems of use value, time is lived,
> organic, heterogeneous, integral, biological and intrinsic. In the mode of
> exchange value, time is conceptual, homogeneous, mechanical, extrinsic
> and independent. There is a fundamental shift from quality to quantity
> brought on primarily by the introduction of abstract value and abstract
> labour, each unit of which is necessarily worth precisely the same as the
> next. In capitalist societies we live by the clock and measure our lives
> by the intervals, all of equal weight and value, the minutes and hours
> marked out by the clock.

The developmental psychologist, Klaus Riegel, also takes a jaundiced view of the
effect of time regulation on our lives, saying that we are 'subordinated to an
impersonal and alienated concept' (1977, p. 8).

The development of industry and the need on the part of owners and employers
to regiment the workforce were, then, the motor behind the new dominance of the
clock and the emergence of a new meaning of time as a commodity which could
be bought, spent, wasted and saved. Our days are no longer shaped by the rising
or setting of the sun or by the weather but by the clock. Our lives are similarly
measured out by conceptions of productivity and worth in relation to the needs of
the state. Thus ageing, for men and women, is seen in industrialized societies as
associated with a decline in worth, in contrast to those societies where ageing was
and is valued as a correlate of wisdom and experience.

As Kohli (1986) suggests, a more complex and centralized society also needs to regulate the lives of its citizenry across time and to structure the life course in terms of the roles expected from its individual members according to their age. The modern state exerts control over the patterning of the life course to an extent unheard of before the rise of industry and capitalism. It is for this reason that the claims by some commentators (see e.g. Hagestad and Neugarten, 1985) that age is increasingly becoming irrelevant do not ring true. Compared to what or when? Kohli considers that the shape of the life course in modern societies is structured around employment (1986). There are thus three main periods related to work in the life course: preparation for work via education and training, work activity, and retirement from work. This is clearly a pattern which has more salience in men's lives but is increasingly becoming applicable to women.

In a 1997 paper, Richard Settersten comments that 'new hopes for a more flexible life course have surfaced' (p. 226). Some commentators have argued that the rigid age restrictions of modern societies are now being dismantled in the postmodern age. For example, career patterns are increasingly discontinuous, and lifelong learning and retraining are becoming common. Age constraints are breaking down in terms of norms and expectations. I suspect, however, that those who claim the lack of societal constraint and the irrelevance of age are the privileged in society, who have the resources to challenge or disregard conventions.

Life periods

Neugarten claims that people think about the life cycle in terms of 'a succession of life periods' (1979, p. 888). This popular perspective on the life cycle does not come about accidentally, and it is informative to ask what social and political purpose is served by the division of the life course into defined periods. The term 'periodization' of the life course is used by some scholars (e.g. James and Prout, 1997). It is a term which has a slightly more specific reference than the more general term 'chronologization'.

What are these divisions and how do they affect women's lives? There has been a long tradition in the West of thinking of the life course in terms of stages, the most famous early example being Shakespeare's piece on the seven ages of man in *As You Like It,* which runs from the first, 'the infant, mewling and puking in the nurse's arms' to the seventh age of 'second childishness, and mere oblivion, sans teeth, sans eyes, sans taste, sans everything'.

However, the way we divide the life course varies from historical period to historical period. For example, adolescence as a distinct period of life seems to have been a construction of the late nineteenth century. The period before a child (or adolescent) is recognized as an adult has been lengthening gradually across the twentieth century, in line with the need for a highly educated workforce. Recently, Jeffrey Arnett made a quite convincing suggestion that we should distinguish a period between adolescence and adulthood which he labels 'emerging adulthood' (Arnett, 2000).

A number of forces have combined to alter the periodization of the life course. Biological changes have been brought about by improved nutrition and health. Girls enter adolescence earlier these days than they did fifty years ago because of the reduction in the average age of menarche, as discussed in Chapter 5. As the requirement for lengthy schooling has increased, more and more girls stay in school until 18, or 19 in some European countries. Thus the period of social irresponsibility and exclusion from some adult privileges has extended to cover all the teenage years. At the same time teenagers are becoming sexually active earlier and pre-teen girls are dressing like little adults in 'sexy' clothes unimaginable on the 9-year-old growing up in the 1950s. In this way, some commentators advise, we are witnessing the end of childhood as we once knew it (Postman, 1982).

The periods marking out the life course have changed in adulthood also. The postponement of having children until the late twenties has been accompanied by an increasing number of women waiting until they are well into their thirties before they have the first of their (two) children. Medical advances now permit women in their fifties and sixties to have children, although this is still extremely rare. More women are living on into very old age.

Middle age seems at some levels to be simply a descriptive category, but writers like Richard Shweder (1998) argue that it should be regarded as a cultural fiction or construction. Margaret Gullette is the author of *Safe at Last in the Middle Years*, which explores the depiction of middle age in the modern novel (1988). She is also a contributor to Shweder's book on middle age where she argues that the middle-aged need to be liberated from current discourses on middle age. The safe, secure, sober citizen of common currency needs to be subverted and resisted. Shweder's book seems to provide evidence for a number of contemporary cultures like Japan and India where middle age is not recognized or spoken of as a distinct life period except among those citizens who are very Westernized.

Even in the West, what is meant by middle age is subject to change. In comparatively recent times the ages encompassed by the term 'middle age' seem to have changed. Middle age was defined by Jung in the 1950s as starting at age 35. Most of today's women of that age would strenuously resist being labelled as middle-aged. Middle age would be seen by many people as starting at least ten years later (Mitchell and Helson, 1990).

Better healthcare and nutrition have led to an extension of the average life expectancy in the West, for women in particular. Old age is now a very long period, and the entry into old age in terms of self-labelling resisted and delayed. Taking Ireland as an example, life expectancy for women was 57 in 1925, and 78 in 1995. A long period of life as an old woman is thus much more likely and it is probable that the culture and social structures are ill-prepared for this kind of rapid shift. When I ask my students how many years a woman aged 60 would expect to live, I am surprised by how often they say twelve or fifteen years. They are clearly basing this calculation on their knowledge about average life expectancy, not taking into account the fact that this statistic is based on average life expectancy at birth. The average life expectancy of a woman of 60 is about 22 years and is increasing. This long period of life needs to be anticipated and plans made as how to best cope with it and enjoy it. All told, both the manner in which the life course is dissected and the meanings attached to being in one period of the life course rather than another are constantly changing.

'Periodization' serves society's need to regulate the lives of its citizens. Different rights and laws apply to people according to their age and stage of life. Thus most Western societies have compulsory schooling until age 16 and most enforce compulsory retirement around 60 to 65. Ages are established for when people can get driving licences, when they can marry and when they can vote. Transitions from stage to stage are marked by state certificates: of examination results, marriage, birth, divorce, pensioner status and death. In many Western societies, people do not mix much with those who belong to separate generations or life periods. Travellers will remark on the way Mediterranean families still go out for meals in multi-generational groups, since such mixing is increasingly rare in English-speaking countries.

Social clocks

An important concept which is helpful in understanding the social construction of the life course is the 'social clock', which is a term coined by Bernice Neugarten (1968). The social clock is a phrase which refers to the strongly held norms in a society which dictate the age-appropriateness of activities and concerns for both men and women. Neugarten suggests that most of us have our own mental social clock which tells us where we are in terms of the 'expectable life cycle'. People can readily recite the expectations for their own culture in terms of what 'the best age' is to marry, have a child or retire, and of what personality characteristics are suited to what age group. This widespread shared understanding extends also to habits of dress, leisure activities and so on. It is assumed by researchers who use this concept not only that people have a clear idea about their local social clock, but that it also matters to them and has a significant influence on their behaviour.

The social clock is an internalization at the level of the individual of social norms to do with timing, with when things should happen. It is linked to the broader set of rules and assumptions about both the periodization of the life course and the timing of publicly significant events within it. Many of these events may be conceived as transitions or turning points in the life course, although for any individual what actually represents a turning point or transition may be much more personal and idiosyncratic than the public events or transitions associated with the social clock.

Ravenna Helson and her colleagues have explored the concept of the social clock with reference to women's lives. Helson *et al.* (1984) coined the term 'social clock projects' to refer to the life commitments which were expected of women, such as marriage and having children. In a sample of college-educated women who had grown up in the late 1950s, it was found that most adhered to what the researchers identified as 'the feminine social clock'. A few followed a 'masculine occupational clock' and a few were 'late' in terms of the expected schedule. Those following the feminine social clock were more responsible and nurturant but also had lower levels of confidence and self-esteem. Those following the masculine social clock were more confident, independent, assertive and effective. The most troubled were those who, at age 30, had not conformed to any recognized social clock, having neither married nor established a career.

The expectations in terms of social clocks are no doubt different for different cohorts. However, being out of time or off time still seems to cause problems, even if the deadlines have changed. In most Western countries the age at which women have their first child is typically later than it was in the 1950s, so that a young woman today, who is age 30 and has not had a child, would not feel out of time or off time. As well as operating as a constraint, clear-cut age norms can offer some sense of security and predictability which today's more fluid lifestyles do not have. The longer time on the social clock between leaving school and 'settling down' may leave some young people at a loss. Jeffrey Arnett (2000, p. 469) quotes a young woman of 22 living in the USA who compares her life to that of her mother:

> When our mothers were our age they were engaged. . . . They at least had some idea of what they were going to do with their lives . . . I, on the other hand will have a dual degree in majors that are ambiguous at best and impractical at worst (English and Political Science), no ring on my finger and no idea who I am, much less what I want to do.

Evidently this young woman still thinks of her major and defining life event as marriage, whereas for many young women today marriage is not the most important goal.

Arnett comments that in 1970 the median age of marriage in the United States was 21 for women and that by 1996 it was 25. The USA has a tradition of early marriage in comparison to many European countries. Ireland, for example, has been noted throughout the twentieth century for late marriage, for a large minority of people who never married and for a high birth rate. In Ireland, the average age of marriage was 26 in 1992 and is now (in 2001) 27. The average age for the birth of a first child to a married woman was 30 in 1992. In 1965 the average family size was four; it is now two. Similarly, in the European Union as a whole, the average age of women at the birth of their first child was 24 in 1980 and 28 by 1993. In Ireland the fertility rate of woman was halved between the late 1960s and the early 1990s. This change has been accompanied by a large increase in the number of women in the workforce. Between 1971 and 1996, 90 per cent of the general growth in employment was due to growth in women's employment.

The demographic changes impacting on the pattern and timing of women's lives are occurring across the developed economies of the world. These aggregate changes point to a dramatic transformation at the level of the individual woman's life experience. The life of a woman who has spent time in her twenties establishing a career before having a small family in her thirties and who continues to pursue that career until her sixties, is very different from that of a woman who married in her twenties and who, without the opportunity to develop a career, devoted her life to caring for a large number of children and working in the home. More women are remaining child-free and more are choosing not to marry, to marry late or to marry more than once. Dramatic social changes in the position of women in a society translate into very significant differences in the daily lived experience of women within that society, and in their attitudes to themselves and their current and future expectations.

Neugarten commented in the late 1970s that there were indications that in the USA 'age is losing its customary social meanings and the trends are toward the fluid life cycle and the age irrelevant society'. Undoubtedly historical periods vary in the precision of their social clocks and the rigidity with which they are applied, but how reasonable is it to argue that age is becoming irrelevant? Some characterize the era of postmodernity as one where people have more freedom to choose, to play with ideas about age and the way one lives one's life. However, I would side with those who see much of our freedom of choice as more apparent than real.

Undoubtedly there is some truth in what Neugarten says about the increased fluidity of the life cycle and, by the same token, the diminished precision of the social clock. Women of my generation who grew up in the 1950s can readily recall the strict norms about age-appropriate behaviour which obtained in relation to relatively trivial matters like dress and hairstyle, let alone about one's proper role in life. A matron in her forties was expected to have her hair short and permed and to wear clothes very different from those worn by her daughter. In contrast many middle-aged women of today wear jeans and keep their hair long. Concepts such as lifelong learning have opened the doors of third-level institutions to many older people who would have been thought of as 'past it' only a few decades ago.

However, I would argue that the social clock persists in many aspects of women's lives. Some of these timing restrictions are essentially imposed by the biological clock, others are socially enshrined and impose expectations about what people are supposed to be doing and to have done at various ages. The markers on the social clock may have changed and the timing may have shifted, but the social clock is still with us. Young women today may feel more anxious about their failure to establish themselves in a career at age 30 than their failure to 'catch' a man. As society places more value on the possession of youth or youthfulness, many older women seem to be engaged in a struggle to *stop the clock*, refusing to be seen to enter the next phase, whether it be middle age or old age. Neugarten remarks on the importance of timing relative to others. This concern is encapsulated in the question, 'How am I doing for my age?' It is obvious that in youth-centred, time-pressured societies such a question can readily become a major preoccupation.

Being off time can entail being ahead or behind schedule. A 14-year-old who passes university entrance examinations is off time and ahead of schedule in a way that may be applauded, whereas a 14-year-old who is pregnant is off time and ahead of schedule in a way that is likely to meet with disapproval. Being off time, either ahead or behind, can have major repercussions.

To take the example of teenage pregnancy; very few societies exist in the West where teenage pregnancy is not seen as undesirable. One study of African American families in Los Angeles tracked the long-term, mainly negative repercussions in families of the birth of a baby to a girl in early adolescence (Burton and Bengston, 1985). The event was seen as an affront to 'how life should be lived', to use the words of one parent. As Elder (1995) elucidates it, the birth of a child to a girl who is still in early adolescence may result in her leaving school and ending up with poor employment prospects. The long-term consequences of this off-time event are predictable, if not always inevitable, to parents and researchers alike. As Elder points out, in the Burton and Bengston study some of the young women who were helped to stay in school had much more positive later outcomes. Similar work conducted by Michael Rutter (1989) and by David Magnusson (1995) shows how an initial event can set a person on a path or trajectory which may have an inevitable quality about it. Such chains of events, where one event is linked to the next probabilistically are one way in which developmentalists describe and account for continuities in development. Being off time is just one kind of negative starting point which can precipitate a negative spiral.

Paul Baltes has made a distinction between normative age-graded, normative history-graded and non-normative life events, all of which interact to influence development (Baltes *et al.*, 1979). Normative age-graded events are those that are highly correlated with chronological age. For Baltes these include both biological processes and those which are connected with socialization. History-graded influences are those experienced by a particular cohort, and non-normative influences are those which are not typical or general. Non-normative events are unanticipated either in terms of their rarity (e.g. being shipwrecked) or their timing (getting cancer at age 33). A major source of distress is when people think they have their lives planned out and either events don't happen when they should, such as when the carefully planned first child does not arrive for years or at all, or when chance events, such as winning the lottery, occur which are not on the schedule and therefore disrupt all plans and timetables for good or ill.

Women's time?

In terms of the social construction of the life course and the social norms relating to the timing of life events, there is considerable evidence that women are expected to have a different relationship to time and the life course than men.

However, it is important to see the social structuring of women's life course in a historical context. In the era prior to industrialization, neither women nor men were regulated by the clock and by the rigid periodization of the life course necessary to the industrial state. The acute division in life pathways which we sometimes call *traditional* is in fact a modern invention. These pathways ensured that the man could work in the public domain until no longer useful and that the woman would produce and rear children and keep house. By this token, the life course for women was not mapped out in terms of paid work or career in the three periods which Kohli (1986) described. At the same time, even though the *traditional* woman of the modern era did not have a career, she very often worked outside the home, and the life course of those women who did not work outside the home would be influenced by the working life of their husbands.

During the historical period when women were not typically caught up in the rhythms of paid work or career, a view emerged that women had lives which were more contingent, less predictable and more discontinuous. Settersten (1997) comments that 'the temporal experience of the family sphere seems non-linear'. Men and women, he suggests, live in different kinds of time and these temporal modes clash as individuals move between work and family spheres. Settersten's view of modern family life seems somewhat out of touch, as women who work in the home also have to struggle to get children to school on time and to and from after-school activities. They must also regulate their own lives to fit in with their partner's schedules, and organize their day and year according to multiple timetables.

Clearly, as more and more women enter paid employment and seek to combine work with having a family, the patterning of the life course is changing. Women's life course today follows the pattern established for the male worker in industrialized society, while also having to keep an eye on the biological clock. Unfortunately traditional discourses on the role of women and the irrelevance of a career for their lives still persist and contribute to the lack of support many women experience in the workforce.

Settersten's empirical study of the salience of age in the lives of men and women in Chicago (1997) indicated that the women in his sample were acutely aware of the biological clock in terms of their capacity to have children, an awareness which their male counterparts did not share. Settersten concludes on the basis of his 1990s data that 'Women's lives are more fluid, unpredictable and discontinuous, their occupational trajectories are typically more disorderly than those of men' (p. 277). To use the term 'disorderly' implies dereliction on the part of women and indicates the author's lack of awareness of the very real difficulties women face in maintaining the multiple facets of their working and domestic lives. Even in their role as workers, women are being judged by the dubious working practices and structures of twentieth-century working men.

Psychological visions of the life course of women which restrict her to the role of wife and mother are clearly of little relevance or use to the twenty-first-century girl or woman. Freud's perspective on women's life course as cited earlier gave

129

little scope for change and fulfilment in the later years after she achieved her life goal of becoming a mother. Freud was struck by the psychological rigidity of women in their mature years. Even at his most benign, the best he could do was to describe women as in youth 'an adored darling and in mature years an adored wife' (1905, p. 130). In his theory he was clearly reifying the truncated life course of the women of his time. Phillida Salmon commented much later, in 1985, that in societal terms the latter half of women's lives was 'virtually unscripted'. In contrast the lives of young girls and women are heavily scripted in terms of their preparation to be good women, wives and mothers.

Despite the contemporary importance of qualifications and a career to girls and young women, women are surrounded by these traditional messages. From childhood they hear fairy stories which end when the heroine secures the prince and the couple 'live happily ever after'. The remainder of life in fairy stories is a blank, the excitement finished. Girls' comic books and magazines focus relentlessly on 'getting a man' as the be all and end all in terms of life goals (Walkerdine, 1991). Contemporary magazines for girls may talk about boys as sex objects and sexual partners in ways that would have been unacceptable a generation ago but the emphasis is still on being attractive to the opposite sex.

Conclusions

The shape and pattern of lives are discursively and structurally produced and constructed. Developmental psychology has traditionally paid little attention to the structuring influence of social norms, leaving such considerations largely to sociology and anthropology. This appears to be changing. As part of a growing recognition of the importance of locating the person in her wider historical context, developmental psychologists are taking on board the impact of historical events and processes on individual psychology and the way in which social structuring of the life course serves to construct life experiences, and the individual's relationship to time and the mapping out of the life course.

Women's lives have been heavily constrained by normative assumptions about the course their lives should take and the organization of their commitments over time. In Chapter 8 I will discuss the ways in which women can and do resist these constraints and the implications of examination of women's location in time for the life span developmental psychology of girls and women.

8

THINKING ABOUT TIME AND THE PSYCHOLOGICAL DEVELOPMENT OF GIRLS AND WOMEN

Thinking more about time reveals both the way it is used to constrain and the way it may be used to liberate. However, the first thing to say, perhaps, is that it is not easy to think about time and it is not easy to understand time.

Great minds, from Heraclitus and Parmenides in Ancient Greece onwards, have struggled to understand what time is. The attempt to understand is still ongoing. There are many ways of theorizing time, some of them conflicting. A recent book by Julian Barbour is entitled *The End of Time: The Next Revolution in our Understanding of the Universe* (1999). As I understand it, Barbour argues that time as conceived by the human mind is nothing but change and that all of what we experience as change is present in the moment. It is clear, as Barbour expounds his point of view, that he is not expecting to convince all his readers. He also appreciates that his view is in major conflict with other scientific theories of time. Time, evidently, is one of the great puzzles which has confronted philosophy and physics. The philosopher Alfred North Whitehead after a great deal of deliberation on this topic concluded that 'it is impossible to meditate on time and the mystery of the creative passage of nature without an overwhelming emotion at the limits of human intelligence' (cited in Whitrow, 1975). I certainly cannot pretend to having either extensive knowledge about the philosophy of time or the physics of time. What I will focus upon is the psychological significance of time in developmental perspective.

Conceptions of time: a psychological perspective

Klaus Riegel asserts, 'what objects are in space, events are in time . . . events involve objects and objects change' (1977, p. 7). Although Riegel was one of the few developmental psychologists to attempt an understanding of the significance of time in human development, he espouses a view of time which is objective, linear and measurable. This is the view of time as the fourth dimension, which has its own existence – independent of us and our mortal doings. Our thinking about time as an independent dimension or force may be subdivided further into two primary metaphors: time as the space we are moving within and time as the space which is moving past us. Lackoff and Johnson have elegantly elaborated on the extent to which we use metaphor in our thinking about time (1999). As they say, 'we ask how time is conceptualized, we do not get very far before we encounter conceptual metaphor. It is virtually impossible for us to conceptualize time without metaphor' (p. 139). The use of metaphors in developmental psychology is an issue I will return to later in this chapter. For the moment, I will focus on our everyday thought and language in relation to our psychological experience of time.

Lackoff and Johnson describe the Time Orientation Metaphor in terms of the Moving Time Metaphor and the Moving Observer Metaphor. When we think of time as moving in space we use phrases like 'Christmas is coming' or 'That time has passed'. The motion of events is how we register the passing of time. When we think of ourselves as moving through time we would use phrases like 'I have nearly reached my fiftieth birthday' or 'She passed the time pleasantly'. The motion of the observer becomes the way of registering the passage of time. According to this way of thinking about time, we are *in* time, whether we see it as moving or ourselves as moving.

A further aspect of this metaphorical thinking in which we orient ourselves relative to time is that we think of time as we think of space. The future is either ahead of us or advancing towards us. The past is behind us, moving away from us or we are moving away from it. Thus time either moves through or past us or we move through time.

Lackoff and Johnson also identify a further metaphor which is of particular importance in the way we think about time and which is, as argued in Chapter 7, very much a feature of economically developed societies. That is the metaphor of time as a resource. They say, echoing Lichtman (1987), that 'one of the most striking characteristics of Western culture is that time is conceptualized in general as a resource and in particular as money' (Lackoff and Johnson, 1999, p. 161). Our thinking about our life course is permeated with time orientation metaphors and time as resource metaphors. Thus, we speak of our life course using expressions like 'She is just starting out', 'My time is running out', 'I have wasted my life'. Lackoff and Johnson conclude that 'human institutions can impose such metaphorical understanding and create metaphorical truths'.

In Chapter 7 I argued that social structures constrain and order our use of time. The power of social structures and institutions is greatly strengthened when it enters discourse and influences our language and our thoughts. We barely recognize any more that we employ metaphors in thinking about time, partly because it is almost impossible to think about time without the use of metaphor. Nonetheless, we need to question the implications of adopting any particular metaphorical system. Where does it come from and what does it lead us to?

As mentioned in Chapter 1, Jaan Valsiner (2000), writing as a developmental psychologist, considers that there are two main views of time which are relevant to psychological development. The first is time as an independent dimension or entity in which objects are located as in space. It is this image of time that Lackoff and Johnson focus upon. Time as commodity would be another conceptualization of time as an independent entity. The second is the idea of time as inherent to the life of the organism. This view of time is most strongly associated with the philosophy of Henri Bergson (1911). Bergson's notion of duration identifies the living being's experience of time (durée). Duration may only be experienced in the present, caught, it is assumed, between the past and the future. Bergson makes a distinction between empirically measurable objective time and the subjective experience or intuition of time as duration. Time as experienced by the biological organism is irreversible. As Valsiner expresses it, 'Developing organisms do not develop in time but with time' (2000, p. 7). Given the dominance of time as space metaphor it is very difficult for us to think of the developing person as changing with time rather than in time.

By trying to measure time as a separate dimension, the duration notion is lost and time becomes presented in ways similar to space, and can be measured out in its linear form as we measure space. Newton's view of time typifies this perspective. In 1687 he stated, 'Absolute, true and mathematical time of itself and from its own nature, flows equally without relation to anything exterior.' I am leaving aside all ideas about time and relativity because they do not impinge on our psychological experience of time in the same way as conventionally measured time and biological time. As biological organisms time is central to what we are, it defines the ultimate rhythm and pattern of our life, its beginning and its end.

If we become fixated on time as an independent dimension or substance, we can lose sight of the importance of our own immediate experience of time as duration. According to Bergson, we can also lose sight of the fact that we are always in the process of becoming and can never be fixed or defined by what has gone before. Thinking of ourselves as things which move in time rather than with time reinforces a view of self as static entity. Time too becomes entified. We begin to talk about time as though it is an entity that can be moved around.

We use expressions like 'saving time', implying that time can be used later, or 'losing time', as though one can find time again. In fact, as biological organisms we are inexorably committed to an irreversible ongoing relationship with time. Life is time. Committed though we are to relentless movement from birth to death, at a psychological level we can play all sorts of tricks with time and alter our experience of time. This is the paradox of our relationship with time; we are both biological and psychological beings with distinct biological and psychological relations to time.

What Henri Bergson points us to is our existence as process. For Bergson, temporality must be taken into account in any attempt to understand the world or human existence within it. Our metaphors of time lead us to think of time as something with an existence that is separate from us – this is a fallacy, and one which may prevent us from connecting at a fundamental level with the inextricable binding together of our life and time.

Resisting time

Although we can have only direct experience of the present of time, as human beings we have the capacity to remember actual events or to create pasts and futures for ourselves. The primary mechanism which sustains this process is language, although it would seem that the extent to which we focus on what is past or future is variable according to culture and disposition. Our cognitive capabilities permit us to escape the immediacies of time and in some ways to resist the passage of time or our inevitable time-bound procession.

In our imagination, we can be any age. As Proust said, 'for man is that creature without any fixed age, who has the faculty of becoming in a few seconds, many years younger'. We can also act our age or act older or younger than our age, feel our age or feel older or younger than our age. The mind can transport us back or forward in time.

As Milton wrote in *Paradise Lost:*

> A mind not to be changed by place or time
> The mind is its own place and in itself
> Can make a Heav'n of Hell, a Hell of Heav'n.

It would seem that one of the first human reactions to the understanding of the inevitability of one's own personal death was the quest for immortality, which has taken many forms. Some would see religion as at heart a refusal to accept the inevitability of the extinction of one's life, since in many religions life after death is a central promise. Throughout most of history, as far as we can tell from our written history, it has been men rather than women who have been preoccupied with ensuring their own 'immortality' – an immortality to be gained not via life after death but by their name living on after they are gone. It has been assumed that women do not need the reassurance of immortality through their works since they have the reassurance of immortality through their children. However, why this same reassurance does not satisfy men, who are also progenitors of future generations, is unclear. Perhaps women have not had the same encouragement in vanity. As women enter the public world in greater numbers, they too will come under pressure to succeed not just in terms of money and status in this world but in terms of making their mark in a way that ensures a measure of 'immortality'.

The writing or telling of one's own life story can be a creative way of resisting time. Few of us doubt that there is a reality to our own histories, that events actually happened in a certain manner and a certain sequence, that we had thoughts at certain specified times and behaved in certain ways that could theoretically have been faithfully recorded contemporaneously and kept as a record. We select what it is we attend to in the present and this is much more true of how we reflect on the past. The distortion of time and events in time as we tell our life story is well known.

In a recent book, Adam Phillips talks about Freud's views on autobiography, among other things. Freud took the view that we are locked in a struggle to present an acceptable story of our lives to others and to ourselves, but that our actual lives keep breaking through; that is, our true desires and impulses. Phillips suggests, 'the life story was, in part, the ways in which a person avoided having a life story. How we escape from our lives is our life; and how our lives tend to resist our stories about them was what interested Freud' (Phillips, 1999, p. 83).

There is a great deal of discussion and research at the moment on narrative and its role in human meaning-making and interpersonal communication. Researchers from various different perspectives are making use of the concept of narrative theoretically and as a research tool. Some of this work is very naive in that there seems to be an assumption that the story a person tells about their life is a veridical representation of that life. Such an assumption was common in the early qualitative work on women's experience and women's lives, where it was thought that the woman herself was the only person who really knew about her life. One thing that Freud should have changed for ever was the delusion that we know all there is to know about ourselves or that we are able to tell it. Phillips comments, 'What is narrative about, if it is not about objects of desire and the detours and obstacles and dangers entailed in their acquisition?' (p. 83). He quotes Freud's comment from a letter written in 1936 to Arnold Zweig: 'Anyone who has written an autobiography is committed to lies, concealment, hypocrisy, flattery and even to hiding his own lack of understanding, for biographical truth does not exist.'

Work on memory also informs us about a further distortion in our view of our own history. As older people look back on their lives, memories are not equally available to them. Events in early adulthood are typically most numerous and vivid, what has been called the 'reminiscence peak', which follows, for most people, the relative amnesia about the events of childhood and is succeeded by the unmemorable regularities of mature adulthood.

We select and refashion our memories and plans to fit our current purposes. This is a powerful way in which we can resist time, by selective use of memory and imagination. Occasionally, as in post-traumatic stress reactions or the experience of intense dread, the mechanisms we use to protect ourselves from the past and the future break down, but most of the time our memories and our anticipations assist us in keeping a level of optimism and self-worth which sustains our personal equilibrium and motivation. We need, it would appear, to fashion a life story that we can live with and which makes sense. The story may not necessarily flatter us but it usually excuses us.

Michael Lewis, the developmental psychologist, has argued that developmental psychology presents a false picture of the power of the past, of history, in the making of human selves (1997). He argues, 'we can alter our lives by wishing, hoping, planning and remembering'. By these means, we – to all intents and purposes – alter our fate. This happens, according to Lewis, 'every day' (1997, p. 10). Lewis' view that 'our actual histories have little bearing on our development' (p. 55) is only partly true. In some crucial ways it is clearly not true. As discussed in the next section, developmental psychology has an unhealthy preoccupation with the past, but it is dangerous to claim that we are entirely unaffected by our actual history and that all that matters is what we construe our life to be here and now.

For Lewis, our current mental constructions are everything, a point of view that veers dangerously close to solipsism. It also presents a reckless disregard for the evidence that events, positive and negative, can have a lasting effect on individuals. Certainly, how we think about events at the time that they happen and then later when we recollect them can make a huge difference in how we deal with them and in the extent to which they impinge on our lives. But to advocate that the past is totally irrelevant is a giant step too far. Where does such a perspective leave the young woman who has been a childhood victim of abuse? Does the promotion of the view that all that matters is her thoughts about the matter here and now (which she should work on in order to put the best possible light on things) totally exonerate her abuser?

I have argued that we are very capable of mentally relocating ourselves in time. Through drugs, through absorption in art and in other ways we can experience time as though it has slowed down, speeded up, or stopped altogether. Our perception of the passage of time appears to change also across the life course, not necessarily in a way which we find welcome. For example, the sense of time speeding up with age appears to be widespread and is nicely described in this passage from *The Patchwork Planet* by Anne Tyler. The elderly Ms Glynn is speaking to a younger character:

> You'll find out for yourself one day. Personal time works the opposite way from historical time. Historical time starts with a swoop – dinosaurs, cavemen, lickety-split! – and then slows and takes on more detail as it gets more recent: all those niggling little four year presidential terms. But with personal time, you begin with a crawl – every leaf and bud, every cross-eyed look your mother ever gave you and you gather speed as you go. To me it's a blurry streak by now.

There is some evidence for a biological basis to this phenomenon. Riegel cites the work of Kety (1956). Kety claimed that the slowing of oxygen consumption in ageing organisms resulted in their experiencing time as passing more quickly. But perhaps some of this phenomenon is due to habituation or satiation. As we age we do not notice things as much, and perceptions lose their freshness and novelty. However, experience of later life as 'a blurry streak' is probably not necessary, even given a possibly slower level of oxygen consumption. Meditation practices can help adults slow their experience of the passing of time, and those who know they have a limited time to live appear often to find a renewed appreciation of the present and an appreciation of the richness in life, which serves to fill their days with immediate meaning and thus effectively slows time.

Life may appear to pass more quickly with age but the present and the quality of life in the present may become more important. Laura Carstensen argues that as we move through the life course and our future life span gets shorter we focus more on the here and now and on reliably gratifying relationships and occupations (1995). Empirically there is evidence that this phenomenon applies to those who know they have a terminal illness as well as those who are older. Both groups, she suggests, cannot afford to give up on immediate satisfactions for the sake of long-term goals in the way a young adult might do.

The difficulties many people find in living fully and comfortably in the present may be a reflection of Western society's preoccupation with progress. Each of us is expected to be working towards a better life in the future, none more so than children who are regarded as radically incomplete as persons. James and Prout have argued that we need to discover and value the present in our view of children and their lives (1997). So much of our rhetoric about children presents them as incomplete becomings rather than complete beings. Children are 'our hope for the future'. We are told that if we invest in our children we are investing in the future of our society. The argument that James and Prout make, about the need to value children as the people they are right now, has great merit, but in some ways it could be applied to adults too. In our modern view of the person, aided and abetted by formal discourse, such as life span developmental psychology, we fail to value the present experience of the adult also. Adults are meant to be progressing, moving on, getting better, acquiring more. Our romantic view of childhood is that the child unlike the adult has time to 'stop and stare'. In reality, both child and adult are being chivvied into a constant preoccupation with what comes next. Much of this has to do with our society's conception of time.

Having said that, there is another way in which adult and child are alike in that we are both *beings and becomings*. We need to see ourselves as *becoming*, but not in the sense that we place more value on who we might be in the future rather than who we are now. We need to resist the tyranny of the future as the time in which we can be better and life can be better than it is now. We are *becomings* in the sense that we are always caught up in time and change and, contrary to so many psychological theories, what we will become in the future is not predictable from what we were in the past.

To conclude this section, I am arguing that we are both inevitably constrained by the realities of our biological existence in and with time but that the way we think about time can radically alter our relationship with time as experienced. Many of our social structures and habits of thought promote an unhelpful, sometimes unhealthy view of ourselves in time. As Riegel stated in 1977, 'We are subordinated to an impersonal, alienated concept' (p. 9). I would continue, however, to take issue with Kristeva's view that linear time is essentially masculine time. Since the preoccupation with linear time is a comparatively recent emergent, it is a function not of the *archetypal masculine* but of the *modern expression of the masculine* through capitalism and consumerism. In the daily lives of many women it has, perforce, become feminine time. Women need to secure their own hold on time, so that they are not 'subordinated to an impersonal, alienated concept of time' but instead can move towards a relationship with time in which each of us can truly 'take her own time'.

I will turn next to developmental psychology and how the reflections on time and change, which have been presented in this chapter and chapters 6 and 7, might contribute to a more adequate developmental perspective on the psychology of girls and women.

Developmental psychology and its construction of women's time

The wrong metaphors

The work of Lackoff and Johnson was discussed earlier in relation to our metaphorical understanding of time. It is also the case that developmental psychology is permeated with metaphors. There is a very strong reliance on metaphor in the conceptualization of both time and development. When developmental theorists grapple with conceptualizing development they arrive at metaphors such as the life course, pathways, journeys, trajectories.

The metaphors we use matter. Phillida Salmon proposes, 'it is through the metaphorical interpretations we place upon the life cycle that we come to experience the deepest meanings of our lives' (1985, p. 8).

Ellin Scholnick has examined the different metaphors and assumptions that underpin developmental theory from a gender perspective. She asks, 'Whose thought is global, undifferentiated, intuitive, context sensitive, subjective and concrete? And whose thinking is articulated, logical, abstract, objective, scientific and hypothetical? Most developmental psychologists would immediately associate the first set of attributes with children and the second with adults' (Scholnick, 2000, p. 29). And of course, some would immediately identify the first set of attributes with females and the second with males. Scholnick asks whether the child is the stereotypical female and the adult the male. Her interest is in asking whether this implies that development (e.g. cognitive development) is construed as a movement from the feminine to the masculine. The conjunction of the feminine with childishness or with actually being a child could also imply that child and woman occupy inevitably the territory of *the Other*, in de Beauvoir's terms, and that from a developmental perspective the female is condemned not to develop into full adult status. The girl child is doubly fixed as the archetypal child, since she is unambiguously feminine and fated not to be transformed into complete adulthood, unlike her boy peer.

Scholnick notes that 'when the end point of development is considered to be the emergence of the scientist or technician, masculine imagery of aggression, competition, control and hierarchical domination is used to characterize developmental trajectories' (ibid., p. 31). She gives four examples of masculine metaphors of development – argument, survival of the fittest, the arrow, and the building. In contrast, she gives four feminine metaphors for development – friendship, conversation, apprenticeship, and narrative. The latter supposedly more feminine metaphors are certainly more evident in feminist scholarship and in some areas of developmental psychology and the psychology of women, as explored earlier in this book.

From the perspective of time and how it is construed, two of the masculine metaphors have a strong relationship to linear time and steady advance or progression – the arrow and the building. The argument metaphor and the survival of the fittest are more dialectic; here the masculinity of the metaphor resides in its promotion of conflict as the mechanism driving change and onward movement and a resolution is found only when a winner emerges triumphant.

In relation to the feminine metaphors, the focus is less on progress and more on emergence. Scholnick claims that feminine images are relational, concrete and nonlinear. The first three metaphors Scholnick lists are basically variations on the theme of relationship and its importance in prompting and supporting development. Concepts such as co-construction, mutuality, reciprocity and bi-directionality belong to this perspective. As I argued in Chapter 2, we have seen a radical shift in developmental psychology over the past two decades to an appreciation of context and the role of the other and of relationships in psychological development. Such models are, at heart, more compatible with a feminist vision of the social world and women's place within it. However, one does not need to see women as relational and men as not. It is more a matter of refocusing on the processes entailed in development, and therefore arriving at recognition of the importance of relationships and culture in the psychological development of both men and women.

The last metaphor, which Scholnick lists, is that of narrative. Narratives organize events in time but not necessarily in a linear sequence. Scholnick claims that narrative is a feminine metaphor and not linear. On this I would disagree, in that many of the traditional narrative forms, which have their place in the iconography of traditional developmental thinking, are indeed linear: the standard male autobiography tells a linear story. The heroic quest may be interrupted by obstacles but the hero's path is ever onward and upward. As Liz Stanley (1992, p. 12) states,

> the dominant current in autobiography provides readers with exemplary lives . . . it inscribes what a life should look like, the form in which (written and spoken) lives should be told and actual lives should be lived. These lives are linear, chronological, progressive and individualist and follow highly particular narrative conventions.

Many women and men will have been encouraged over the years to shape their life stories according to this rubric. Shaping the life story occurs both in prospect, in terms of plans, hopes and dreams, and in retrospect, in terms of formal and informal telling of the life story. Women's life stories and narratives, it has been argued, typically take a different form to that of men. First, since they rarely fit the bill in terms of heroism, their lives are seen as less worthy of telling. Second, they may not follow the heroic path but be fragmentary, discontinuous and prone to detour. The pattern of the narrative is thus gendered, in the way the life story is gendered. But there is nothing intrinsically feminine about narrative.

Nonetheless, the kinds of stories girls are told about the female life and its desirable course and the kinds of stories that they come to tell themselves do matter greatly. It is in this regard that developmental psychology joins with informal and literary stories as yet another set of stories (this time sanctioned by 'science') about how women should live their lives.

In this book, I have argued that in relation to theorizing the psychological development of girls and women, the existing theories require further critical analysis and deconstruction. Many aspects of our thinking in relation to female development, as psychologists, as social scientists and as feminists, are permeated with unnecessarily constricting ideas about development and age.

The primary fault is due to a fixation on the past as the determinant of the future course of development. A corollary is that the future is seen as a predictable unfolding of intrinsic processes, originating in biology or in personal history. The traditional developmental theory is obsessed with prediction. Predicting the future from our knowledge of the past entails an implicit fixing of the properties that will emerge in the future. There is little room in such historical accounts for the emergence of novel forms, for new ways of being. In actuality, developmental psychologists are very poor at predicting someone's life course. They are much better at reconstructing causes and determinants in retrospect. As I outlined in Chapter 2, science in general and developmental science in particular are converging on a view which aspires to take account of the existence of emergence as a defining property of self-organizing systems.

In relation to theories about the origins of women's personality it is important not to forget the powerful influence of evolutionary psychology currently. Evolutionary psychology advocates a highly reductive explanation of male and female behavioural differences based on a belief in their genetically fixed origins. As discussed in Chapter 3, there is reason for concern that this form of biological determinism is gaining ground within mainstream psychology and in the other social sciences. Thoughtful and informed critiques of evolutionary psychology are available (e.g Segal, 1999; Rose and Rose, 2000) but it remains to be seen whether these compelling critical perspectives will prevail against the popular bias in favour of naive, biological explanations. I predict that ultimately the inadequacies of genetic determinism will become apparent, although history would inform us that there is always a risk that such theoretical models will promote and be promoted by reactionary political movements and institutions (Greene, 1999). It is the case, then, that biological, historical and social forms of determinism have widespread currency as explanations of the genesis of female behaviour.

It is because of the conceptual constriction in traditional developmental thinking that I have argued that feminists and others interested in women's psychology, and, crucially, in the capacity for change in women's psychology, have not been well served by either traditional developmental psychology in its various expressions or by the favoured, women-centred developmental accounts.

Although developmental psychology claims to be about change in time, it is all too often trapped by the discipline's desire to fix the human being and deal with her as though she had properties which can be described and understood in a timeless, context-free framework. As many of the more radical developmental psychologists recognize, this old-fashioned, positivist view of human psychology is inadequate to its subject. Much psychological language consists of the entification and stabilization of processes, which are not fixed in time. As Valsiner says, 'all biological, psychological and social systems can be considered to be in a permanent process of change' (2000, p. 9). More than that, the traditional approach is a prescription for conservatism and maintenance of the status quo.

Situating women in time, with time, helps us to see that when we talk about development we are talking about emergence and about possibility. Inevitably, we are talking also about constraints – the constraints of history, place and the demands of the mortal body. However, what we can dismantle are the unnecessary constraints such as limiting theories about women's life course commitments and about their capacity for change. The manner in which our lives are dictated by the political and social structures of our society is also open to challenge and to change (see e.g. Moane, 1999).

In developmental psychology, a long-standing axiom is that age is an empty variable. This means that stating that someone is a particular age explains nothing. This is in part true since, if one is seeking explanation, it is necessary to look to events or processes in time. The fact that a child is age 7 does not necessarily tell you what she can do or why. But the axiom is also in a very significant sense incorrect; for age is an extremely loaded variable, as I have argued in this book.

Changing developmental thinking

As stated in the Introduction, I am not arguing for a new life span developmental psychology of women but for the incorporation of a revised developmental perspective, such as the one outlined in this book, into the study of the psychology of girls and women, and ultimately into that of boys and men also. This perspective entails viewing developmental psychology as the study of change across the life span and developmental change as a constrained but, ultimately, radically indeterminate consequence of ongoing exchange between the human person and her material and cultural environment.

In her (1990) paper Mary Gergen uses the phrase 'the refurbishment of the life-span psychology of women'. This book is a contribution to that refurbishment process. Gergen has argued cogently that 'the social constructionist position as a form of postmodernism, seems particularly relevant to the refurbishment of the life span psychology of women' (1990, p. 481). I agree with this viewpoint and have tried to draw out in various ways the importance of discourse and socio-cultural processes in the active construction of the self. The social construction-ist movement has effectively challenged the naturalistic assumptions so central to traditional developmental psychology. However, I feel that social construction-ism alone is an inadequate theoretical base for understanding the psychological development of women. It is an important part of the theoretical armamentarium, but it is incomplete and therefore unhelpful if used as the only theoretical frame-work. As I have commented earlier, the major problem for a social constructionist approach is its obliteration of the psychological and of the active agentic capaci-ties of the individual. A further problem is that it minimizes the material and non-discursive aspects of our existence.

A revised developmental perspective such as the one I am advocating in this book combines elements of social constructionism and dynamic systems perspectives with an acknowledgement of the psychological 'realness' of the person and her lived life. I would argue that such a combination of theoretical perspectives is necessary. The push to account for diversity and for complexity has given rise to more complex, in the sense of multiple, theoretical frameworks. For example, Martin and Sugarman label their theoretical perspective, one which I find highly compatible, 'dynamic socio-cultural-psychological interactionism' – a label which does not trip easily off the tongue. 'Dynamic interactionism' is premised on an 'emergent, dynamic psychological ontology' (1999, p. 4) and also upon a view of societies and cultures as 'ever-mutable and engaged in a con-stant working through of patterns of interaction' (p. 13). It locates the person in her collective, socio-cultural context but resists the view that the individual is 'reducible to the sociocultural' (p. 5). Socio-cultural practices act so as to both enable and constrain 'the emergence of a genuinely reflexive psychological self'.

Dynamic, systemic perspectives such as those offered by Martin and Sugarman, by Lerner (1998), and by Lewis (2000) and an increasing number of others are both more faithful to the changing, complex nature of our psychology and more likely to provide a liberative theoretical framework for understanding the nature of our potential for growth and change. Michael Levenson and Cheryl Crumpler (1996) label their favoured developmental approach, which is based on dissatis-faction with the reductionism and determinism of both ontogenetic and socio-genic theories (as discussed in Chapter 2) *counterdeterministic*. Neither they nor the dynamic systems theorists mentioned above deny the existence of constraints on development but they recognize the limits of constraint and the role the person can take in shaping the course of their own development.

It is important that this approach is not seen as advocating a view of the person as utterly autonomous and free of constraint. Indeed I have been at some pains to identify some of the many sources of our subjugation to context and to culture. I recall some years ago listening to a famous American psychologist, known for his work on helplessness, saying that we must convince people that they have control over their lives. On the contrary, we need to understand the extent to which our circumstances and our culture define and restrict us. All of us are caught up and enmeshed in circumstances and in cultural frameworks which are part of what we are. The extent of freedom does vary however. There are still many millions of women in the world who live lives not far removed from slavery. Only some of us have the great privilege of exploring the boundaries of our own agency.

In the following and final section I will attempt to delineate some of the consequences of adhering to deterministic models of development and some implications of the adoption of a revised model which centres on emergence and possibility.

Developmental psychology – working for girls and women

The theoretical approach, described above, challenges current fashionable perceptions of developmental psychology within feminism and the psychology of women. First, it answers the criticisms of the anti-developmentalist critics who have dismissed developmental psychology as unsalvageable. While recognizing the validity of these critiques in relation to developmental psychology as traditionally promoted and practised, I believe that recent attempts to theorize life span psychological change hold considerable promise. They can incorporate the contingent, dynamic, situated character of the processes, which we might still venture to label as developmental. The outright rejection of a developmental perspective can lead to an approach to psychology that fails utterly to take on board the significance of our dynamic existence in time, of our specific location in the life course, and of the crucial influence of our personal interpretation of time and age.

Second, it is important to challenge the adherence of those feminists who do adopt a developmental perspective to outdated developmental models. Feminists worked hard over the twentieth century to question the assumptions of the natural and social sciences, and yet in relation to psychology they have fallen into some of the oldest traps. One trap is making phenomena that are processes into entities, another is historicism and another is being in thrall to the idea of prediction. As I hope I have managed to argue throughout this book, such theories are inadequate and unhelpful. They have pernicious practical consequences.

For example, object relations theory encourages women to find the causes of their psychological problems in their first relationship with their mother. This serves to perpetuate the mother-blaming deeply enshrined in Western culture and in many psychological theories (Caplan, 1989). It neglects the formative influence of other members of the family and the wider social context, which has been so fully explored by developmentalists working from ecological and cultural perspectives. It is, in its most extreme form, profoundly fatalistic. A recent book edited by Gerd Fenchel entitled *The Mother–Daughter Relationship: Echoes Through Time* (1998) is representative of this type of approach. Many of the chapters in the book focus on a view of the mother–daughter relationship as unhealthily symbiotic, defined by rivalry, conflict and a struggle for ascendancy or for individuation. No doubt some mother–daughter relationships are like this;

but others are positive and sustaining, and also very often not central to the definition of a woman's personality for life. The multiple other influences on a woman's life apart from the maternal are thoroughly neglected.

The fixation on the woman's first relationships is central to the focus of many current forms of psychotherapy. Analytic therapies are totally preoccupied with the past, with early life experiences and with primary relationships. Backward-looking theories divert attention from the importance of understanding the nature of women's life course change and the multiple influences on that change. They fix and universalize the origins of female personality and limit the scope for change. So, when the focus is on first relationships, political and discursive contingencies are disregarded. When a theory is deterministic in this way, the role of chance, emergence and agency is not considered.

There is a further danger lurking in deterministic or essentialist theories which is that their proponents may cease to be aware of the need to constantly revise our understanding of women's psychology in the light of historical change. When historical change is given due regard, unqualified pronouncements such as 'middle-aged women are like this' or 'older women are like that' become simply untenable. Feminists have become acutely aware in recent years of the dangers of generalizations about women and the need to take account of difference in relation to ethnicity, nationality, class and sexuality. Age must be added to that list, but not simply age: cohort is a further crucial category. Age and cohort are – to further complicate the picture – thoroughly enmeshed with the other dimensions which constitute each woman's individuality. Thus, what it means to be a 70-year-old woman living in rural Ireland is both different from what it meant to be a 70-year-old rural woman living in Ireland fifty years ago and what it means to be a 70-year-old woman living in Tokyo. Such statements seem obvious but the literature is still replete with misconceived over-generalizations about women's lives and psychology.

Theories about women's psychology which fail to highlight the open-endedness and potential for change which many contemporary life span theorists would see as the hallmark of development are perpetuating stereotypes about ageing and about the aged.

To take old age as an example, there has been a recent upsurge in research on the elderly woman. Uncharitably, one might see this as a function of the age of many of those feminists, in psychology and other disciplines, who were students or young women in the 1960s or 1970s. Betty Friedan is one famous feminist who has written what is in fact a very useful and insightful book on old age (Friedan, 1993). However, more research which focuses on diversity of pathways, on the potential for transformation and the constraints on living the fullest life possible, is needed. Elderly women are invisible not only in the media but also in the pages of many feminist texts. Developmental psychologists such as Labouvie-Vief, Neugarten and Baltes have carried out empirical studies on older men and women which convey a good news story about ageing, not a rose-tinted story, but solid evidence of a degree of competence and potential for growth which belies popular stereotypes. Kastenbaum, for example, has explored the way in which our expectations can have a dramatic effect on how we age (1984). He argues that people become old and set in their ways not because they are old but because they become set in their ways. Unless we are careful to remain open to change, we are liable to become prone to 'hyperhabituation'– failing to recognize and respond to challenge. Research on growth and change in later life is the kind of developmental research which deserves much greater dissemination and publicity. It should form the basis for action by women and by policy-makers and practitioners.

Action should be taken to undermine the dread many women experience in relation to ageing and old age, and to challenge unhelpful discourses on women and age. The barriers to a happy old age such as poverty and loneliness need to be tackled as a matter of priority, not seen as a sad fact of life. Given their relative longevity, women, even more than men, need to appreciate fully the sheer amount of time they are likely to spend as an old person and prepare accordingly. There is both more time than people think there is and less. Time takes on new meaning in old age because there is less of it in the sense of there being fewer years left to live, and inevitably the chances of becoming a concert pianist or a champion skier are drastically more limited than they were at age 20. However, there are many achievements that remain possible and many different ways of being that are still open.

Such considerations about receptivity to change do not apply only to the aged. Traditional developmental psychologists have been in thrall to the notion of within-person constancy throughout the life course. As noted in Chapter 2, critiques of the various constancy hypotheses within developmental psychology have brought us to a recent understanding of the open-endedness of development and the potential for change at any point in the life course. Combined with an understanding of the extent to which the person might change in her behaviour and reactions in different contexts, the idea of the fixed and determined self is radically undermined in our current understanding.

There are major consequences of this shift in developmental thinking for theories about the psychology of women. It directs us away from the *early formation* determinism of psychoanalysis and object relations theory. It directs us away from the *woman in relation* models of Gilligan and Baker Miller, as fundamentally conservative in their definition of what it means to be a woman. On the other hand, it directs us towards a vision of women's lives as both constrained by biology and context and yet open to transformation. A historical view reminds us of the multiple ways women have already found of making their way through their lives. A temporal perspective reminds us of the necessity of our relationship to time and how bringing time to the forefront of our developmental thinking can demonstrate how it too can serve to constrain or to liberate our ideas about how best to live our lives.

Elizabeth Grosz says, 'Determinism is the annulling of any concept of temporality other than the one structured by the terms and conditions of the past and present' (1999, p. 4). A transformative developmental psychology of women provides a new perspective on our potential for change and our relationship to time.

I have argued in this book that what women have been offered to date by developmental psychology and what feminists have chosen to select from developmental psychology provide a prescriptive and restrictive account of development. Although it is a book about theory, it is also, in the end, about policy. I would argue that theory matters in relation to the practicalities and realities of our daily lives. Developmental psychology's theories have been popularized and made available to the non-academic community since it became a distinctive and well-established discipline at the end of the nineteenth century (Greene, 1997a). Developmental theories – those of Freud, Piaget, Erikson, Bowlby, Gilligan and many others – have been taken up and used by policy-makers and by practitioners, whether they be teachers, social workers, psychotherapists or parents. Developmental psychology has been one of those disciplines which has played a role in constructing our sense of who we are. As Broughton stated in 1987, 'Developmental psychology sets goals and formulates ideals for human development and provides the means of realising them. Rather than simply observing development, it develops us . . . it enters into the realm of the private, participating in our formation as subjects' (p. 2). It is therefore vitally important to us as women and full human beings that the theories which impinge on our lives and which instruct us about our lives reflect both our complexity and diversity and our potential for change throughout the life course.

REFERENCES

Ainsworth, M. D. S. (1989) 'Attachments beyond infancy'. *American Psychologist* 44: 709–716.

Alexander, C. E. and Langer, E. (eds) (1990) *Higher Stages of Human Development.* Oxford: Oxford University Press.

Alwin, D. F. (1995) 'Taking time seriously: social change, social structure and human lives'. In P. Moen, G. H. Elder and K. Luscher (eds) *Examining Lives in Context.* Washington, DC: American Psychological Association.

Angier, N. (1999) *Woman: An Intimate Geography.* London: Virago.

Anthony, M. (1990) *The Valkyries: The Women around Jung.* Dorset: Element Books.

Arnett, J. J. (2000) 'Emerging adulthood: a theory of development from the late teens through the twenties'. *American Psychologist* 55: 469–480.

Astington, J. W. (1993) *The Child's Discovery of the Mind.* Cambridge, MA: Harvard University Press.

Baltes, P. B., Cornelius, C. W. and Nesselroade, J. R. (1979) 'Cohort effects in developmental psychology'. In J. R. Nesselroade and P. Baltes (eds) *Longitudinal Research in the Study of Behaviour and Development.* New York: Academic Press.

Bandura, A. (1977) *Social Learning Theory.* Princeton, NJ: Prentice-Hall.

Barbour, J. (1999) *The End of Time: The Next Revolution in our Understanding of the Universe.* London: Phoenix.

Barkow, J. H., Cosmides, L. and Tooby, J. (eds) (1992) *The Adapted Mind: Evolutionary Psychology and the Generation of Culture.* Oxford: Oxford University Press.

Barnett, R. C. and Baruch, G. K. (1978) 'Women in the middle years: a critique of research and theory'. *Psychology of Women Quarterly* 3: 187–197.

Beal, C. R. (1994) *Boys and Girls: The Development of Gender Roles.* New York: McGraw Hill.

Becker, E. (1970) *Denial of Death.* New York: Free Press.

Belenky, M. F., Clinchy, B. McV., Goldberger, N. R. and Tarule, J. M. (1986) *Women's Ways of Knowing: The Development of Self, Voice and Mind.* New York: Basic Books.

Bem, S. (1993) *The Lenses of Gender: Transforming the Debate on Sexual Inequality.* New Haven, CT: Yale University Press.

Benhabib, S. (1999) 'Sexual difference and collective identities: the new global constellation'. *Signs* 24: 335–361.

Bergson, H. (1911) *Creative Evolution.* New York: Holt.

Beyenne, Y. (1992) 'Menopause: a biocultural event'. In A. S. Dann and L. L. Lewis (eds) *Menstrual Health in Women's Lives.* Urbana: University of Illinois Press.

Bijou, S. W. and Baer, M. (1961) *Child Development: A Systematic and Empirical Theory.* New York: Appleton-Century-Crofts.

Bohan, J. S. (1993) 'Regarding gender: essentialism, constructionism and feminist psychology'. *Psychology of Women Quarterly* 17: 5–21.

Bowie, M. (1991) *Lacan.* London: Fontana.

Bradley, B. S. (1989) *Visions of Infancy; A Critical Introduction to Child Psychology.* Cambridge: Polity Press.

Bradley, B. S. (1993) 'The future of developmental theory'. *Theory and Psychology* 3: 403–414.

Bradley, B. S. (1998) 'Two ways to talk about change: "The child" of the sublime versus radical pedagogy'. In B. M. Bayer and J. Shotter (eds) *Reconstructing the Psychological Subject: Bodies, Practices and Technologies.* London: Sage.

Bronfenbrenner, U. (1979) *The Ecology of Human Development: Experiments by Nature and Design.* Cambridge, MA: Harvard University Press.

Bronfenbrenner, U. (1994) 'Nature–nurture reconceptualized in developmental perspective: a bioecological model'. *Psychological Review* 101 (4): 568–586.

Bronfenbrenner, U. (1995) 'Developmental ecology through space and time: a future perspective'. In P. Moen, G. H. Elder and K. Luscher (eds) *Examining Lives in Context.* Washington, DC: American Psychological Association.

Brooks-Gunn, J. and Ruble, D. N. (1983) 'The experience of menarche from a developmental perspective'. In J. Brooks-Gunn and A. C. Petersen (eds) *Girls at Puberty.* New York: Plenum Press.

Broughton J. (ed.) (1987) *Critical Theories of Psychological Development.* New York: Plenum Press.

Brown, L. M. (1994) 'Standing in the crossfire: a response to Tavris, Gremmen, Lykes, Davis and Contratto'. *Feminism and Psychology* 4: 382–398.

Brown, L. M. and Gilligan, C. (1992) *Meeting at the Crossroads: Women's Psychology and Girls' Development.* Cambridge, MA: Harvard University Press.

Bruch, H. (1973) *Eating Disorders; Obesity, Anorexia Nervosa, and the Person Within.* New York: Basic Books.

Bruner, J. (1986a) 'Discussion of Kaplan paper'. In L. Cirillo and S. Wapner (eds) *Value Presuppositions in Theories of Human Development.* Hillsdale, NJ: Erlbaum.

Bruner, J. (1986b) 'Value presuppositions of developmental theory'. In L. Cirillo and S. Wapner (eds) *Value Presuppositions in Theories of Human Development.* Hillsdale, NJ: Erlbaum.

Bruner, J. (1990) *Acts of Meaning.* Cambridge, MA: Harvard University Press.

Burman, E. (1992) 'Feminism and discourse in developmental psychology: power, subjectivity and interpretation'. *Feminism and Psychology* 2: 45–60.

Burman, E. (1994) *Deconstructing Developmental Psychology.* London: Routledge.

Burman, E. (ed.) (1997) *Deconstructing Feminist Psychology.* London: Sage.

Burton, L. M. and Bengston, V. L. (1985) 'Black grandmothers: issues of timing and continuity of roles'. In V. L. Bengston and J. F. Robertson (eds) *Grandparenthood.* Beverly Hills, CA: Sage.

Buss, D. (1994) *The Evolution of Desire: Strategies of Human Mating.* New York: Basic Books.

Buss, D. (1995) 'Psychological sex differences: origins through normal selection'. *American Psychologist* 50: 164–168.

Butler, J. (1990) *Gender Trouble: Feminism and the Subversion of Identity.* London: Routledge.

Butler, J. (1994) *Bodies that Matter: On the Discursive Limits of 'Sex'*. London: Routledge.

Caplan, P. J. (1989) *Don't Blame Mother*. New York: Harper and Row.

Carstensen, L. (1995) 'Evidence for a life-span theory of socio-emotional selectivity'. *Current Directions in Psychological Science* 4: 151–156.

Chafe, W. H. (1972) *The American Woman: Her Changing Social, Economic and Political Roles 1920–1970*. New York: Oxford University Press.

Chodorow, N. (1978) *The Reproduction of Mothering: Psychoanalysis and the Sociology of Mothering*. Berkeley: University of California Press.

Chodorow, N. (1989) *Feminism and Psychoanalytic Theory*. New Haven, CT: Yale University Press.

Cixous, H. (1981) 'The laugh of the Medusa'. In E. Marks and I. de Courtivron (eds) *New French Feminisms*. New York: Schocken Books.

Clarke, A. M. and Clarke, A. D. B. (eds) (1976) *Early Experience: Myth and Evidence*. London: Open Books.

Clarke, A. M. and Clarke, A. D. B. (1984) 'Constancy and change in growth of human characteristics'. *Journal of Child Psychology and Psychiatry* 25: 191–210.

Clarke, A. M. and Clarke, A. D. B. (2000) *Early Experience and the Life Path*. London: Jessica Kingsley.

Coupland, N., Coupland, J. and Giles, H. (1991) *Language Society and the Elderly: Discourse Identity and Aging*. Oxford: Blackwell.

Crawford, M. and Unger, R. (2000) (3rd edn) *Women and Gender: A Feminist Psychology*. New York: McGraw Hill.

Croghan, R. (1991) 'First-time mothers' accounts of inequality in the division of labour'. *Feminism and Psychology* 1 (2): 221–246.

Cross, L. W. (1993) 'Body and self in feminine development: implications for eating disorders and delicate self-mutilation'. *Bulletin of Menninger Clinic* 57 (1): 41–68.

Cross, S. and Markus, H. (1991) 'Possible selves across the lifespan'. *Human Development* 34 (4): 230–255.

Curtis, R. (1991) 'Towards an integrative theory of psychological change in individuals and organisations: a cognitive-affective regulation model'. In R. Curtis and G. Stricker (eds) *How People Change: Inside and Outside Therapy*. New York: Plenum Press.

Cushman, P. (1990) 'Why the self is empty: toward a historically situated psychology'. *American Psychologist* 45: 599–611.

Damon, W. (ed.) (1998) *Handbook of Child Psychology*. New York: Wiley.

Dan, A., Wilber, J., Hedricks, C., O'Connor, E. and Holm, K. (1990) 'Lifelong physical activity in midlife and older women'. *Psychology of Women Quarterly* 14: 531–542.

Dancey, C. (1990) 'Sexual orientation in women: an investigation of hormonal and personality variables'. *Biological Psychology* 30 (3): 251–264.

Dannefer, D. (1984) 'Adult development and social theory: a paradigmatic reappraisal'. *American Sociological Review* 49: 100–116.

Daston, L. (1996) 'The naturalized female intellect'. In C. F. Gaumann and K. J. Gergen (eds) *Historical Dimensions of Psychological Discourse*. New York: Cambridge University Press.

Dawkins, R. (1989) *The Selfish Gene 2nd Edition*. Oxford: Oxford University Press.

Dawkins, R. (1998) *Unweaving the Rainbow: Science, Delusion and the Appetite for Wonder*. London: Allen Lane.

de Beauvoir, S. (1997) *The Second Sex*. London: Viking. Originally published 1949.

Deutsch, H. (1925) *Psychoanalysis of the Sexual Function in Woman*. Vienna: Internationaler psychoanalytischer Verlag.

Deutsch, H. (1944) *Psychology of Women*. NewYork: Grune and Stratton.

Eichenbaum, L. and Orbach, S. (1982) *Understanding Women: A Feminist Psychoanalytic Approach*. New York: Penguin Books.

Elder, G. H. (1974) *Children of the Great Depression: Social Change in Life Experience*. Chicago, IL: University of Chicago Press.

Elder, G. H. (1986) 'Military times and turning points in men's lives'. *Developmental Psychology* 22: 233–243.

Elder, G. H. (1995) 'The life course paradigm: social change and individual development'. In P. Moen, G. H. Elder and K. Luscher (eds) *Examining Lives in Context*. Washington, DC: American Psychological Association.

Elder, G. H. (1998) 'The life course as developmental theory'. *Child Development* 69: 1–12.

Engel, S. (in press) 'What children's stories tell us about children'. In S. Greene and D. Hogan, *Researching Children's Experience: Approaches and Methods*. London: Sage.

Erikson, E. H. (1950) *Childhood and Society*. New York: W. W. Norton.

Erikson, E. H. (1964) 'Inner and outer space: reflections on womanhood'. *Daedalus* 93 (2): 582–606.

Erikson, E. H. (1968) *Identity Youth and Crisis*. New York: W. W. Norton.

Erikson, E. H. (1982) *The Life Cycle Completed: A Review*. New York: W. W. Norton.

Erikson, E. H., Erikson, J. M. and Kronick, H. Q. (1986) *Vital Involvement in Old Age*. New York: W. W. Norton.

Fagot, B. (1978) 'The influence of sex of child on parental reactions to toddler children'. *Child Development* 49: 459–465.

Fagot, B. (1985) 'Beyond the reinforcement principle: another step towards understanding sex role development'. *Developmental Psychology* 21: 1097–1104.

Farrington, B. (1951) *Francis Bacon: Philosopher of Industrial Sciences*. London: Lawrence and Wishart.

Faulconer, J. E. and Williams, R. N. (1985) 'Temporality in human action: an alternative to positivism and historicism'. *American Psychologist* 40: 1179–1188.

Fausto-Sterling, A. (1985) *Myths of Gender: Biological Theories about Women and Men*. New York: Basic Books.

Favazza, A. R. and Conterio, K. (1996) *Bodies Under Siege: Self-mutilation and Body Modification in Culture and Psychiatry*. Baltimore, MD: Johns Hopkins University Press.

Featherman, D. C. and Lerner, R. M. (1985) 'Ontogenesis and sociogenesis: problematics for theory and research about development and socialisation across the lifespan'. *American Sociological Review* 50: 659–676.

Feldman, W., Feldman, E. and Goodman, J. T. (1988) 'Culture and biology: children's attitudes towards thinness and fatness'. *Pediatrics* 81: 190–194.

Fenchel, G. H. (ed.) (1998) *The Mother–Daughter Relationship: Echoes Through Time*. New Jersey: Jason Aronson.

Fine, M. (1985) 'Reflections on a feminist psychology of women'. *Psychology of Women Quarterly* 9: 167–183.

Fine, M. (1988) 'Sexuality, schooling and adolescent females: the missing discourse of desire'. *Harvard Educational Review* 58: 29–53.

Fine, M. (1992) *Disruptive Voices: The Possibility of Feminist Research*. Ann Arbor: University of Michigan Press.

Flax, J. (1990) *Thinking Fragments: Psychoanalysis, Feminism and Postmodernism in the Contemporary West*. Berkeley: University of California Press.

Foucault, M. (1975, 1977 in English) *Discipline and Punish: The Birth of the Prison*. London: Allen Lane.

Foucault, M. (1980) *Power/Knowledge*, New York: Pantheon.

Fox, D. and Prilleltensky, I. (eds) (1997) *Critical Psychology: An Introduction*. London: Sage.

Franz, C. and Stewart, A. (eds) (1994) *Women Creating Lives: Identities Resilience and Resistance*. Boulder, CO: Westview Press.

Freeman, M. (1993) *Rewriting the Self: History, Memory, Narrative*. London: Routledge.

Freud, S. (1905) 'Three essays on the theory of sexuality' (Vol. VII, Standard Edition). London: Hogarth Press.

Freud, S. (1925) 'Some psychical consequences of the anatomical distinction between the sexes' (Vol. IXX, Standard Edition). London: Hogarth Press.

Freud, S. (1933) 'Femininity' (Vol. XXII, Standard Edition). London: Hogarth Press.

Friedan, B. (1963) *The Feminine Mystique*. New York: Norton Press.

Friedan, B. (1993) *The Fountain of Age*. New York: Simon and Schuster.

Gadamer, H. G. (1975) *Truth and Method*. New York: Seabury Press. Originally published 1960.

Galambos, N. L., Almeida, D. M. and Peterson, A. C. (1990) 'Masculinity, femininity and sex role attitudes in early adolescence: exploring gender intensification'. *Child Development* 61: 1905–1914.

Gannon, L. R. (1994) 'Sexuality and menopause'. In P. Y. L. Choi and P. Nicolson (eds) *Female Sexuality: Psychology, Biology and Social Context*. London: Harvester Wheatsheaf.

Gannon, L. R. (1999) *Women and Aging: Transcending the Myths*. London: Routledge.

Garrison, D. (1981) 'Karen Horney and feminism'. *Signs: Journal of Women in Culture and Society* 6: 672–691.

Gatens, M. (1983) 'A critique of the sex/gender distinction'. In T. Allen and P. Patten (eds) *Beyond Marxism: Interventions after Marx*. Sydney: Intervention Press.

Geary, D. C. (1998) *Male, Female, The Evolution of Human Sex Differences*. Washington, DC: APA.

Geertz, C. (1973) *The Interpretation of Cultures*. New York: Basic Books.

Gergen, K. J. (1982) *Toward Transformation in Social Knowledge*. New York: Springer-Verlag.

Gergen, K. J. (1985) 'The social constructionist movement in modern psychology'. *American Psychologist* 40: 266–275.

Gergen, K. J. (1988) 'If persons are texts'. In S. B. Messner, L. A. Sass and R. L. Woolfolk (eds) *Hermeneutics and Psychological Inquiry*. New Jersey: Rutgers University Press.

Gergen, K. J. (1991) *The Saturated Self: Dilemmas of Identity in Contemporary Life*. New York: Basic Books.

Gergen, K. J. (1992) 'Toward a postmodern psychology'. In S. Kvale (ed.) *Psychology and Postmodernism*. London: Sage.

Gergen, K. J. and Gergen, M. (1987) 'The self in temporal perspective'. In K. P. Abeles (ed.) *Life-Span Perspectives and Social Psychology*. New Jersey: Erlbaum.

Gergen, M. (1990) 'Finished at 40: women's development in the patriarchy'. *Psychology of Women Quarterly* 14: 470–493.

Gergen, M. (2001) *Feminist Reconstructions in Psychology: Narrative, Gender and Performance*. London: Sage.

Gesell, A. and Ilg, F. (eds) (1946) *Child Development*. New York: Harper and Row.

Gilligan, C. (1979) 'Woman's place in man's life cycle'. *Harvard Educational Review* 49 (4): 431–447.

Gilligan, C. (1982) *In a Different Voice; Psychological Theory and Women's Development*. Cambridge, MA: Harvard University Press.

Gilligan, C., Brown, L. M. and Rogers, A. (1990) 'Psyche embedded: a place for body, relationships and culture in personality theory'. In A. I. Rabin, R. Zucker, R. Emmons and S. Frank (eds) *Studying Persons and Lives*. New York: Springer.

Gilligan, C., Lyons, N. and Hanmer, T. (1990) *Making Connections; The Relational Worlds of Adolescent Girls at Emma Willard School*. Cambridge, MA: Harvard University Press.

Goldberger, N. R. (1998) 'Looking back, looking forward'. In N. R. Goldberger, M. F. Tarule, B. M. Clinchy and J. M. Belenky (eds) *Knowledge, Difference and Power: Essays Inspired by 'Women's Ways of Knowing'*. New York: Basic Books.

Gottlieb, G. (1992) *Individual Development: The Genesis of Novel Behaviour*. Oxford: Oxford University Press.

Gould, E., Reeves, A. J., Graziano, M. and Gross, C. (1999) 'Neurogenesis in the neocortex of adult primates'. *Science* 286 (1): 548–552.

Gould, S. J. (1996) *The Mismeasure of Man*. New York: Norton Press.

Greenberg, D. E. (1996) 'The object permanence fallacy'. *Human Development* 39: 117–131.

Greene, S. (1997a) 'Child development: old themes and new directions'. In R. Fuller, P. Noonan Walsh and P. McGinley, *A Century of Psychology: Progress, Paradigms and Prospects for the New Millennium*. London: Routledge.

Greene, S. (1997b) 'Psychology and the reevaluation of the feminine'. *Irish Journal of Psychology* 18: 367–385.

Greene, S. (1999) 'What makes a person a person? The limits and limitations of genetics'. In M. Junker-Kenny (ed.) *Designing Life? Genetics, Procreation and Ethics*. Aldershot: Ashgate.

Greer, G. (1999) *The Whole Woman*. New York: Doubleday.

Grosz, E. (1999) *Becomings: Explorations in Time, Memory and Futures*. New York: Cornell University Press.

Guisinger, S. and Blatt, S. (1994) 'Individuality and relatedness'. *American Psychologist* 49: 104–111.

Gullette, M. M. (1988) *Safe at Last in the Middle Years; The Invention of the Mid-life Progress Novel*. Berkeley: University of California Press.

Gutmann, D. L. (1975) 'Parenthood: a key to the comparative study of the life cycle'. In N. Datan and L. Ginsberg, *Life-span Developmental Psychology: Normative Life Crises*. New York: Academic Press.

Gutmann, D. L. (1987) *Reclaimed Powers: Toward a New Psychology of Men and Women in Later Life*. New York: Basic Books.

Hagestad, G. and Neugarten, B. (1985) 'Age and the life course'. In E. Shanas and R. Binstock (eds) *Handbook of Aging and the Social Sciences* (2nd edn). New York: Van Nostrand and Reinhold.

Hall, G. S. (1904) *Adolescence*. New York: Appleton.

Hall, G. S. (1922) *Senescence, the Last Half of Life*. New York: Appleton.

Hardyment, C. (1983) *Dream Babies: Three Centuries of Good Advice on Child Care*. New York: Harper and Row.

Harter, S. (1999) *The Construction of Self: A Developmental Perspective*. New York: Guilford Press.

Haste, H. (1994) *The Sexual Metaphor*. Cambridge, MA: Harvard University Press.

Hayslip, B. and Panek, P. (1993) *Adult Development and Aging* (2nd edn). New York: HarperCollins.

Heidegger, M. (1962) *Being and Time*. New York: Harper and Row. Originally published 1927.

Helson, R., and Moane, G. (1987) 'Personality change in women from college to midlife'. *Journal of Personality and Social Psychology* 53: 176–186.

Helson, R., Mitchell, V. and Moane, G. (1984) 'Personality and patterns of adherence and non-adherence to the social clock'. *Journal of Personality and Social Psychology* 46: 1079–1096.

Henley, N. M. (1977) *Body Politics: Power, Sex and Nonverbal Communications*. New Jersey: Prentice-Hall.

Hill, A. and Robinson, A. (1991) 'Dieting concerns have a functional effect on the behaviour of nine-year old girls'. *British Journal of Clinical Psychology* 30: 265–267.

Horney, K. (1926) 'The flight from womanhood'. *International Journal of Psychoanalysis* 7: 324–339.

Horney, K. (1967) *Feminine Psychology*. London: W. W. Norton.

Hyde, J. (1996) *Half the Human Experience: The Psychology of Women* (5th edn). Lexington, MA: D. C. Heath.

Hyde, J., Rosenberg, B. G. and Behrman, J. A. (1977) 'Tomboys'. *Psychology of Women Quarterly* 2: 73–75.

Irigaray, L. (1985, in French 1977) *This Sex Which Is Not One*. Ithaca, NY: Cornell University Press.

James, A. and Prout, A. (1997) 'Representing childhood: time and transition in the study of childhood'. In A. James and A. Prout (eds) *Constructing and Reconstructing Childhood: Contemporary Issues in the Sociological Study of Childhood*. London: Routledge/Falmer.

Johnson, N. G., Roberts, M. C. and Worell, J. (1999) *Beyond Appearance; A New Look at Adolescent Girls*. Washington, DC: APA Books.

Jordan, J. (1997) *Women's Growth in Diversity*. New York: Guilford Press.

Jordan, J., Caplan, A., Miller, J. B., Stiver, I. and Surrey, J. (1991) *Women's Growth in Connection*. New York: Guilford Press.

Josselson, R. and Lieblich, A. (Series eds) (1993) *The Narrative Study of Lives*, Vol. 1. London: Sage.

Joy, M. (1993) 'Feminism and the self'. *Theory and Psychology* 3: 275–302.

Jung, C. G. (1953) 'Anima and animus'. In *Two Essays in Analytical Psychology*. New York: Meridian.

Jung, C. G. (1954) 'The archetypes and the collective unconscious'. In *Collected Works Volume 9, Part One*. Princeton, NJ: Princeton University Press.

Jung, C. G. (1964) 'The stages of life'. In *Collected Works Volume 8: The Structure and Dynamics of the Psyche*. Princeton, NJ: Princeton University Press.

Karraker, K. Vogel, D. and Lake, M. (1995) 'Parents' gender-stereotyped perceptions of newborns: the eye of the beholder revisited'. *Sex Roles* 33: 687–701.

Kastenbaum, R. (1984) 'When aging begins'. *Research on Aging* 6: 105–117.

Katz, L. and Rubin, M. (1999) *How to Keep Your Brain Alive*. New York: Workman.

Kessen, W. (1979) 'The American child and other cultural inventions'. *American Psychologist* 34: 815–820.

Kessen, W (1990) *The Rise and Fall of Development*. Worcester, MA: Clark University Press.

Kestenberg, J. (1975) *Children and Parents: Psychoanalytic Studies in Development*. New York: Jason Aronson.

Klein, M. (1937) *Love, Hate and Reparation*. London: Hogarth Press (with J. Riviere).

Kogan, N. (1979) 'A study of categorisation'. *Journal of Gerontology* 34: 358–363.

Kohlberg, L. (1966) 'A cognitive-developmental analysis of children's sex role concepts and attitudes'. In E. E. Maccoby (ed.) *The Development of Sex Differences*. Palo Alto: Stanford University Press.

Kohlberg, L. (1976) 'Moral stages and moralisation: the cognitive-developmental approach'. In T. Lickona (ed.) *Moral Development and Behaviour: Theory, Research and Social Issues*. New York: Holt, Rinehart and Winston.

Kohli, M. (1986) 'The world we forgot: a historical review of the life course'. In V. Marshall, *Later Life*. Beverly Hills, CA: Sage.

Kohli, M. and Meyer, J. W. (1986) 'Social structure and social construction of life stage'. *Human Development* 29: 145–180.

Kristeva, J. (1981) 'Women's time'. *Signs: Journal of Women in Culture and Society* 7 (1): 13–35.

Kuhn, D. (1995) 'Introduction'. *Human Development* 38: 293–294.

Labouvie-Vief, G. (1994) *Psyche and Eros: Mind and Gender in the Life Course*. Cambridge: Cambridge University Press.

Labouvie-Vief, G. and Chandler, M. (1978) 'Cognitive development and life-span developmental theory: idealistic vs contextual perspectives'. In P. Baltes (ed.) *Life Span Development and Behaviour*, Vol. 1. New York: Academic Press.

Lacan, J. (1977) 'The mirror stage as formative of the function of the I'. In J. Lacan, *Écrits: A Selection*, trans. A. Sheridan. London: Tavistock Publications.

Lacan, J. (1978) *The Four Fundamental Concepts of Psychoanalysis* (ed. Jacques-Alain Miller). New York: W. W. Norton.

Lackoff, G. and Johnson, M. (1999) *Psychology in the Flesh: The Embodied Mind and its Challenge to Western Thought*. New York: Basic Books.

Lederman, R. P. (1996) *Psychosocial Adaptation in Pregnancy*. New York: Springer.

Lerman, H. (1986) *A Mote in Freud's Eye: From Psychoanalysis to the Psychology of Women*. New York: Springer.

Lerner, R. M. (1993) 'The demise of the nurture–nature dichotomy'. *Human Development* 36: 119–124.

Lerner, R. M. (1998) 'Theories of human development'. In R. Lerner (ed.) *Handbook of Child Psychology*, Vol. 1. New York: Wiley.

Levenson, M. R. and Crumpler, C. A. (1996) 'Three modes of adult development'. *Human Development* 39: 135–149.

Levinson, D. (1978) *The Seasons of a Man's Life*. New York: Knopf.

Levinson, D. (1996) *The Seasons of a Woman's Life*. New York: Knopf.

Lewin, M. (ed.) (1984) *In the Shadow of the Past: Psychology Portrays the Sexes*. New York: Columbia University Press.

Lewis, M. (1992) 'Commentary on Lerner and von Eye'. *Human Development* 35: 44–51.

Lewis, M. (1997) *Altering Fate: Why the Past Does Not Predict the Future*. New York: Guilford Press.

Lewis, M. (2000) 'The promise of dynamic system approaches for an integrated account of human development'. *Child Development* 71: 36–43.

Lichtman, R. (1981) 'Notes on accumulation, time and aging'. *Psychology and Social Theory* 1: 69–76.

Lichtman, R. (1987) 'The illusion of maturation in an age of decline'. In J. Broughton (ed.) *Critical Theories of Psychological Development*. New York: Plenum Press.

Lock, M. (1986) 'Ambiguities of aging: Japanese experience and perceptions of menopause'. *Culture, Medicine and Psychiatry* 10: 23–46.

Lock, M. (1993) *Encounters with Aging: Mythologies of Menopause in Japan and North America*. Berkeley: University of California Press.

Lykes, M. B. and Stewart, A. S. (1986) 'Evaluating the feminist challenge to research in personality and social psychology'. *Psychology of Women Quarterly*: 10: 393–412.

McAdams, D. (1990) 'Unity and purpose in human lives: the emergence of identity as a life story'. In A. Rabin, R. Zucker, R. Emmons and S. Frank (eds) *Studying Persons and Lives*. New York: Springer.

McNeill, E. (1994) 'Blood, sex and hormones: a theoretical review of women's sexuality and the menstrual cycle'. In P. Choi and P. Nicolson, *Female Sexuality: Psychology, Biology and Social Context*. London: Harvester Wheatsheaf.

Magnusson, D. (1995) 'Individual development; a holistic integrated model'. In P. Moen, G. H. Elder and K. Luscher (eds) *Examining Lives in Context*. Washington, DC: American Psychological Association.

Magnusson, D., Stattin, H. and Allen, V. J. (1986) 'Differential maturation among girls and its relation to social adjustment: a longitudinal perspective'. In P. B. Baltes, D. Featherman and R. M. Lerner (eds) *Life Span Development Volume 7*. New York: Academic Press.

Maracek, J. (1997) 'Disappearances, silences and anxious rhetoric: gender in abnormal psychology textbooks'. In M. M. Gergen and S. N. Davis, *Toward a New Psychology of Gender: A Reader*. London: Routledge.

Markus, H. and Nurius, P. (1986) 'Possible selves'. *American Psychologist* 41: 954–969.

Martin, J. and Sugarman, J. (1999) *The Psychology of Human Possibility and Constraint*. Albany: State University of New York Press.

Martin, J. and Sugarman, J. (2001) 'Interpreting human kinds: beginnings of a hermeneutic psychology'. *Theory and Psychology* 11 (2): 193–208.

Matlin, M. (2000) *The Psychology of Women* (4th edn). Fort Worth, TX: Harcourt Brace.

Mead, M. (1935) *Sex and Temperament in Three Primitive Societies*. New York: Morrow.

Mercer, R. (1995) *Becoming a Mother: Research on Maternal Identification – Rubin to the Present*. New York: Springer.

Miller, D. (1994) *Women Who Hurt Themselves*. New York: Basic Books.

Miller, J. B. (1976) *Toward a New Psychology of Women*. Boston, MA: Beacon Press.

Miller, P. H. and Scholnick, E. K. (2000) *Toward a Feminist Developmental Psychology*. London: Routledge.

Mitchell, V. and Helson, R. (1990) 'Women's prime of life. Is it the 50s?' *Psychology of Women Quarterly* 14: 451–470.

Moane, G. (1999) *Gender and Colonialism: A Psychological Analysis of Oppression and Liberation*. London: Macmillan.

Mooney-Somers, J. and Ussher, J. (2000) 'Young lesbians and mental health: the closet is a depressing place to be'. In J. Ussher (ed.) *Women's Health; Contemporary International Perspectives*. Leicester: British Psychological Society Books.

Morss, J. (1990) *The Biologising of Childhood Developmental Psychology and the Darwinian Myth*. Englewood Cliffs, NJ: Erlbaum.

Morss, J. (1996) *Growing Critical: Alternatives to Developmental Psychology*. London: Routledge.

Mumford, M. D., Stokes, G. S. and Owes, W. A. (1990) *Patterns of Life History: The Ecology of Human Individuality*. Englewood Cliffs, NJ: Erlbaum.

Nelson, K. (ed.) (1993) *Narratives from the Crib*. Cambridge, MA: Harvard University Press.

Neugarten, B. (1968) 'Adult personality: towards a psychology of the life course'. In B. Neugarten (ed.) *Middle Age and Aging*. Chicago, IL: Chicago University Press.

Neugarten, B. (1977) 'Personality and aging'. In J. E. Birren and K. W. Schaie (eds) *Handbook of the Psychology of Aging*. New York: Van Nostrand Reinhold.

Neugarten, B. (1979) 'Time, age and the life cycle'. *American Journal of Psychiatry* 136: 887–894.

Neugarten, B. and Datan, N. (1973) 'Sociological perspectives on the life span'. In P. B. Baltes and K. W. Schaie (eds) *Life-span Developmental Psychology: Personality and Socialisation*. New York: Academic Press.

Orbach, S. (1986) *Hunger Strike*. London: Faber and Faber.

Ostertag, P. A. and MacNamara, J. R. (1991) 'Feminization of psychology: the changing sex ratio and its implications for the profession. *Psychology of Women Quarterly* 15 (3): 349–369.

Oyama, S. (1993) 'How shall I name thee? The construction of natural selves'. *Theory and Psychology* 3 (4): 471–496.

Paludi, M. A. (1998) *The Psychology of Women*. New Jersey: Prentice-Hall.

Parke, R. D., Ornstein, R. A., Rieser, J. J. and Zahn-Waxler, C. (eds) (1994) *A Century of Developmental Psychology*. Washington, DC: American Psychological Association.

Parlee, M. B. (1973) 'The premenstrual syndrome'. *Psychological Bulletin* 83: 454–465.

Parlee, M. B. (1979) 'Psychology and women'. *Signs: Journal of Women in Culture and Society* 5: 121–133.

Perry, W. (1968) *Forms of Intellectual and Ethical Development in the College Years*. New York: Holt, Rinehart and Winston.

Peterson, S. and Kroner, T. (1992) 'Gender bias in textbooks for introductory psychology and human development'. *Psychology of Women Quarterly* 16 (1): 17–36

Phillips, A. (1999) *Darwin's Worms*. London: Faber and Faber.

Piaget, J. (1970) *Structuralism*. New York: Harper and Row.

Pilcher, J. (1998) *Women of their Time: Generation, Gender Issues and Feminism*. London: Ashgate.

Pinker, S. (1994) *The Language Instinct*. London: Allen Lane.

Pinker, S. (1997) *How the Mind Works*. New York: W. W. Norton.

Plomin, R. (1994) *Genetics and Experience: The Interplay Between Nature and Nurture*. Thousand Oaks, CA: Sage.

Postman, N. (1982) *The Disappearance of Childhood*. New York: Delacorte.

Rama, R., Habermas, J. and Nurmer-Winkler, G. (1987) 'Psychological approaches to understanding the self'. In J. Broughton (ed.) *Critical Theories of Psychological Development*. New York: Plenum.

Rich, A. (1976) *Of Woman Born: On Motherhood as Experience and Institution*. New York: W. W. Norton.

Ricoeur, P. (1991) 'Narrative identity'. *Philosophy Today* 35 (1): 73–81.

Riegel, K. (1977) *'The dialectics of time'*. In N. Datan and H. W. Reese, *Life-span Developmental Psychology: Dialectical Perspectives on Experimental Research*. New York: Academic Press.

Riger, S. (1992) 'Epistemological debates, feminist voices: science, social values and the study of women'. *American Psychologist* 47: 730–740.

Risman, B. J. (1987) 'Intimate relationships from a microstructural perspective: men who mother'. *Gender and Society* 1: 6–32.

Rogers, A. (1994) *Exiled Voices: Dissociation and Repression in Women's Narratives of Trauma*. Wellesley, MA: Stone Center Working Papers Series.

Rogers, A. (in press) 'Relational methods'. In S. Greene and D. Hogan, *Researching Children's Experience: Approaches and Methods*. London: Sage.

Roland, A. (1991) 'The self in cross-civilizational perspective: an Indian–Japanese–American comparison'. In R. Curtis (ed.) *The Relational Self: Theoretical Convergences in Psychoanalysis and Social Psychology*. New York: Guilford Press.

Rorty, R. (1979) *Philosophy and the Mirror of Nature*. Princeton, NJ: Princeton University Press.

Rose, H. and Rose, S. (2000) *Alas Poor Darwin: Arguments Against Evolutionary Psychology*. London: Jonathan Cape.

Rose, S. (1997) *Lifelines: Biology, Freedom, Determinism*. London: Allen Lane.

Rossi, A. (1977) 'A biosocial perspective on parenting'. *Daedalus* 106 (2): 1–32.

Rossi, A. (1980) 'Life-span theories and women's lives'. *Signs: Journal of Women in Culture and Society* 6: 4–32.

Rousseau, J. J. (1762, in English 1974) *Emile*. London: Dent.

Ruddick, S. (1989) *Maternal Thinking: Towards a Politics of Peace*. London: The Women's Press.

Rutter, M. (1989) 'Pathways from childhood to adult life'. *Journal of Child Psychology and Psychiatry* 30: 23–51.

Ryff, C. (1985) 'The subjective experience of life span transitions'. In A. Rossi (ed.) *Gender and the Life Course*. New York: Aldine.

Ryff, C. (1991) 'Possible selves in adulthood and old age: a tale of shifting horizons'. *Psychology and Aging* 6: 286–295.

Salmon, P. (1985) *Living in Time*. London: Dent.

Sampson, E. E. (1985) 'The decentralization of identity: toward a revised concept of personal and social order'. *American Psychologist* 40: 1203–1211.

Santrock, J. (1992) *Life-span Development* (4th edn). Dubuque, IA: Wm. C. Brown.

Santrock, J. (1999) *Life-span Development* (7th edn). Boston, MA: McGraw Hill.

Sarbin, T. (1986) *Narrative Psychology: The Storied Nature of Human Conduct*. New York: Praeger.

Sayers, J. (1992) *Mothering Psychoanalysis: Helene Deutsch, Karen Horney, Anna Freud, Melanie Klein*. London: Penguin Books.

Sbisa, M. (1996) 'The feminine subject and female body in discourse about childbirth'. *European Journal of Women's Studies* 3: 363–376.

Scarr, S. and McCartney, R. K. (1983) 'How people make their own environments; a theory of genotype-environment effects'. *Child Development* 54: 424–435.

Scholnick, E. K. (2000) 'Engendering development: metaphors of change'. In P. H. Miller and E. K. Scholnick (eds) *Towards a Feminist Developmental Psychology*. New York: Routledge.

Sears, R. R. (1975) 'Your ancients revisited: a history of child development'. In E. M. Hetherington (ed.) *Review of Child Development Research*, Vol. 5. Chicago, IL: University of Chicago Press.

Segal, L. (1999) *Why Feminism?* Cambridge: Polity Press.

Seifert, K., Hoffnung, R. and Hoffnung, M. (1997) *Lifespan Development*. New York: Hayster Mifflin.

Serbin, L., Powlishista, K. and Gulko, J. (1993) *The Development of Sex Typing in Middle Childhood*. Monographs of the Society for Research in Child Development 58 (serial no. 232).

Settersten, R. (1997) 'The salience of age in the life course'. *Human Development* 40: 257–281.

Sharpe, S. (1994) *Just Like a Girl*, 2nd edn, Harmondsworth: Penguin.

Sharpe, S (2001) 'Going for it: young women face the future'. *Feminism and Psychology* 11: 177–181.

Shweder, R. (1998) *Welcome to Middle Age*. Chicago, IL: University of Chicago Press.

Smith, G. J. (1985) 'Facial and full-length ratings of attractiveness related to the social interactions of young children'. *Sex Roles* 12: 287–293.

Smith, M. B. (1994) 'Selfhood at risk: postmodern perils and the perils of postmodernism'. *American Psychologist* 49: 405–411.

Squire, C. (1989) *Significant Differences: Feminism in Psychology*. London: Routledge.

Squire, C. (1997) 'AIDS panic'. In J. Ussher (ed.) *Body Talk: The Material and Discursive Regulation of Sexuality, Madness and Reproduction*. London and New York: Routledge.

Stanley, L. (1992) *The Autobiographical I: Theory and Practice of Feminist Autobiography*. Manchester: Manchester University Press.

Stevens, R. (ed.) (1996) *Understanding the Self*. London: Sage.

Stewart, A. J. (1994) 'Women's lives'. In A. Lieblich and R. Josselson (eds) *Exploring Identity and Gender: The Narrative Study of Lives*, Vol. 2. London: Sage.

Stewart, A. J. and Healy, J. M. (1989) 'Linking individual development and social change'. *American Psychologist* 40: 30–42.

Stewart, A. J. and Ostrove, J. (1998) 'Women's personality in middle age: gender, history and midcourse corrections'. *American Psychologist* 53: 1185–1194.

Strawson, G. (1996) *Mental Reality*. Cambridge, MA: MIT Press.

Tangri, S. and Jenkins, S. (1993) 'The University of Michigan Class of 1967: the women's life paths study'. In K. D. Hulbert and D. T. Shuster, *Women's Lives through Time*. San Francisco, CA: Jossey Bass.

Taylor, C. (1989) *Sources of the Self*. Cambridge, MA: Harvard University Press.

Teo, T. (1997) 'Developmental psychology and the relevance of a critical metatheoretical reflection'. *Human Development* 40: 195–210.

Thelen, E. and Smith, L. B. (1994) *A Dynamic Systems Approach to the Development of Cognition and Action*. Cambridge, MA: MIT Press.

Thompson, C. (1950) 'Some effects of the derogatory attitude towards female sexuality'. *Psychiatry* 13: 349–354.

Thompson, C. (1964) *Interpersonal Psychoanalysis: The Selected Papers of Clara Thompson*. New York: Basic Books.

Tolman, D. (2000) 'Femininity as a barrier to sexual health for adolescent girls'. In J. M.

Ussher (ed.) *Women's Health: Contemporary International Perspectives*. Leicester: BPS Books.

Tong, R. (1989) *Feminist Thought*. London: Routledge.

Triandis, H. C. (1989) 'Cross-cultural studies of individualism and collectivism'. In *Nebraska Symposium on Motivation*, Vol. 37. Lincoln: Nebraska University Press.

Trivers, R. (1972) 'Parental investment and sexual selection'. In B. Campbell (ed.) *Sexual Selection and the Descent of Man*. Chicago, IL: Aldine.

Tuana, N. (1993) *The Less Noble Sex*, Bloomington: Indiana University Press.

Turner, P. J., Gervai, J. and Hinde, R. A. (1993) 'Gender-typing in young children: preferences, behaviour and cultural differences'. *British Journal of Developmental Psychology* 11: 323–342.

Unger, R. (1997) 'The three-sided mirror: feminists looking at psychologists looking at women'. In R. Fuller, P. Noonan Walsh and P. McGinley, *A Century of Psychology: Progress, Paradigms and Prospects for the New Millennium*. London: Routledge.

Urwin, C. (1985) 'Constructing motherhood. The persuasion of normal development'. In C. Staedman, C. Urwin and V. Walkerdine (eds) *Language, Gender and Childhood*. London: Routledge & Kegan Paul.

Ussher, J. M. (1989) *The Psychology of the Female Body*. London: Routledge.

Ussher, J. M. (1997) *Fantasies of Femininity: Reframing the Boundaries of Sex*. London: Penguin.

Vaillant, G. (1977) *Adaptation to Life*. Boston, MA: Little Brown.

Valsiner, J. (2000) *Culture and Human Development*. London: Sage.

van Mens-Verhulst, J., Schreurs, K. and Woertman, L. (1993) *Daughtering and Mothering: Female Subjectivity Reanalysed*. London: Routledge.

Vasta, R., Haith, M. M. and Miller, S. A. (1999) *Child Psychology: The Modern Science* (3rd edn). New York: Wiley.

Vygotsky, L. (1978) *Mind in Society: The Development of Higher Psychological Processes*. Cambridge, MA: Harvard University Press.

Walker, A. (1998) *The Menstrual Cycle*. London: Routledge.

Walkerdine, V. (1984) 'Developmental psychology and the child-centred pedagogy'. In J. Henriques, W. Hollway, C. Urwin, C. Venn and V. Walkerdine (eds) *Changing the Subject: Psychology, Social Regulation and Subjectivity*. London: Methuen.

Walkerdine, V. (1988) *The Mastery of Reason; Cognitive Development and the Production of Rationality*. London: Routledge.

Walkerdine, V. (1991) *Schoolgirl Fictions*. London: Virago.

Walkerdine, V. (1993) 'Beyond developmentalism?' *Theory and Psychology* 3: 451–469.

Wapner, S. (1993) 'Parental development: a holistic, developmental systems-oriented perspective'. In J. Demick, K. Bursick and R. diBiase (eds) *Parental Development*. Englewood Cliffs, NJ: Erlbaum.

Watson, J. B. (1925) *Behaviourism*. New York: W. W. Norton.

Waugh, P. (1989) *Feminine Fictions: Revisiting the Postmodern*. London: Routledge.

Wehr, D. (1988) *Jung and Feminism: Liberating Archetypes*. London: Routledge.

West, C. and Zimmerman, D. H. (1987) 'Doing gender'. *Gender and Society* 1: 125–151.

Wetherell, M. (1986) 'Linguistic repertoires and literary criticism: new directions for a social psychology of gender'. In S. Wilkinson (ed.) *Feminist Social Psychology*. Milton Keynes: Open University Press.

Whitrow, G. J. (1975) *The Nature of Time*. London: Penguin Books.

Wilcox, S. (1998) 'Age and gender in relation to body attitudes: is there a double standard of aging?' *Psychology of Women Quarterly* 21: 549–565.

Wilson, E. O. (1978) *On Human Nature*. Cambridge, MA: Harvard University Press.

Wilson, R. A. and Wilson, T. A. (1963) 'The fate of the non-treated post-menopausal woman: a plea for the maintenance of adequate estrogen from puberty to the grave'. *Journal of the American Geriatric Society* 11: 351–356.

Wine, J. (1985) 'Models of human functioning: a feminist perspective'. *International Journal of Women's Studies* 8: 183–192.

Winnicott, D. W. (1958) *Collected Papers*. London: Tavistock.

Woollett, A. and Marshall, H. (1996) 'Reading the body; young women's accounts of the meaning of the body in relation to independence, responsibility and maturing'. *European Journal of Women's Studies* 3: 199–214.

Young-Eisendrath, P. C. (1984) *Hags and Heroes: A Feminist Approach to Jungian Psychotherapy and Couples*. Toronto: Inner City Books.

AUTHOR INDEX

SUBJECT INDEX